# NEW WORLD WISDOM
## Book Three

# ALSO BY LORI TOYE

*A Teacher Appears*

*Sisters of the Flame*

*Fields of Light*

*The Ever Present Now*

*New World Wisdom Series*

*I AM America Atlas*

*Points of Perception*

*Light of Awakening*

*Divine Destiny*

*Freedom Star Book*

*I AM America Map*

*Freedom Star Map*

*6-Map Scenario*

*US Golden City Map*

# New World

# *Wisdom*

## Teachings from the Ascended Masters

Book Three

# LORI AND LENARD TOYE

I AM AMERICA PUBLISHING & DISTRIBUTING
P.O. Box 2511, Payson, Arizona, 85547, USA.
www.iamamerica.com

I AM America Maps and Books have been marketed since 1989 by I AM America Seventh Ray Publishing and Distributing, through workshops, conferences, and numerous bookstores in the United States and internationally. If you are interested in obtaining information on available releases please write or call:
I AM America, P.O. Box 2511, Payson, Arizona, 85547, USA. (928) 978-6435, or visit:

www.iamamerica.com
www.loritoye.com
www.loritoye.org

Graphic Design and Typography by Lori Toye
Editing by Elaine Cardall and Betsy Robinson

*Love, in service, breathes the breath for all!*

10 9 8 7 6 5 4 3 2 1

*"Within your heart lies the gentle revolution
which can redirect the course of such events."*

~ MASTER K. H.

# CONTENTS

CHAPTER FOURTEEN

## Conscious Immortality • 179

CHAPTER FIFTEEN

## Map Review • 191

CHAPTER SIXTEEN

## *Africa* • 215

CHAPTER SEVENTEEN

## Exchanges • 235

CHAPTER EIGHTEEN

## The Celebration of Shamballa • 243

CHAPTER NINETEEN

## Birth Changes • 251

CHAPTER TWENTY-TWO

## The Key  •  293

CHAPTER TWENTY-THREE

## Earth Changes  •  309

# Preface

I have often thought about H. P. (Helena) Blavatsky or Alice Bailey meeting their Master Teachers for the first time. Fortunately Helena was only a child, so it is possible when she spoke about her beloved *Azahulama*, which means "the blue teacher," mom and dad probably raised their eyes and whispered to themselves, "Another imaginary playmate." Alice did not have the excuse of childhood fantasy when a tall man dressed in European clothing and a huge white turban walked into her drawing room on a Sunday afternoon. She was a young woman, just fifteen years old, and during the brief interview he let her know that there was some work planned. If she gave up being an "unpleasant little girl" and developed a measure of self-control, she would spend the rest of her life traveling about the world, "doing your Master's work all the time."

These same Master Teachers, El Morya and Kuthumi, are two of the sponsors of this Earth Changes material for Europe and Africa. It is obvious why they have this job, as they are undoubtedly experienced.

Beloved Lady Nada, the third sponsor for this material, has been instructing humans longer than they have. Since she has been in the ascended state for more than 2,700 years, the ancient priestess of Atlantis holds a focus for the healing of mankind. Like Helena and Alice, Lady Nada was contacted for instruction as a small human child. Her teacher, a beautiful lady in pink who carried the fragrance of roses, taught her how to work with nature, flowers, and birds. It is likely that Lady Nada at one time instructed El Morya and Kuthumi before they became world servants.

In early 1990, after I had been similarly contacted and subsequently had been working as a mystic channeler for two years, my Master Teacher, Saint Germain, introduced me to this trio, calling them the Master Teacher Sponsors for Europe and Africa. Before then, I knew little about El Morya and Kuthumi, but they had been introduced by Saint Germain in previous prophecies.

El Morya, the prophesied teacher of the Golden City of Gobean, works with the Blue Ray and holds the focus for the transformation of humanity's will through the experience of harmony. He is the consummate teacher, and has a timely and ordered nature. Tall and stately, his eyes are a piercing azure blue, although some esoteric texts claim they are an intense brown. Sometimes his aura crackles with currents of cobalt blue energy. Maybe that is why Helena called him her "Blue Teacher."

Kuthumi, the prophesied teacher of the Golden City of Malton, works with the Ruby Ray, and holds the focus for the renewal and fruition of the nature kingdoms in the Golden Age. Alice originally confused Kuthumi with Jesus Sananda, as their energies are very similar—soft, gentle, and loving. Years later she would write, "Everything that he told me came true and I discovered that he was not Master Jesus, as I had naturally supposed, but a Master of whom I could not possibly have heard and one who was totally unknown to me." He would appear for our teachings carrying a rabbit or a small nest full of baby birds. Sometimes his eyes changed color, reflecting the blue of the sky or the gold rays of the Sun.

Lady Nada is the prophesied teacher of the Golden City of Denasha. Previous accounts of the beautiful Lady Mistress state that she is the shortest of the Master Teachers; however, in her appearance for these teachings she was always extremely tall, stately, and graceful. Nada works with the Yellow Ray of Wisdom, but quite often her aura glows with a tint of aquamarine that carries the energies of the new Eighth Ray. Her skin is fair and her hair is golden. She holds a symbolic red rose to honor her previous teacher, and sometimes, before or after her teachings, you can detect this faint fragrance.

The beginning of this book features a set of introductory lessons from a trilogy of Spiritual Teachers who purposefully combined their energies for the teaching. When asked who should be defined as the Master Teachers, they replied, "Master K. H." This Master is well known in theosophical circles as the Mahatma Koot Hoomi, (aka Kuthumi). Apparently his identity would morph for these teachings as a trinity of energies to include the Ascended Master along with two of his trusted helpers. Originally we had not planned to include these lessons in this book, but it became apparent, after the first edit of this material, that their inclusion would be extremely helpful in understanding the teachings for Europe and Africa.

My husband, Lenard Toye, and I joined forces for the channeled works featured in this third book of channeled wisdom, teachings, and prophetic warnings. This adds a depth to this work through the metaphysical blend of both feminine and masculine energies, a spiritual theme throughout these teachings as consciousness is prepared to actualize their child, the Christ. And if you've read the I AM America Trilogy, you may have read how Len had psychic tendencies since he was a small child and had seen Earth Changes Maps—especially Europe. His ability to remotely view this map in clairaudient trance is featured in this book, and this adds vivid detail and insight regarding some of the most extreme prophecies that include possible ice age (Abrupt Climate Change) and nuclear detonations.

The Earth Changes Map for Europe, the Middle East, and Africa is known as the "Map of Exchanges," and according to its prophets, Earth is literally readied to anchor an energetic heaven on Earth. Through this celestial exchange, human consciousness furthers its potential for Ascension through the ONE and the Unity Consciousness of Unana. And the final chapters of this book include an extensive Earth Changes update from our I AM America archive. This important information focuses on global warming, with a focus on the United States and Europe. This spiritual knowledge places an emphasis on our global shift into accelerated light frequencies, the times after the Earth Changes, and the prophesied new souls who will later inhabit the New Earth.

These radical changes may be necessary to incite a spiritual rebirth and deepening that is prophesied to transform our cultures, our global politics, and above all, each and every one of us. The Spiritual Teachers remind us, yet again, that our potential for tragedy or transcendence lies in our own personal harmonization process. I leave you with this inspirational passage from Master K. H.—his invitation to join the effort for the spiritual upliftment of all:

"Let us join in wisdom to extinguish ignorance and inequity.

Let us join in love to extinguish suffering.

Let us join in service to extinguish greed and avarice.

Let us join in charity to extinguish poverty.

Let us join in harmony to extinguish disease.

As our ears are opened and our eyes begin to see,

Let us join as ONE Light in our hearts and minds."

Yours in love and service,

*Lori Toye*

# Seven Life Sources

*"The potentials and possibilities of consciousness must be finely
cultivated in order to create strength of character."*
- MASTER K. H.

*Three Master Teachers have joined forces to channel the lessons on the
Rays. The speaker for each teaching is the Ancient Tireless One. This
teacher, remaining in the Third Dimension, is a practicing physical immortalist and resides in a mountain retreat in India. He is assisted by
his servant and co-worker, a Shaman of energy movement who carries
the symbolic feather; this feather represents the sustaining power of
flight for birds and angels as the intermediary position between Source
and man. This nameless servant gives assistance for the movement of
each telepathic wave of consciousness. The information is translated
from eastern consciousness into western consciousness by the Ascended
Master Teacher Kuthumi. The trinity of these energies calls itself "K. H."*

Perhaps the first thing that we should begin to address is not
the origin of man's body, but the origin of God. Referred to as
Source in the hierarchical sense of the word, God is represented
through many personalized names throughout history. For
reference in this work, we will refer to God as Source, meaning
Light, and tarry not over idiosyncrasies that happen to match

the languages of present day biological evolution. Source is that which is untouched by chaos or worldly order, knowing within Itself, the ONE Omnipresence. In a manner of untouchability and yet union with all things, it begins to enter into congestion, pushing and pulling, waving between order and chaos. Source moves, filling and allowing space with the Omnipotent Life.

At the moment of Life, Source mirrors, and yet this mirroring is a cohesive part of the Omnipresent ONE. This Life is the bi-product of Source and the result of movement within the ONE eternal. As each wave moves, it is still obedient to the ONE that it is and becomes qualified (which is the best terminology that language can offer to express the Omnipower contained within the Source). For instance, you cannot separate a high wind from the surrounding air and yet, there is a distinctive difference between the two. The high wind arises from the essence of the surrounding air and although distinct, they are ideally known as ONE. The wind could not exist without the air to fill its being-ness, and the air does not place limitation on the movement of itself. It is simply the qualification of life through the principle of Omnipower, and this forms the basis of Life through cohesive natural law.

The next virtue of Source is appearance, and while it is the one phenomenon that perplexes the minds of humankind, it is based on simplicity. Appearance is the bi-product of order and cohesion, and deifies the pattern of the will force. Again, following the pattern of Life, quality and appearance manifesta-tions of form fill with the breath of Source, and although quite limited, still reflect the Omnipower through the display of Omniscience. From this is derived the category of thought known as science and the aim of man in this endeavor is to determine and learn from the created world about him. All forms draw their substance from the Omnipresent and Omnipotent Light, and carrying throughout them in this present scheme of worldly expression, the septenary qualities and subsequent patterns.

Throughout the world of forms, man treads the path of Light, searching for meaning in small victories and expressing a vision of the Source which created him. Knowing so little of the ONE that permeates his true essence and yet, defined in being through the indirect cause of its movement, man is qualified and filled with the movement of order. We shall pay attention to the order within the being as it too reflects the order from without, and it also aggregates and stimulates the many patterns that bring harmony and joy to those lovers of Life. Played upon seven strings, our universal order and harmony are voiced through the qualities of Seven Life Sources, known as Rays.

As we have taught in many schools before this presentation, the Seven Rays are the first place we will start. We ask that you consider them as your point of departure and the first of a mapping to understand the trail of consciousness. Consciousness follows the quality of the Ray Forces and so impresses the world of forms in which the Omnipotent overviews free will, much like a system of checks and balances. Free will is the gift to choose understanding within the perimeters of natural law. The devoted student seeks to apply the natural laws as a servant and lover of the Omnipresent ONE. It is with steadfast devotion and a love for the giver of the law, that I present again, the sevenfold aspects of creation.[1]

THE SEVEN ASPECTS OF CREATION

**Three Sacred Rays.** Each, a single Ray Force, qualify as the holy trinity of Life: Power, Love, and Wisdom.

BLUE RAY is the first qualification of Light. Ray One is seen as electrical impulse. Shattering and yet penetrating, this Ray Force is the closest to Source and reflected as the prodigal son, celebrated on its return. Standing for truth and power, this Ray carries also the essence of the destroyer with the promise of re-creation, and knows first the Will of Light and then carries forward its purpose.

PINK RAY is the second qualification. Ray Two knows only love and carries the first deification of the female or feminine aspect of creation. It is a Ray Force which attracts and attaches creation to the ONE of all, in strict contrast to Ray One which, through the course of natural law, strays and then returns. The second of the three Sacred Rays announces its arrival by the accompaniment of sound and thus rules that creation. It is the force which qualifies all music and many have come to know this Ray Force as the Light of Harmony, the tie that binds all. It is the force of the home quality and rules all families in form and always remains connected to the ONE. This connection is the vibration of love and all forms carry this quality to a lesser or greater degree.

YELLOW RAY is the third qualification. Ray Three carries the Omnipresence of illumination to creation. It assures that the substance of Light is utilized and held within the purpose of Source. This qualification is also defined as the Wisdom Ray. This Ray sheds the Light on all creations which serve purpose and connects those creations through love into the scheme held of the varying patterns through wisdom. Actively utilizing the Presence of Intelligence, Light is shed on all who create and Light is seen for all to choose accordingly. As the most active servant of the Source, it is also the taskmaster of the forces, examining and scrutinizing form into the plan of the "best and highest good," placing its hand upon the forehead and stating "So Be It."

[Editor's Note: The sequence of the numbering of the Pink Ray (Two) and the Yellow Ray (Three) can be reversed in some teachings; as in the sequence for manifesting, where the Divine Idea within the Blue Ray expands into the details of the "best and highest good" of the Yellow Ray, and then is nurtured with the magnetic force of Pink Ray of love. The sequence presented here by the Master Teacher K. H. follows the sequencing of the Rays as one is incarnating, where the Blue Ray descends first as the masculine principle, then the Pink as the feminine, and thirdly, at the time of birth, the Yellow Ray of Wisdom enters.]

**Four Servile Rays.** These Rays hold the combination of two Sacred Ray Forces, such as the Green Ray, containing Blue and Yellow; the Violet Ray, containing Blue and Pink; and the Ruby

Ray, containing Pink and Yellow. The White Ray acts like a Sacred Ray, having its own twin Ray Force.

WHITE RAY is known by many as the Ray of Purity. The teaching of the Fourth Ray is harmony achieved through conflict and is associated with creative energy. It is a Ray that is misunderstood and achieves its focus from the ability to heal and harmonize through turmoil, war, and suffering. The mystic teaching that only "pain will kill pain," opens the potential in the student to utilize this Ray Force in order to achieve bliss. One of the most challenging Ray Forces to deal with, once disciplined, Ray Four produces tremendous contributions to humanity. It governs the process of birth on planet Earth and is the Ray which carries the tone of the "Holy Comforter." "Purification through fire" yields the strongest steel, able to sustain and carry the mission of the heart.

GREEN RAY activates the intelligence of the higher consciousness and is thus known as the ruler of humanity. Its energy and teaching glistens as the star, lighting the path we follow in human form, ruling the healing arts, technology, and the sciences. Associated with the pineal gland, the Fifth Ray Force rules electromagnetics and the ability of the consciousness to travel through dimensions. "Look within and see without," as the force asks us to surrender all worldly possession, so as to find true value and worth. Then the hidden is revealed. This is the Ray Force that built the pyramids, aggregates molecules into patterns, and is referred to in teaching circles as the building force of the universe, the "grand architect." It is the sponsor of Free Masonry, most mystery schools, and higher institutions which benefit humanity, such as colleges and research hospitals. It is the Ray Force of music composition and its higher color is Indigo.

RUBY RAY is known as the Ray of Devotion. Traveling from the urgings deep within the heart, it is first felt as desire and later expresses itself as devotion to cause. This is the Ray which developed the many religions on the face of the planet and, as it is fully developed, will evolve the first group of world servers. The teaching contained within its force is vital and potent. "Hear within the great longings of the heart, letting each one play and die, now facing this new day washed and desireless, ready to serve." The Sixth Ray governs life force on this planet and rules the life force in the body. It is the Ray of Destiny that the soul treads during physical embodiment and often is misread as chance or fortune. "All things happen for a reason" is the keynote of the Sixth Ray, as it is the force that "prepares a place for us," unmistakably guiding the path we tread onward to the service of the Light. The Sixth Ray, when properly utilized, produces endless and abundant energy for he who has the ability to do and the commitment to serve.

VIOLET RAY is known as the Ray of Alchemy. It is a force that transmutes in order to achieve and, although closely related to the Fourth Ray, the Seventh Ray carries the energy of mysticism, miracles, and magic. Governing the voice, it is the Ray Force that unlocks the consciousness of sound and the power of the spoken word. "Let the voice sing and reveal the glory of the heavens. Let the heart heal and join hands with its brethren" is the key phrase to understanding the Seventh Ray. Its purpose is to empower consciousness to ask and receive, governing the art of diplomacy, world governments, and uniting the planet as a Brotherhood/Sisterhood. Often called the Violet Flame of Mercy and Forgiveness, it is able to instantly transmute, apply energy known as spiritual fire, and create a sense of sparking and crackling, much like electricity. The Seventh Ray became the overtone Ray in 1857 and now serves as the current Ray of order (influence).

[Editor's Note: To understand the dynamic of how the subtle force of a Ray overtone affects conditions and events on the planet, the overtone of the Violet Ray produced many historical events that emphasized Brotherhood, freedom, open communications among peoples, unity and the Alchemy of the sciences for the good of humanity.[2]]

## SPIRITUAL TEACHINGS CONTAINED IN EACH RAY

Follow the Rays and use them much like steps, as they each contain a spiritual teaching. For instance:

Blue Ray ............. TRUTH
Pink Ray ............. LOVE
Yellow Ray ......... WISDOM
White Ray .......... PURITY
Green Ray ........... REASON
Ruby Ray ............ DEVOTION
Violet Ray .......... FORGIVENESS

It is the nature of a spiritual teaching to yield a result, often favored by the student. For example:

TRUTH: The ability to grow strong and healthy and always able to return to the Source of All.

LOVE: Our connectedness to ourselves and the gift of life, mirrored through the wants and needs of others.

WISDOM: Experience alone is the teacher. Stay open to its gifts, as it reveals the synchronicities and joy in life.

PURITY: Stay innocent and willing to accept trial and tribulation to achieve a higher goal.

REASON: Keep all things simple and develop the highest of all human senses, common sense.

DEVOTION: Duty and responsibility reveal our inner strengths and discipline the soul for all conditions.

FORGIVENESS: The nature of grace is not meted or granted, but given to all of humanity, ensuring Brotherhood and peace.

USING THE RAY FORCES IN MEDITATION

There are many uses for the Seven Rays, such as techniques for visualization, meditation on a particular Ray Force, and the application of their exoteric use in daily living.

In the teachings of this Lodge (The Great White Light Lodge)[3], Ray Forces are always doubled, or used in combination to increase their efficacy and latent potency. "Why?" you may ask. We have noted that in the physical realm, based on the theme of duality, that the patterns of two strengthen the cause. In this instance, one Ray Force nurturing and disciplining the female side while the other Ray Force, harmonizing and assimilating the process of the male. It isn't always necessary, but recommended, to choose harmonizing Rays. For instance, Blue, Yellow, Green, and Violet Rays (One, Three, Five, and Seven) often times vibrate together effectively and Pink, White, and Ruby Rays (Two, Four, and Six) work well together. Remember, this is not a rule, only a recommendation, and highly suggested for those students who have just awakened to the path of spiritual disciplines.

To utilize Ray Forces in your daily meditation, simply visualize the color vibration associated with the Ray Force. If you are having problems with patience and tolerance, focus on the White Ray and the Ruby Ray. As always, keep it simple, as each color is qualified with the magnetic vibration assigned to it. Within five to eight days of continuous application, you will note your desired effect. Ray Forces can also be directed through prayer and for the adjustment of the group or collective consciousness. Many a time I have led group discussions, following after a full hour meditation of the Yellow and Green Rays. For the novice, having a difficult time holding mental attention on the Rays, simply find a sheet of paper or cloth of the desired color and hold it within the eye's vision. Nothing more is needed. Beads the color of the desired Ray Forces may also be held while their vibration peaks the consciousness and allows the qualities of light to perform their attributes.

Remember always that the activity of the Rays within the being must be activated throughout the day, through your conscious demonstration and activity. Consider your meditation time as the time you seed the Ray throughout your being and throughout your day. That seed must be watered, sufficiently lit, shaded, weeded, and nurtured. You are the tender of your garden. The potentials and possibilities of consciousness must be finely cultivated in order to create strength of character, a loving and open heart, and a servant, whose presence blesses the purpose of the Master and the Lodge. The seeds given in this presentation will yield the finest results.

# Ray Harmonics and Self Unity

*"The days of the guru are now ending and the spark of Life which was planted ages past has germinated into consciousness to be lead directly by the ONE Omnipresence."*
**- MASTER K. H.**

The interplay of the Rays produces a homogeneity that is conducive to biological, mental, and subsequently, spiritual development. As the Rays find themselves on the threshold of Life, quality makes its contribution to appearance, arching the Life Force, Light, from the ONE Omnipower. With the increase of Light Source, the biological and mental bodies of man, and his ability to assimilate spiritually, increases and effects evolutions of lifestreams on the planet. The continuous interplay of the Ray Forces evolves all life, from Mineral, Vegetable, Animal, and Human Kingdoms. Each Ray, accompanied by its overtone, seeks the Will of Life, conditioning the world of form to its particular quality of Light. Evolution is always tended by the careful guardianship of two Rays. One Ray expresses the male force, soul, and the overtone expresses the female source, spirit. Other Rays offer their qualities. Manifestations of form carry the interplay of the Rays. Each appearance is a combination of many Ray Forces, sounds, and conscious will. All is harmonized into purpose by the master conductors.

Third Dimension is continuously under the guidance and authorship of the male and female unions, expressing the authority of the ONE and offering fertile experience of the birthing processes. Co-creatorship unites the Source within all Life to the potential of free will. Without exception, the union of Source and free will follows this pattern:

DESIRE...caused by the interplay of the two conducting Rays.

VISUALIZATION...activated by the intelligence.

CONCEPTION...in most cases, in the world of form, activated by instinct.

GESTATION...the subservience of all Life to Divine Will.

APPEARANCE...form/forms.

COMPLETION...the free gifting of choice.

As you will note, this process of Life, quality, and appearance is ruled by the Ruby Ray Force. This Ray charges the process with the frequency required for this planetary scheme and for the particular placement of this planet in relationship to its position from the Sun. As male and female forces unite in the Co-creation processes, the influences of other qualities of force play their roles after the inception of choice. These forces find their ways from the solar source, arching throughout the planetary schemes, and filling appearance with their delightful, unique, and useful personality. Individuality unites then with the forces of the Rays, arching their qualities from the planets identified with our consciousness.

MARS ................Ruby Ray

JUPITER .............Pink Ray

VENUS ...............Green Ray

SATURN.............Yellow Ray

MERCURY..........White Ray

URANUS ............Blue Ray

MOON ................Violet Ray

NEPTUNE ..........Pink Ray

SUN....................Blue Ray

PLUTO ...............White Ray (overtoned by the Violet Ray)

## ASTROLOGY AND RAY FORCES

Each Ray Force finds its path to the Earth and mirrors from the planet the Ray Force qualities to the individual. Again, the refraction of the Ray Force subtly overtones the personality with the qualification from the refracting planet and pronounces certain qualities inherent, which do align with current Astrology. The science of the interplay of Ray Forces on our planet is known as Astrology and our current system is adapted from the Chaldean Method, brought to our planetary scheme from the Dahl Universe. [Editor's Note: The Dahl Universe is a galactic star cluster that is said to exist beyond the Pleiades, approximately 415 light years away.] Taught by these wise and loving teachers of truth, the people who inhabited the valley among the Tigris and Euphrates Rivers perfected and modeled the first science into the application we utilize today. It is a science which has seen several evolutions, as always, flowing through the consciousness which it naturally serves.

[Editor's Note: Astrology is one of the oldest sciences known to humanity and there is evidence of its influence in every religion of the world. The word "zodiac" is derived from the Greek word, *zodiakos*, which means a circle of animals. The Chaldeans, Phoenicians, Egyptians, Persians, Hindus, and Chinese all had zodiacs that were much alike. There is also evidence that the Central and North American Indians had an understanding of the zodiac. Astrology is estimated to be over five million years old and originated from Atlantean and possibly Lemurian civilizations. The Ancients saw the zodiac as a means to define each crucial stage in man's evolution, recognizing all life as being in various stages of becoming: humans evolving to planets, planets to solar systems, solar systems to cosmic chains. One stage between the solar system and the cosmic chain was called the zodiac and was seen as the solar system breaking up into a zodiac.]

Blue Ray.........Leo and Aquarius
Pink Ray.........Sagittarius and Pisces
Yellow Ray......Capricorn
White Ray.......Gemini, Virgo, and Scorpio
Green Ray ......Taurus and Libra
Ruby Ray........Aries
Violet Ray.......Cancer (Scorpio overtone)

## THE SACRED RAYS

Blue Ray: *Leo* represents the return of the son. *Aquarius* represents the departure, or journeying Ray Force.
Pink Ray: *Sagittarius* represents the love of home and family.

*Pisces* represents the feminine love, always attached to the Source.

Yellow Ray: *Capricorn* represents the student and the teacher, the force of authority in all plans. It is an examining and scrutinizing force, often misidentified with the Law of Karma, and best known as the taskmaster of the forces.


THE SERVILE RAYS


White Ray: *Gemini* represents purity through fire, (achieved through duality). *Scorpio* represents the creative energy of the Ray Force. *Virgo* represents the discipline and order as the bridge to harmony.

Green Ray: *Taurus* represents the green portion of this Ray Force, offering the Mastery of worldly possession, through the assessment, attainment, and surrender of all worldly forms. *Libra* represents the human dynamic in all sciences and identifies with the healing force achieved when practiced with higher consciousness and common sense.

Ruby Ray: *Aries* represents the individualization of consciousness to the planet in all things as streaming from the Source of All, the I AM. Because all Life on the planet Earth contains this Ray Force, the presence of Aries personifies the planting of the spark of Life in all expressions in the world of form.

Violet Ray: *Cancer* represents the mysticism of the Seventh Ray Force, personifying the gifts of receivership through inner connection with Source. The overtone of the Seventh Ray presents itself in the Scorpio personality, achieving Mastery of the Law of Transmutation and the Laws of Forgiveness, Mercy, and Compassion.

## "KNOW FIRST THYSELF"

In exploring the guardian forces of the individual, the student first begins to understand his or her place in the Universe, the plan in which each and everything is an active part. In the roles that all are playing, each part plays an integral part, not one of them insignificant. It is the duty of the student to listen to the urgings within, noting the rhythm and cause, and to follow with appropriate action. Living in a time of turbulent change, it is important to keep both feet planted firmly on the path, ready and willing for the movement to serve the plan when it is required.

Harmony with soul and spirit results in a healthy body and a useful mind. These are the natural traits of the student of the Lodge, held through the efforts and activity of the student, and based on the teachings of the Master. In the past, students were held in the watchful gaze of the Master Teacher and much of their movement was guided and held within the magnanimous electromagnetic pulse of the teacher's own force.[4] This was done in large part to insure the purity of evolution at critical times and fulfilled the need at that particular point of expansion. However as time moves needs change, and humanity has reached that point of emergent evolution that requires sovereign experience, personal choice, and responsibility. Feeding a starving man is an act of compassion. Teaching him how to grow his own food and prepare it himself is a contribution to the greater ONE and unites his sense of dignity, self worth, and honor.

The days of the guru are now ending and the spark of Life which was planted ages past has germinated into consciousness to be lead directly by the ONE Omnipresence, which guides and directs all Life. It is always held within the heart of the teacher that each word will find an opening in the students' ears, eyes, and hearts, intentionally seeding a new strain of thought or fertilizing an old one. Personal experience is now the teacher and guide which all must follow to tend and enjoy the Garden, and this places the tools in the hands of each one to utilize and properly employ.

The first of these tools is knowledge, and as said by my own Master Teacher, "Know first thyself." We will not spend time on scrutinous self examinations, our failings and weaknesses; however, we will explore ourselves by considering Omniscience, our True Being, the nature of its force, and its positing and gift to Life. The science of self knowledge is founded on three principles contained in all schools dedicated to ageless wisdom: To Do, To Dare, and To Be Silent.

Experience prepares one for many challenges on the path. Accept each challenge with the love, the enthusiasm, and the openness with which you accepted your first Master Teacher. Laugh at the harmless, work with the strength of ten, and take time to rest. It is the balance of these three principles that prepares and works the consciousness with the seeds of truth. Let the Tree of Truth grow throughout humanity, providing shade on warm days, ample fruit at harvest, and be strong enough to survive the highest of winds and coldest of seasons.

Unifying the self through the teaching of the Rays requires more than the words you are about to read. It requires the wisdom attained through a selfless desire and motivation to serve a greater good. Following this light, the self emerges as a collective group, each portion of self now identified, seasoned, and conditioned for world service. Let each of these facts awaken your slumbering counterparts. Condition, prepare, and attend to them, if you will.

## THE FEMININE GUARDIAN RAY: VENUS

We will begin with the female or feminine energy of the self. The Ray of Appearance is the first Ray that enters the physical dimension upon embodiment. Cloaking the manifestation of the Divine Spark, the arch of the Ray of Appearance is carried from the planet Venus[5] and imbues the character with certain personality traits. Located on the left side of the physical form, it twists along the Golden Thread Axis and forms one half of what is called, and now known from prior teachings, the Kundalini. [Editor's Note: Also known as the Vertical Current, the emanation of the Divine Spark connecting to the central core of this planet.] The determination of the Ray Force is chosen before the descent into matter and on the first breath after birth, the Ray current is activated.

Current tabulations, provided by an accurate ephemeris, determine the zodiacal sign in which Venus is overshadowed in that moment. For example, if the birth occurs with the Venus emanation overshadowed by Aries, the Ruby Ray (Six) is the feminine or personality Ray of that self. If the birth (or better stated, first breath) occurs with the Venus emanation overshadowed by Taurus, the Green Ray (Five) is the Personality Ray. The table is as follows, if the Venus is overshadowed by:

Aries.................Ruby Ray (Six)
Libra.................Green Ray (Five)
Taurus .............Green Ray (Five)
Scorpio ............White Ray (Four)*
Gemini .............White Ray (Four)
Sagittarius.......Pink Ray (Two)
Cancer..............Violet Ray (Seven)
Capricorn ........Yellow Ray (Three)
Leo ...................Blue Ray (One)
Aquarius..........Blue Ray (One)
Virgo................White Ray (Four)
Pisces ...............Pink Ray (Two)
*overshadowed by Violet Ray (Seven)


## YOUR BODY, EMOTIONS, AND INSTINCTS

The Personality Ray cloaks the Divine Being during its incarnation on Earth, ensuring protection of the monadic spark and attracting thereafter, the necessary Rays to build the proper form, the body. This is a body that suits the tasks required of the soul incarnating, the path of the soul force, and the lessons it chooses to complete during the Earth sojourn. The Ray qualities that determine the body also determine aspects such as physical and emotional health, intelligence, ability to assimilate attributes from other Kingdoms (Elemental, Mineral, Vegetable, and Animal), and the electromagnetic force surrounding the system and it's ability to attract or repel. As the Personality Ray rules the form aspect itself, its presence is temporary and held for the term of the incarnation. Its Ray vibration aligns to the energies of the soul force, developing its latent qualities, utilizing its strengths, and always complementing and assisting its mission.

Since the nature of the personality is feminine, it rules such matters, overshadowing the personality with the qualities of the Ray birthing its form: the physical body and it's attributes, such as hair and eye color; the instinctive nature of the person; the ability to utilize and integrate intuition and intelligence; the emotional force of the body; the ability to sense and feel, ruling responses according to the qualities of the Ray Force.[6] The Personality Ray rules both the Law of Attraction and the Law of Repulsion. This gives the incarnating person tremendous and ample opportunity to bring forward the lessons needed in the service of life. The Personality Ray rules all aspects of the form, including the astral body and assists the soul force in the ascent of matter after the close of the physical embodiment. Incarnation is the process of the Personality Ray cloaking Divine Form and ends with the return of the breath into the ONE.

It can be readily said and observed that the Personality Ray rules all senses, from the tactile ability to grasp, or touch, smell, taste, hear, and see, to the compelling senses that attract or repel such feelings/emotions as anger, lust, passion, and joy. Moreover, those subtle senses that integrate intelligence through the intuition, such as memory, déjà vu, precognizance, and psychic experience are also ruled by the Personality Ray. The Personality Ray Force, through the previous animal experience, rules instincts such as protection, survival, the ability to nest and procreate (in higher forms family and home) and territorial instincts, which determine the degree and amount of war and violence induced on a society. It is said the time that humanity is experiencing now is one of the most violent; however, it is a time that the aspects of the Personality Ray are most pronounced.

"Energy goes where attention flows," is a concept that must be heeded while traveling the path. Societies are no exception. Societies that continuously guide energy into competitiveness awaken the animal nature of the form that has long dropped into a conscious slumber, and if over utilized, this force inhibits the finer qualities of integrating intelligence. The results? Violence, self-destructiveness, degradation of the home and upcoming generations. The solution is based on the flow of energy returning to the assimilation process, which integrates the instinct with intelligence. This requires the bridge known as the intuition and you will note that during the healing of any person or society, the intuitive experience is quite noticeable. It is always the sign of an ensuing Age of Peace, when a society accepts the intuitive arts as essential and normal and welcomes their presence into accepted practice.

## THE LAW OF INVOLUTION

The Personality Ray, thusly, rules this process in the individual: Instinct + Intuition = Active Intelligence, known as the Law of Involution. The success of this process is overshadowed by the qualities of the Ray Force. For instance, a Ray Four (White) personality will walk a distinctly different path to union than that of the Ray Six (Ruby) personality. Please understand that while the union is Omnipotent and essentially Omniscience, they differ in appearance and their return to the ONE is distinctive and individually poignant. Ray Four achieves union through a sense of ruling the creative force. Therefore, its personal path to union may be described as forces uniting to achieve, each force experienced, explored, and Mastered, resulting in a contrast of experience, brilliant and appearing chaotic. However, on completion, a synergy of experience produces harmony and the creative forces yield art, music, literary works, plans and schemes of a greater good, all of which are synergistically activated to serve all members of the Lodge.

Ray Six, follows a path colored with earnest devotion. Finding a strength in numbers, it seeks first to unite through cause, then protects and hides the cause from destruction of the union it has created to bring it forward. We find the Sixth Ray ruling many world religions, world governments and organizations. As the hidden cause is slowly revealed through outer experience, sincerity, purity, and devotion evolve the presence of cause. Soon the needless falls away, leaving only the glowing ember of the fire to serve the fire of desireless devotion.

# The Soul Ray of Purpose

*"Only the soul can rule its own life force and
stabilize its own creations."*
**- MASTER K. H.**

Masculine energy rules the appearance of the Soul Ray. It is
the determining factor for an individual on our planet according
to the position of Mars at the time of birth. The Soul Ray rules
purpose and will. As each occult student knows that only the
Omnipotent Source of All rules and guides the will. We refer to
will in the context of incarnation. The Soul Ray rules the life
force within the body, arching energy currents in the direction and with the force required for all subsequent guardians
to interchange and interplay. This allows biological functions
to begin. It becomes the leading force of the appearance, and
sometimes quiet and unnoticed in its reign, directs the energy
of the Monad to serve the plan, to align to the will of God.

## AGES SEVEN THROUGH TWENTY-TWO

The ruling energy of soul keeps most of its leadership roles confined to biological and systematic life until the age of seven, when the child announces sovereign status and begins the steps of its individual journey. Entrusted with the plan, the soul knows and enacts the purpose of all life, directing and guiding the child through the many lessons, perils, and schemes that this schoolhouse provides. Around the age of eleven to fourteen, the awakening occurs, signifying specific biological functions through the Personality Ray, and initiating a pattern which the soul will follow throughout its sojourn on the planet. From the ages fourteen to eighteen, the years of initiation ensue, and the being begins to integrate the great plan of Life he or she must follow. By the twenty-second year, transfiguration occurs. The soul is ready to stand to meet the world and places the plan into the world of forms, utilizing all the attributes of the Personality Ray.

During the period of transfiguration, the soul activates the power of the Monad, and pulsing to optimum capacity (according to the evolution of the soul and its integration with the Personality or feminine Ray) distributes the solar Ray which overshadows it (determined again, at breath of birth). Dispensing a series of waves throughout the Earth Plane, each wave is activated throughout the incarnation of the soul, by the soul. Only the soul recognizes the harmony, synchronism, and sattva (the harmonious response to vibration) required to unlock its life force. There are no exceptions to this rule. Only the soul can rule its own life force and stabilize its own creations.

## THE RISE OF THE SPIRITUAL BEING

From the twenty-eighth to the thirty-second year, the ascent of the wave and the rise of its purpose is clearly seen by the individual and through union of the guardian Rays, the rise of the spiritual being begins. By the thirty-third year, as the union increases in potency and clarity, the Soul Ray clearly shines, revealing its leadership, gentleness, and attention to the life it serves. [Editor's Note: It is said that Jesus Sananda ascended on his thirty-third year, called a Master Year[7]] This cycle repeats throughout the term of incarnation, although less extreme, due to the continuous integration of the male and female Rays activated in the lifestream. Let me tabulate these stages for your knowledge:

| AGE | KEYNOTE | PURPOSE |
| --- | --- | --- |
| 7 | Individualization | Energy becomes sovereign and in service to the plan it serves. |
| 14-18 | Initiation | The individual begins to Master the force of the guardian and group Rays, the resulting energy, learning and assimilating the great plan. |

| AGE | KEYNOTE | PURPOSE |
|---|---|---|
| 22 | Transfiguation | Activation of the Monad through the solar Ray emits the waves that only the soul can retrieve, unlock, and utilize. |
| | | This emission occurs several times during the incarnation; however, the first carrying the greatest impact (as it carries the life purpose of the solar Ray), subsequent emissions supporting that first great emanation. |
| 29-32 | Ascension | The ascent of the first wave emitted, the soul learns the value of that which it creates in the world of forms. The ascent of the cresting wave generally runs for four years. |

| AGE | KEYNOTE | PURPOSE |
|-----|---------|---------|
| 33 | Union | The integration of the guardian Rays is seen for the first time, throughout the incarnation. The individual can now draw on the marriage of the female and the male forces, allowing for the gentle leadership of the male and the nurturing support of the female. |

The Soul Ray leads the first cycle of the soul's purpose, and on completion of the thirty-third year, finds at its side, the harmonious presence of the Personality Ray. Until that moment, their awareness of one another is limited, as the urgings of the body and outer forms are sometimes in stark contrast to the plan and leadership of the soul. Up to the ascent of union, many individuals fall by the side, choosing to union in the less denser fields of created realities, for example, the astral and the devachan (the ideal heaven state). Perhaps the sattva of their soul will find another opportunity to descend into the world of forms. It is true that only the strongest of steel will temper its consciousness in the world of dual senses. "It was never promised to be easy," my Dear teacher would often remind me. I pass these words to you. Hold them and know.

[Editor's Note: The devachan, also known as Summerland, is where the karma (of evil) steps aside for the time being and the karma of good (dharma) is manifested. Each desire quickly manifests its hopeful, optimistic side. In this heaven of our dreams, there are magnificent mountains, lakes, gardens, and thought-forms suited to our individual concepts of Paradise.]

## THE SIDEREAL YEAR

The relationship of the Soul Ray serves the greater plan of the planetary schemes, riding a greater wave which serves the Divine Plan. The idea of race comes from the concept of Rays, in the plural sense, as each race fulfills the appearance and purpose of the Rays in guardianship. A race rules the incoming guardianships for approximately 25,000 years, known as a sidereal year. Each race evolves the appearance of life, and often quite drastic in the servile planets. [Editor's Note: Earth is known as a servile planet, allowing itself to be utilized for evolving lifestreams. Sacred planets contain only the qualities of one Ray Force and appearance limits to that Ray quality. Servile planets arch Ray Forces according to the dispensations of the sacred planets.] Presently, on the Earth, evolving lifestreams of humanity have experienced three sidereal years, each serving a combination of Ray Forces.

Sidereal Year One.....Lemuria....Blue Ray
Sidereal Year Two....Atlantis.....Pink Ray, Overtone, Ruby Ray
Sidereal Year Three...Aryan.......Green Ray, Overtone, Pink Ray

Inasmuch as each sidereal year is directed by certain Ray Forces, the Soul Ray directs the energy of the embodiment, orchestrating the group, or better known as Servile Rays, into a harmony with the planetary Rays. The Father Rays appear with the qualities of protection and leadership. Their ability to conduct the group to serve the plan of "the best and highest good," best describes the presence of the Soul Ray.

The Soul Ray of the individual is overshadowed by the time of birth, focusing the qualities of a particular Ray into the leadership role and demonstrating the qualities it carries. For instance, BLUE RAY souls are often found in careers that require investigation and limitless energy. Here we find many of our researchers and scientific leaders. PINK RAY souls are leaders of the Source and we find many teachers and caretakers of incoming generations of all life, mineral, vegetable, animal, and human. YELLOW RAY weaves intelligence into a plan that can be utilized. Here we find many philosophers, writers, and keepers of wisdom. WHITE RAY finds a leadership role creating harmony and beauty. Politicians, artists, and entertainers focus the qualities of the Soul Ray through its arc. GREEN RAY blends the knowledge of the Yellow Ray with the purpose of the Blue Ray, producing leadership between medicine and health and displaying always a "common sense" that serves humanity's body, mind, and spirit. RUBY RAY produces the leaders of social and religious causes. As devoted servants, they ensure the protection of the masses, sometimes at great personal sacrifice. VIOLET RAY of Alchemy produces the leaders and lovers of peace. Here we find leadership in diplomacy and the ability to utilize ceremony for sacred means. It is the Ray of the mystic leader, the miracle worker who has gained wisdom from the unseen depths.

Let us close by stating that the Soul Ray carries the potency of the heavens and anchors that plan through its marriage to form, leading, guiding, and directing the servant to the sacred, unbound, and ever-present Truth.

# *Mastering Your Ray Chart*

*"Moving from the un-conscious to the ONE-conscious requires steadfast devotion to the love that flows from heart to heart."*
**- MASTER K. H.**

As you begin to Master the energy of your personality (feminine) and soul (masculine), you may want to identify and Master the Rays which arc from other planets. These Rays are known as the group Ray Force, and although servile in their presence, they help to identify the focus and attention of the embodiment. The Sacred Rays of spirit and soul stay throughout the incarnation, and in most cases, the Soul Ray never strays while attention is placed in the Earthly schoolroom. Should the Ray Force change qualities, the Ray evolves, and in this case, attracts the qualities of another Ray Force, blends those qualities, and emerges as a new Ray Force altogether. For instance: Blue Ray attracts Pink Ray, for purposes only the individual could reveal, and soon the Blue Ray soul is now considered a Violet Ray individual. Simply, here is the table:

Blue Ray + Pink Ray = Violet Ray
Blue Ray + Yellow Ray = Green Ray
Pink Ray + Yelllow Ray = Ruby Ray

Computation of the group will help to determine the evolution of the soul, as well as providing direction for the individual and their service in the Lodge. First, addressing the astrological chart, find the corresponding planets, in the same manner that the location of Venus and Mars is computed. Using the table:

Aries......................Ruby
Libra......................Green
Taurus..................Green
Scorpio................White*
Gemini ................White
Sagittarius ..........Pink
Cancer.................Violet
Capricorn............Yellow
Leo.......................Blue
Aquarius .............Blue
Virgo ...................White
Pisces ..................Pink
*overshadowed by Violet Ray

Place now in position the planets from the astrological chart. In this case, we will use a student's chart for example:

SACRED RAYS:
Venus/Virgo...........White Ray
Mars/Virgo.............White Ray

SERVILE RAYS:

Sun/Virgo ........................... White Ray
Moon/Leo .......................... Blue Ray
Mercury/Virgo ................. White Ray
Jupiter/Sagittarius .......... Pink Ray
Saturn/Scorpio ................. White Ray and Violet Ray
Uranus/Sagittarius .......... Pink Ray
Neptune/Sagittarius ........ Pink Ray
Pluto/Libra ....................... Green Ray

As you will note, there are eight Rays which form the group and center themselves in the center of the Heart Chakra and are known as the Eight-Sided Cell of Perfection. In this particular group chart, you will note that the Ray from Saturn is overshadowed by another Ray (Violet). It is included for interpretative purposes, although the two Rays intertwine, forming one homogeneous Ray, which seeds itself into the heart.

Interpreting this chart is quite easy. In looking at the focus of the group, we see the Omnipresence of the White Ray, which through no coincidence, follows the leadership of the Sacred Rays, both defined as Ray Four. This is a student, brought to bring the purity of service, perhaps working as a bridge among those who do not completely understand the mission of the Lodge, but will respond to someone with an open heart and deep sincerity, which is emanated through the Pink Ray. This student will bring pure service to the planet in the form of caretaking one or several of the kingdoms of Earth, most likely choosing a career in the White Ray. This service of caring for the planetary kingdoms is expressed politically, artistically, or through the field of entertainment. This group also benefits from the focused attention of Blue Ray, adding will and the ability to work untiringly, and as it is over-toned by the Violet Ray, giving the grace to function in public. The Sacred Rays, arcing the qualities of the White Ray, give added attention and leadership typical of the Fourth Ray servant.

## THE STUDENT'S CHOICE

It is important to understand, that while tendencies and qualities may be defined with stunning accuracy for the student on the path, once a Mastery of the Ray Forces is achieved, it is the choice of the student to use the forces for good or for bad. The Third Dimension is a plane of dual forces and, as it is stated from the Great Masters of Wisdom, "When the Light appears, the dark attracts." The leadership of the soul, expressing itself through the septenary qualities, must keep the focus and attention on the group force, as well as the needs of the Lodge, in bringing forth the perfect service to the Earth Plane and Planet. The personality, or form characteristics, find their service in complementing the soul through the spark of spirit and allow the soul an ease of manifestation, duty, and clarity.

It is important to understand how easily Light may cloud or slip into darkness once choice develops. The contrary sides of the leadership of the soul are mentioned in the following only to warn and assist the student in their endeavors for the Lodge, seeking only "the best and the highest good," and keeping their feet firmly on the path of Light.

Be quiet and be still earnest seeker, for the path can be paved with deception and distraction. Know thyself well and the Light of God will Never Fail.

## THE CONTRARY FORCE OF THE RAYS

BLUE RAY: Appearance (manifestation) without qualification or energy output. The leader Ghandi taught that all who ate must also work and that work was described as "bread fare." In other words, work produced a good or a product; it was not merely the result of mind or intellect. In the times humanity is now experiencing, little attention is given to the idea of adding value to anything; rather, we simply hold on to or pass something on until it has increased in value and a profit can be seen. Welfare and government handout programs bankrupt societies that contain good and able-bodied persons, whose self-esteem would rise through their own "work value." Getting rich quick does not solve the problems, unless you are willing to place a value on your own energy and your own ability to work. Beware of the promises of quick and easy wealth, which require little of your energy, effort, and labor.

[Editor's Note: Mohanda Karamchand Gandhi (1869-1948) was known as the Mahatma, great soul, who brought about India's emancipation in the 1940's. For Gandhi, bread-labor is a minimum physical labor which must be performed by everyone. This is a service to others, providing a living and self-actualization. Gandhi also taught that purposely avoiding rough work in order to practice more easy-going occupations created unbalances that crush the weak with overwork. His solutions taught that five to ten percent of our time, devoted to less desirable forms of work, promoted equity among all peoples and opened our hearts to hold compassion for people of all economic states.]

The contrary Blue Ray Force produces inflation, gambling, greed, and inevitably a poverty that all humanity share in. Assimilating and integrating the Blue Ray Force allows the individual to work with endless, fearless energy, always producing something of value to the world of appearances. In the world of leadership, the Soul Blue Ray Forces evolve through the natural laws, new discoveries, products, and inventions that are good for all evolving and incoming generations. In the Personality-assimilated Blue Ray Force gives us the energy to work at all things, small and great, achieving always a satisfaction in a "hard day's work."

PINK RAY: Taking pleasure from life without a conscience. Pink Ray Force is the quality that caretakes and understands that all creations require love and deep caring. Its contrary side shows no concern for life, the inability to assimilate and integrate love, and a failing to consider wastefulness or possible degradation when taking pleasure. The pollution of today's environment shows the reverse of the Pink Ray Force, when societies are unwilling to protect or caretake environments, deemed by those who previously harvested a benefit not to be cost effective. Wake up and stay close to your Source! Someday the world will not even be a fit place to live if you continue on this path. Wake up and love, not for what love will give you, but for what love is, the continuous quality that considers and cares for all kingdoms of Creation.

YELLOW RAY: Intelligence without wisdom. The contrary force of Yellow Ray is an active mind that does not walk the words it talks. If there is no experience to combine with the small amount of knowledge the brain has gained, the character of wisdom fails to appear. "A little knowledge may be a dangerous thing," the Master of Wisdom teaches, "but he who has achieved wisdom has used his knowledge with his hands." The Master Teacher Jesus Sananda always reminded his students to observe the fruits that a tree would bare.[8] A Hopi Indian saying, "Does it grow corn?" is another example that the force of Yellow Ray must be utilized to light a path with useful experience. Weave your intelligence into a cloth to cover your body, wash the face of a child, or shade your head from summer's heat, warm it during winter's nights.

WHITE RAY: Attraction and attention without morality. In the twentieth century, mankind has perfected the statement that the "squeakiest wheel gets the grease." The contrary White Ray Force finds itself in constant motion, achieving very little of the harmony and creative force that it qualifies. The gathering of the White Ray requires that attention is first given to the three Sacred Rays, as their use is intended for the service of the planet. The development of the conscience, or shall we call it, the ability to make a sacred choice built upon the development of consciousness, is held by the White Ray. The White Ray holds for humanity the ability for each student to decide moral qualities based upon their inner development of truth, love, and wisdom.

The light that shines forth and is seen in the eye of the earnest seeker of truth is often the purity of the White Ray, which qualifies the three Sacred Rays into creative innocence. "Be as little children," the Master Teacher has commanded, wherein his intention is to offer that seeker innocence, not childish innocence. The inversion of this Ray Force manifests itself in constant attention-seeking, small vanities, and approval of others only for the sound of applause. Ask if you should question your conscience. "Do my words and actions open eyes and ears to the sacred teachings without injure or intentional offense to others?" The White Quality Ray Force is intended to blend creation, not to separate it for private gain.

GREEN RAY: Science without Omniscience. Science and technology are given to humanity to ease burdens and assist in its spiritual development. When it is used for financial gain and business purposes, the inversion of the Green Ray Force often turns against men and women, creating impossible choices, and horrid, often incurable diseases, the worst of which is the disease of greed. Greed is rooted in holding or leveraging energy for only a select few, or to separate energy from the flow of the universe and slating it only for self-purpose. There is no-one or no-thing that does not find its breath rooted in the Great Cause and purpose of the universe. Omniscience is the presence and purpose of God Source in all things, reflected and mirrored in the fifth quality to serve humanity, to heal all burdens great and small. All technology and science come from this Source and is meant for all to use and enjoy.

When the abundant gifts of the universe are held in one selfish hand, the flow diminishes and all suffer the consequences. The natural resources created on this planet, such as pure water, clean air, and sunlight were intended for all to enjoy, but man-made technological advances that meter these agents for humanity's use, are only inverse uses of the Green Ray quality.

The science of healing is a sacred art meant to be a service to humanity and carries the Omniscience of tomorrow. When this sacred art becomes a business, it shuts doors to tomorrow and to many generations to come. "Think with your soul and not your head," my Master Teacher would often remark. "Gather the light of the four Rays, as fruits that laden the cloth of the feast. Gather the fruits and feed humanity. Do not hoard and store, for another season comes. Gather the light of the four Rays, not as beneath your feet and in servitude to the little self who cries upon its death. Reach above your sight, beyond your sound, and deep into your bloodless heart and there is the place that you may serve through the Green Ray Force."

RUBY RAY: Service without sacrifice. This is a parable: A man who held much wealth was asked to perform the greatest of services for his Lodge. It was an honor to be asked and he had been chosen for his ability to manage and handle the resources he had acquired. Upon completion of this task, it was made clear to him that he would advance along the path and gain a new understanding of life. Before the wealthy man performed the task, he became lost in countless decisions surrounding his empire. Who would handle his livestock, take care of his children, and make sure his money was invested wisely while he was away. He wrote his concerns on a piece of paper and went to his teacher for the answers. The wise teacher was silent as the wealthy man addressed his concerns and when he was finished reading the list, the teacher replied, "Go home and run your household, you are not ready." The man, now shocked by the answer, replied, "But wouldn't you ask? Wouldn't you want to be responsible for your children and your business?" The teacher replied, "Those you were given to prepare you for this moment. Were you ever asked to abandon either? When you can come without question, worry, or doubt, you are ready. Come then with a heart tempered by choice and ready to serve the causeless cause."

VIOLET RAY: Politics without diplomacy. The Age of Cooperation is nearing and the age of competitiveness is soon to close. Of all the Rays present for humanity's use, the Violet Ray has been inverted the most, its contrary force causing much of the war and violence on the planet Earth. [Editor's Note: Since the overtone of the Violet Ray in 1857, the world has experienced two World Wars and the United States has been involved in seven wars since this overtone influence.] Known as the Transmuting Ray, when its qualities are misused, the selfish and little will plays aloud, cornering and captivating economies and social structures into a competitive, violent game. The Age of Brotherhood is built on the principle of cooperation, which guides the greater will of humanity. Diplomacy holds within its grasp the ability to save both civilization and humanity, although at times it would appear only one could survive. How does the student of the path apply diplomacy and Brotherhood without forming political groups? Develop a solution-based conscience that only seeks for all to win and none to lose. Realize that ALL can share in the experience of abundance, and seek that first through your own inner harmony. Your Brother or Sister is clearly your equal. Would you not want the same for yourself?

Moving from the un-conscious to the ONE-conscious requires steadfast devotion to the love that flows from heart to heart. As you have begun to understand that all life flows from ONE Omnipotent Source, you can example this knowledge through daily demonstration. As we asked before, can you separate the wind from the air? It is doubtful that you practically can, but you have isolated the wind through your consciousness. To heal the sickness of non-assimilation of the peaceful, loving Violet Ray, merge the wind back into the air. Discover a sky which holds clouds, birds that fly, and thousands of pollens for colorful flowers. Those kingdoms co-exist inside of you and yet you do not realize them!

I shall close by again reminding all students of this Lodge that the last of the septenary qualities holds the vibration that binds all individuals into groups. Six rods tied together are always infinitely stronger than one. That one rod can snap with a sudden twist and bend in the wind, but the six gathered as one are strong and prepared to weather many conditions in the game of life. [Editor's Note: The Great Seal of the United States contains this spiritual teaching, symbolized through the eagle that holds 13 arrows in its left talons.] Use your group influence to focus energy into the healing of the nations. "Let purpose guide the little wills of men." May that purpose serve the greater good of all humanity. OM SHEAHAH (I AM as ONE).

# The Embodiment and Unfoldment of Incarnation

*"The threefold activity of Power, Love, and Wisdom, are used to begin the incarnation process."*
**- MASTER K. H.**

The first descent of matter into form is at first a lengthy process, which involves many experiences with group soul forces, moving the consciousness through the Elemental, Mineral, Vegetable, and Animal Kingdoms. When the soul reaches the first stage of individualization[9], the group soul force withdraws and the soul evolves into the HU-man. In this chapter, we will discuss thoroughly the HU-man incarnation process and the harmony of Ray Forces required in this magnificent interplay.

When you were a small child, do you remember how long the days would be? You would awaken in the morning, live out an entire morning, take your nap, and then live out, again, an entire afternoon. From the perception of the child, each day seemed like a week. Now, with the perception of an adult, each day resembles a second. How is it that time can alter its affect upon our mind? Time is simply the measuring tool we use to perceptibly measure our length of experience, which is judged by our consciousness as either good or bad. When we were small children, we had little experience to compare with, our consciousness fresh and alive with innocence and wonder. As an adult, we have obtained the temperament created by the many attitudes obtained from our consciousness judging our experience.

When we view the time spent in the physical realm at the close of the embodiment, we have many experiences, some more prevailing to our perception and locked into our memories and some that are faint to our perception and lost to our memory. When the universe perceives time, again, since it retains memory with the Omniscience of the ONE Source, the memory is perfect and every memory, great and small, is stored in the record of time waves. In the physical dimension, each of these time waves carries the record of the experience in vibration and Light, which understand and perceive each experience, not as good or bad, but for the energy each action carries and the effect from that action. When viewing the universe like this, the student begins to understand that each incarnation is much like a day to the child; twenty to thirty incarnations, moving the soul swiftly along the path of Light, aided by the gentle murmur of pulsing time waves.

If we are to follow the understanding of human incarnation like a day in the life of a small child, those students who are now experiencing the slow and tedious physical dimension, akin it much to the child's morning. It is at that break at noon, after lunch and a hard morning of outside play, that the soul naps, dropping the physical body. The death of the physical body, which we have feared with our adult-like grip, is nothing more than taking off our shoes and muddied shirts for a brief nap and we awaken refreshed and ready for the rest of the day.

We resume our play in the Divine Circle of descent and ascent of matter, and fill the early afternoon again with more play, re-clothed again this time in the Emotional, or Astral Body. It is in this time that we release the fervor of our desires and, no longer bound by the need of food and tedious care of the physical body, enjoy the full scope of the astral playtime. We are able to choose our experiences without the tedious temperament demanding bad for all of good experiences, and we use our time for good only, or again, at least that which we perceive to be "good." As all children, who stay too long at a party or eat too much sweet candy, we tire again and become restless. Soon, mid-afternoon requires again a change of clothes, and the soul drops the Astral Body for the Mental Body.

In the Mental Body, the soul is freed again, no longer bound by the need of either good or bad, but is allowed the time to develop the interests which so captivated the play time. It is the time of study, reading, contemplating and meditating with the wonders of creation. During this time of incarnation, the soul gains knowledge for the sake of wisdom, which will assist again a new day with a fresh pair of clothes for morning play. During the incarnation process, the soul spends the longest time in the mental body, absorbing from the ONE universal Source all that is necessary to fulfill the natural interests, intellect, and knowledge that the soul can magnetize. Soon the day must close, and the child, weary from his sojourn in the worlds of created forms, bathes the body for the final time and lays it to rest for the warmth of secure blankets and a good night's rest.

Upon the laying down of the Mental Body, the soul finds itself cradled in the arms of Source in the tender love of the Causal Body. Since this is the body of individuality, the cycle of the descent and ascent of matter is now complete. The soul now rests in the divine, the ONE, the unclothed and unknowable, until such time that it is urged to awaken again to form. That time is determined only by the ONE which is known and served.

And so the soul, which so sought individualization, seeks form through desire and experiences that form much like the playful and sometimes dreadfully long day of a child. Each successive day tempers the child into an adolescent, and onward into a young adult. Soon the child of God wants to Master the purpose of creation. It is for those who seek this Mastery with the intent of service to the ONE Source that we reveal these teachings. Use them, if you will, for the good of humanity and lift another of your Brothers and Sisters to the path of light and the love that is and awaits us all. I will tabulate the following for your understanding:

Physical Embodiment = POWER
Astral Embodiment = LOVE
Mental Embodiment = WISDOM

As you can see, it is the threefold theme which holds the pattern for all incarnations of evolving Life from the Great Central Sun. The theme of Love, Wisdom, and Power is ever-present throughout all experience in all dimensions of appearance; however, they are pointed out for their prevalence in each dimension. During the time of physical embodiment (and this teaching is intended for those who are currently in the morning play period), the Blue Ray of Truth and Power overshadows the dimension. Therefore, electricity is the ruler of the physical plane and all life that appears there carries the electric spark in, through, and around them. It is electricity that moves and aggregates all physical life and when mankind applies this in the world of physical science, the atrocities and degradations to human and Earth life will cease and balance will more quickly resume. As all things happen in their due time, this too shall come when the playground is readied and for those who desire harmony as the next game to Master.


## PLANES OF CONSCIOUSNESS AND THE RAYS

The Astral Plane is identified with the Pink Ray and is therefore, ruled by magnetism, or the Law of Attraction. The Mental Plane is identified with the Yellow Ray and is ruled by the Law of Aggregation. Each of these worlds, while separate and distinct, also overlap one another, and in the physical realm are accessed through sleep, meditation, and spiritual disciplines. Each carries within them an immutable law which they represent and demonstrate in the worlds of appearances, and each of them is qualified with the Ray Force which serves their purpose.

The descent of matter begins with the Blue Ray, and is carried by the force of the soul within the Causal Body. Leaping again from the Source of desire, the soul within the causal form, desiring again the sensation of touch, hearing, laughter, and sound (that only can be sensed in such a way in the physical dimension) finds its way upon the peaceful descent to the Earth Plane and Planet. As it enters within the atmosphere of the physical planet, the light increases and vibrates, giving the planet itself a blue tinge from the masses of incoming souls. For the soul to enter the physical dimension, sponsorship is first required, and a Being of Light is required to hold at the Causal Plane, a continuous balance for the incoming individual. This stream of balanced energy penetrates through each of the successive layers of consciousness, which the incoming soul has to meet through the mental, astral layers, and finally, the meeting of the physical Earth.

Providing a shaft of lighted consciousness and carrying the purpose of the Divine Plan, the shaft, or core of vibral energy, penetrates to the core of the planet, forming an axis [Golden Thread Axis] between the physical world and the Causal Plane. The sponsor at the causal level holds the intent, purpose, and focus for the incarnation, in tandem with and knowing only the Will of God. The sponsor serves the incoming soul for the entire incarnation. This lighted being, known as the Divine Complement of the incoming soul, and though individualized, has found its service based upon the Law of Opposites, or the Law of Balance. Throughout the incarnation, the individualized soul in form, dulled by the cloak of matter, will be filled with impulses from the sponsor. These impulses spark the Laws of Perfection into manifestation and guide and direct the lessons that are fueled by the desire for form. Operating under the guidance and direction of a Hierarchy of evolved love and wisdom, the sponsor functions too under the Law of Grace. It is through this law that the incoming lifestream will never be given or revealed more than he or she can bear in the day spent learning the effects of cause.

THE PERFECT SERVICE OF DIVINE COMPLEMENTS

When the individualized soul returns to the ethers of the Causal Plane, it offers then again the perfect service in return to the sponsor soul and holds from that perfect level of consciousness, the balance of energy required for their individualized descent into form. This game of see-saw, based upon perfection and balance, endures a minimum of 200, and sometimes as many as 500, rounds into the dual planes, until such time that the energy of the manifesting duo attracts the attention and assistance of an Ascended Master. It is at that causal level that the two individualized souls are admitted into the Master's Ashram of Light, and the collective force from the initiated members of the Ashram, or Lodge (as it is known in its physical activity), sponsors the two to simultaneously carry forth perfect service into the physical descents.

These pairs of opposites are allowed many incarnations to provide service for the Ashram of Light, until they attract to themselves knowledge of one another and consciously choosing that Light of service, become sponsored by the breath and energy of one Ascended Master from the Ashram. This Ascended Master becomes known as the Master Teacher and works for both souls with equal effort and energy to unite the pulse and pull of countless centuries of embodiment. If the two are dedicated to the Ashram, its plan and disciplines, the uniting and merging of their energies for perfect service is effortless. The pair of opposites becomes known as Divine Complements, and their arching, or pushing and pulling of Divine Energy, becomes apparent on the planes of matter.

The Blue Ray attaches itself to the vibral core, also known as the Golden Thread Axis, and wraps itself around the vibrating axis forming one half of what is known in many circles as Kundalini (or snake) energy. The Pink Ray arcs from the Causal Plane and makes its descent, wrapping and turning and swirling down the pole of light, forming the other half of the Kundalini energy to be used in full for the entire incarnation. The Pink Ray settles itself first in the location of the heart of the incoming soul and creates first a circle, or swirling cup, that forms later into the first chakra to know physical matter. This swirling ovoid provides a home or cradle for the first infusion of energy from the causal sponsor, be that collective force from the Ashram or from an Ascended Master, and in it is planted as a spark or reflection of the Monad, known as the Unfed Flame of Love, Wisdom, and Power. It is the perfection of this flame that the individual will seek to model throughout the descent and ascent of matter, and attract and repel circumstance and situations according to the Divine Will that the Causal Plane knows and serves. Let me outline this process again for you:

1) Descent from the Causal Plane, the Blue Ray is in tandem with the Golden Thread. The Blue Ray serves to penetrate each layer of form on the descent. The Golden Thread penetrates the core of the planet, forming a perfect connection between the lower planes of appearances and the Causal Plane of perfection.

2) Golden Thread is sponsored by the Divine Complement, not in duo incarnation, or the collective energies of Ashram, or if the Divine Complements seek tandem service for the Ashram, an Ascended Master.

3) The Pink Ray then follows, winding down the axis pole and completes the other half of the Kundalini energies.

4) The Pink Ray forms the first chakra of physical descent, the Heart Chakra.

5) The Unfed Flame, or shadow of the flaming Monad, is planted in the heart, giving purpose and life to the descent into the worlds of form.


## CHOOSING THE FAMILY, CONCEPTION, AND BIRTH

Physical birth has yet to occur, although form has begun to aggregate, and the light substance emanates it own electro (blue) - magnetic (pink) field. It is at this time that impulses from the Causal Plane send wave forces that urge the incoming soul to select the perfect family, social surrounding, and geophysical location that will serve the purpose of appearance. At this moment, the soul has an aggregated form with minimal sensing capability and the presence of the Blue Ray gives the individual access to physical senses and movement. The vibral energy of the Causal, joined with the energy of the core of the Earth, give the individual the sensation of this first embodiment, much like the form of an angelic deva, flying with the ease of the ethers, yet unhampered by the physical body, still to appear. When the perfect conditions have been found for the embodiment, conception occurs, and the energies (perfect, although not completed or matured) anchor themselves into the womb of the Earth sponsor and the development of the infant body begins.

At conception, the Golden Thread Axis ceases its waving motion and anchors itself firmly into location into the physical dimension, drawing itself taunt and rigid for the infusions of energies from the Causal to emit. The mother at this time opens her lowest chakra to receive a complement of energy from the conscious will of the Earth Planet herself and the clay form which will house the precious God Light begins to form its characteristics. In a succession of nine breaths (3 X 3) from the causal sponsor, the Divine Energy of the soul is poured into the gestating form. Until such time that the soul takes its first breath, as the form is completed and the incoming causal energies also completed, the hour of birth into form comes with the appearance and adjoining of the Yellow Ray of Wisdom and Purpose. Within the rising of the Sun or the setting of the Moon, physical labor begins, and the soul makes its final descent down the birth canal. Upon the first individualized breath, each Ray arches from its sacred or servile planet, filling the infant body and knowing soul with influences which develop and nurture the character and assuring a personality to fulfill the Laws of Karma and Harmony.

And, so again, the threefold activity of Power, Love, and Wisdom, the Blue, Pink, and Yellow Rays, are used to begin the incarnation process. Throughout the physical embodiment, the guardian Ray Forces which rule the masculine and feminine currents in the body play their roles, again determined by the first physical breath in correlation to the positing of Mars and Venus within the astrological chart. The Servile Rays also arch their qualities to accompany the process. The interplay of electromagnetic Light Rays emit their purpose and plan throughout the life and incarnation of the soul in the worlds of appearance.

# The Nature of Change

*"Develop love within yourself and you will be
fearless and strong in all endeavors of service."*
**- MASTER K. H.**

Life, quality, and appearance fill each atom that is qualified in
the worlds of form. As we have discussed the nature of Source
Itself, perhaps it will benefit the student on the path to discuss
the nature of movement. Movement and change are qualities
inherent and inevitable in all of life, and of all things to expect,
Dear students, expect change. What is the nature of change and
how can we determine if its function is useful and evolutionary?[10]

"Each man is his own absolute lawgiver; the dispenser of glory
or gloom to himself; the decreer of his life, his reward, his punishment." These words were given to a strong and wonderful
teacher of the ancient wisdoms in the early part of the twentieth century. They are words of truth, and hold within them the
nature of change and the immutable law which governs those
who will to appear. You, through choice and action, are the
keeper of your destinies. There are energies that affect life, and
these energies are of course the Ray Forces and their purpose

for guiding the lifestream along the path of evolution towards the plan of the best and highest good.

There are also patterns that inevitably crop up throughout all of incarnation in rhythm, or sattva, and determine a clocklike persistence in the personality. Sometimes these patterns are natural and healthy for the development of the soul; sometimes these patterns are stagnating and inhibit the natural growth of the soul. We can look at these patterns as streaming from the inevitable Laws of Cause and Effect and bringing with them the momentum of past life experience. We can also use these patterns to show the most obvious course of inner growth and spiritual development.

PAIN, THE STEADFAST FRIEND

Each student on the path knows the truth that cannot be denied: Pain is the dispenser of glory and gloom, and our choices with pain determine its return, or open the doors to bliss. Pain is our steadfast friend and the evolved student welcomes its return without fear or apprehension. When you were a very small child learning to use the senses you had just re-acquired, it took the constant, watchful gaze of your mother to protect you from harm. Her presence, most likely, kept you from many accidents. She became your source of love and comfort and also your source of discernment and restriction.

How a child hates restriction, and waiting for that one free moment that mother's eyes could not catch, you reached for the burning coal, stepped down the first of a flight of stairs, or grabbed a knife on the shiniest end. It was then that the inevitable protector of the universe stepped in to show you what you were not ready for, or what you cared not to repeat again. The stinging burn, bruised forehead, or bleeding finger, yes, are all PAIN! Your friend PAIN, who has stepped in to remind you of your choices; your friend PAIN, who has reminded you to use wisdom in your approach; your friend PAIN, who has clearly said, "No, not yet." Your friend PAIN, your teacher, your guide, and your protector, why do you deny him?

Denying the pain slows the movement on the path. The return of the protector inevitably gives us wisdom, love, and power. Perhaps the student would be well advised that pain holds the Law of Evolution and shows the power and potency in "knowing the difference." Clearly, the student knows the difference between pain and bliss, and using choice before experience is always the wisest of deterrents. Take risks students and be fearless. Perhaps there is a door opening. Don't let fearful pain restrict your way. Instead, use the pain as the key that will unlock the door and place you in new surroundings, experience, and movement into change. Do you want to change who you are? Do you want to change the course of your life? Do you feel stagnate and are you ready for change? Pay attention to the protector of your senses. Perhaps it will lead you to your next move. Or perhaps, if your eyes and ears are open, it will show you where you no longer care to tread and what you no longer care to do.

## THE RAY OF THE HEART: LOVE

As much as pain can be a deterrent, and keep a lasting impression upon the will to choose the path most appropriate for the soul, love refreshes the soul and allows those lasting qualities of love, hope, and faith to develop. If there are any exceptions to rules, love is the exception and provides, not only a lasting power that the member of the Lodge can utilize for cohesion and attraction, but when offered in use like a seamless garment, the energy protects and guides the innocent and wise alike. Love is the gift for all and is the silent peacemaker when all other methods and treaties fail.

After the soul is birthed and opens its eyes for the first time, mother and infant meet and the bond is instant. Their gaze meet in a harmony of need, want, protection, and vulnerability that comprise the early essence of human love. The infant, missing the warmth and safety of the womb, longs again for the vibration that had so securely blanketed its being. The mother, hopeful and wanting, inspects the prize she has just be awarded for her tireless efforts and holds the small bundle that she has filled with her hopes, desires, and secret aspirations. Together they bond all of these aspects in a vibration we know as love, and it will be this first love that is shared that will model the love they will spend an entire incarnation perfecting. Perfect love knows no boundaries, darkness, or shadows. Inasmuch as pain can often restrict, love opens and expands.

Love is the one vibration that stays with us throughout the entire incarnation and expands its dimension throughout the Physical, Astral, Mental, and Causal Planes. Its manifestations differ though in each of the successive planes, and for the student on the path, there are keywords which identify the consciousness of love when working on a particular plane. On the Physical Plane, love always demonstrates itself as cooperation. On the Astral Plane, we have seen countless manifestations of love through devotion. On the Mental Plane, love is manifested again in the mind through inspiration. And the Great Silence of the Causal Plane allows love to be experienced as expansion. Let me tabulate these for you:

Physical Plane  = Love/Cooperation
Astral Plane  = Love/Devotion
Mental Plane  = Love/Inspiration
Casual Plane  = Love/Expansion

## GROUP MEDITATION FOR HEALING THE PLANET

Of course the student on the path may develop some or all of these attributes of love while still embodied on the Earth/Physical Plane and the adept understands, not only the attributes, but demonstrates them on a regular basis for the service of humanity. As all things are perfected and known through their utilization and steadfast demonstration, I encourage all students in the physical embodiment to exercise and employ their use, first through individual meditation and then through practical group exercise. I encourage all individual meditations to begin at either sunrise or sunset. This time is perfect to assimilate the energies of creation as there is a stillness and a peaceful, calming effect that occurs as the Rays of the Sun lessen and arc their energies to herald or close the day. Members of this Lodge practice group meditation at these hours and devote the the bulk of their meditation time for the healing and upliftment of the planet and humanity. We begin in collective thought:

To the planes of form I send my prayer and intention
through the Light of All.
Let Light descend on Earth and
may humanity COOPERATE willingly through it.
Let Light DEVOTE those who are readied
to serve the greater plan.
Let Light INSPIRE our collective mind and
serve the Cause Divine.
Let Light ascend on Earth and EXPAND
the heart of love of all creation,
great and small, united in one service.
OM MANAYA PITAYA, HITAKA!
(I AM the Light of God, So Be It!)

These are the words and thoughts of our Lodge at meditation. Use them, if you will, for the greater plan and the service of Brotherhood and Sisterhood. As the Light expands throughout your being through the disciplined approach of meditation, we encourage you to join collectively in these words throughout your day. Find new ways to cooperate with others, seeking first the motive of love and extending it outward in perfect harmony. Be fervently devoted to the love that you are and demonstrate. Should you lose confidence, remember the many that have tread the path before you. Inspire others as you walk the path with cheerfulness; trust in the Divine Plan; and encourage the God Light within them to be utilized to its fullest potential. Expand the heart of love to all around you. Send love to all Kingdoms of Creation, from Mineral to Vegetable, from Animal to Human. Care for them in the precious God Light that you all share and are created of.

My Master teacher often repeated this phrase, "When everything is said and done, all that is left is love." I have devoted many incarnations to the study of this phrase and I now share my understanding with devoted students on the path. Develop love within yourself and you will be fearless and strong in all endeavors of service. OM SHEAHAH (I AM AS ONE).

# Desire that Co-creates the Love of God

*"Quietly listen and you will hear the call in your heart."*
**- MASTER K. H.**

Many students on the path have argued about desire.[11] Some find it the source of all discomfort, holding their passions in bondage to the Earthly, physical planes. Others find it as the scent of the flower; using desire as the indicator, much like a thermometer on a frozen winter morning, to show the true feelings of the heart. My teacher once spoke of desire, "Desire! The giver and glory of pain and love. Once I Master you, I face the truth of the Universe!" Desire is truly, at all times, the giver and glory of pain and love and is the measure of our spiritual agility. Desire can lead us temporarily off of the path or startlingly push us back on.

Desire inevitably returns us to the creative force, the Omnipresent Source. When we become frozen or weak in our journey here, you can rest assured desire will return us to our Home. All who are created from the love that fills all of life yearn to return to that love. From the point of love within the heart of God, we travel throughout the worlds of form, seeking protection and union through the love that created us. It is the desire for the love of God that I shall begin this lesson. Open your hearts and perhaps you will feel the fluttering of the pure Flame of Desire.

A young student traveled the path until he had met a man he knew would be his guru. He followed the teacher like a lost puppy, begging him to take him into his study. Soon the teacher, wearied by the young man's constant attention, asked him to follow him to the river. Both walking out to waist-deep water, the teacher quickly plunged the head of the young man under until he kicked and bubbled for life-giving air! When he finally let him up, the young student gasped for breath, and after several minutes of shock and disbelief asked the older man, "Why did you do that?" Then the wise man replied, "When you desire God like you desired that breath of air while you were under the water, you are ready then to follow the path with me."

Desire works this way for all of us, leading us innocently into waters, fires, and earthquakes. Desire, which was once fueled by greed, ambition, or avarice, upon reflection and experience, seeks purification. Initiation through desire is the most tempering of fires but also the most essential. There will be many fires that you will walk through while you travel the path. The path is strewn with broken dreams and unfulfilled expectations, all discarded when realized they are the frivolous garments covering the prize inside, the nut of the fruit, the Omnipotent Truth. It is truth that we come to value as stalwart followers of the path and plan.

We are created of this truth and while we desire to hold it unto ourselves, we cannot, for that would destroy us.[12] Yet truth universally brings us all to the understanding of the causeless cause and evolves to hold the spark of desireless desire. When we can serve that cause without expectation or personal desire, we serve from the point that we departed from. This is the point of love and truth and we accept our role as a Co-creator, mirrored in the image and likeness of our Creator.

## THE FIVE-FOLD PATH

Those of you who accept the role of SERVANT, expect but one thing: you will know freedom. Your purpose is to serve the Will of God through humanity and the worlds of form. Your desireless form will know the Christ and you will build the bridge between the worlds of form and spirit. Through your open eyes you will open the doors of the soul. Through your open ears you will attain perception. Carry always the symbol of the star, for you are Divine Man!

Should you walk the path of the TEACHER, profess your service to all of life! Through synchronicity, thought, and meditation, you become the awakener. You will know the ONE, the consciousness of ALL, and there will be your source of inspiration and experience. Allow the upper lid of your all-seeing eye to be the teacher; allow the lower lid to be the student. Be watchful that you do not become too narrow or slanted, but keep your eyes wisely open. Upon your shoulder rests the owl, you who hold the eyes for humanity, to recognize divinity for all.

Should you walk the path of the HEALER, you will hold the keys to understand desire through the development of the senses, compassion, and the intelligence of diagnosis. You will profess to the wholeness of body and mind, as a peaceful warrior who carries a sword of love that applies and directs energy. Your Source is the Mother God, who knows only purification and sacrifice, joined with the great reward of Alchemy. You walk the path in service to divinity, knowing that the light that shines, shines for ALL as ONE. As the healed carry the potency of the healer, you carry the potency of those healed. The swirling circles of Life continuous, the lotus and the rose are your symbols.

Should you walk the path of the PROPHET, know that your purpose is for the healing of the nations. You will constantly be a catalyst who will work with the tool of consciousness for change and choice. Check carefully at all times your intent; dilute it not, for your skill lies in the strength of your balance and interpretation. You know your Source as Spirit and seek the equalization in divinity: As above, so below. Once you choose this path, do not turn back. "Great ones fall back even from the threshold, unable to sustain the weight of their responsibility, unable to pass on. Therefore, look forward always with awe and trembling to this moment and be prepared for the battle." The path of the prophet purposely surrenders all animal desire for the symbol and principle they carry, the dove of peace.

Should you walk the path of the PRIEST, know that your purpose will seal divinity. Through ceremony, prayer, and song you transform and harmonize, knowing your Source as the Father God. You are the leader of groups, who also knows and understands the sound of silence. "Listen only to the voice which is soundless. Look only on that which is invisible, alike to the inner and the outer sense." You flow within and you flow without. You tread the path of the adept, seeking and knowing only perfection.

You are the perfect man, known through ancient numerology in the number nine. You are the animal beast, 666 (6+6+6=18=9), who has chosen to regenerate, 144,000, (1+4+4+0+0+0=9). Your symbol is the Tree of Life and the Philosopher's Stone.

Let me tabulate again this five-fold path of desire, should you choose to tread:

SERVANT ...............The working of the Divine Plan.
TEACHER................The recognition of Divinity.
HEALER ..................The service to Divinity.
PROPHET................The equalization in Divinity.
PRIEST....................The sealing of Divinity.

## THE COURSE OF SERVICE IS REQUIRED

Know that each of these courses is required in the journey on the path. Each of them are steamed and fueled by desire and inevitably lead us back to the source of Creator Love. So that we know the truth of desireless desire, we approach each of these roles through embodiment after embodiment, through the service of the Rays and the roles of desire that we choose. In our mission to know truth, each role, much like the Rays, presents itself in service to the next. For instance, the role of the servant paves the pathway for the teacher; the teacher paves the pathway for the healer; the healer paves the pathway for the prophet; the prophet paves the pathway for the priest; and the priest paves the pathway for the adept, he who listens to the Voice of Silence.

In many instances, we blend the roles of desire, seeking an understanding of Truth and Life, much as the Rays blend their septenary qualities for our sacred mission. To gain a better understanding of the correlation between the Rays and the roles of desire, I present this table:

```
SERVANT ............. Blue and White Rays
TEACHER ............. Pink and Yellow Rays
HEALER ................ Pink, Yellow, and Green Rays
PROPHET ............. Yellow, White, and Ruby Rays
PRIEST ................. Green, Ruby, and Violet Rays
```

The student on the path chooses one or several of these forms of selfless service to understand the role of desire and the evolution of the mighty spark of Omniscience. Gently and gracefully, when the student intentionally chooses to drop self-centeredness to the call of service on the path, he holds the keys to emergent evolution. When the HU-man, Divine God-Being, can no longer be denied expression, the hold that the animal consciousness once held, drops into slumber. This great victory achieved allows a greater service. Then the call of the Lodge, dedicated to the service and spiritual upliftment of humanity, opens your ears.

AN INVITATION

I close by extending an invitation to all of you to join with us. The need is great among humanity today. There is still needless suffering, fueled by the fires of ignorance and deception. Quietly listen and you will hear the call in your heart. We are not a religious group or sect; however, we are a service group of elder Brothers and Sisters who have been known throughout mankind's history as the Great White Lodge. Through the medium of consciousness we have merged our efforts and energies aimed towards the unity of all of life. Our goal is simple and our work is hard. It is never promised to be easy; however, the reward immeasurable. Come through prayer and meditation, if you feel the urge of the mission within.

A new cycle awaits humanity. It is a cycle filled with growth, learning and life. Painfully and lovingly, sometimes this growth is achieved through disease, poverty, and destruction. However, within your heart lies the gentle revolution which can redirect the course of such events. This is a revolution armed with the power of service, charity, and love. If you should turn your back now, know that timelessly we await.

Let us join in wisdom to extinguish ignorance and inequity.
Let us join in love to extinguish suffering.
Let us join in service to extinguish greed and avarice.
Let us join in charity to extinguish poverty.
Let us join in harmony to extinguish disease.

As our ears are opened and our eyes begin to see, let us join as ONE Light in our hearts and minds.

May this Light of Wisdom serve ALL.
May this Light of Truth and Justice prevail.
May the law be written in hearts
And joined through Harmony, Brotherhood, and Love.

Timelessly and agelessly, the unknown poet sings:

"Oh, let not the flame die out!
Cherished age after age in its dark cavern,
In its holy temples cherished,
Fed by pure ministers of love,
Let not the flame die out!"


OM MANAYA PITAYA, HITAKA!
~Master K. H., a member and servant of the Great White Lodge

# Perfect Plan of Purity

*"The Eighth Ray brings the golden clarity of light, life, thought, feeling, action, Oneness, and breath."*
**- ARCHANGEL CRYSTIEL**

Greetings Beloved Children. I AM Sanctus Germanus, the Holy Brother, and I ask your permission to come forward.

Response: "Always Dear Brother, come forth."

It is again that we bring balance to this perfect plan of purity. It is again that we bring forth the great compassion, the great heartfelt yearnings, the great desire of all perfection coming forward. It is once again that the Monad, that is ONE, comes forward. And now we ask you to give this Monad its choice—the choice of perfection.

THE CONSCIOUSNESS OF CHOICE

The choice that we have spoken of as service is a service of perfection of desire. It is truly this perfection that comes forward in your daily lives of thought, in your daily lives of feeling, in your daily lives of action. It is this perfection, this focus, that we ask you to consider as being your heart, as being your desire, as being your action. You and I and all on this planet are ONE Monad, and it is the individual expression of this Monad that gives service to the consciousness of choice. It is the personal expression that you and I have individually chosen, that all our Brothers and Sisters express and act upon in accordance to this Divine Monadic Activity.

Through the perfection of choice is brought this balanced harmony. For as one fits to the other, for as one expresses to the other, so too does this balanced harmony bring forth the great desire of Unana. It is the Oneness that we all truly desire. It is the ONE thought, the ONE feeling, the ONE action, the ONE breath, the ONE Light that we truly are.

Our service comes to this awakening and it is a step-by-step path each of us takes. As you step from one step to another for the higher expansion, look about you and see those who have found the step with you. Look through the great garden . . . look through these great mountain ranges . . . look through these great expressions of this planetary thought, feeling, and action. Look, feel, experience; it is this experience, one step at a time, that each of us brings to you for your consideration. Look, feel, and experience on your own; for then, you may in turn bring this to others. We, as this ONE Body of Light, this ONE Body of Thought, this ONE Body of Being, had this choice. In this choice we individualize, but the choice does not separate our family, does not separate our beingness. Choice only expands our family.

## ONE LIGHT, ONE SOURCE

When you look to a molecule, there are many atoms, but it is one molecule. When you look to this one organ, there are many molecules, but it is one organ. When you look to this one human body, it is one body, but there are many organs, many molecules, and many atoms. Likewise, the ONE Monad that we are, is expressed in the same pattern. The one body, the one organ, and the molecules and atomic structures are all the expression of this ONE Body of Light. For as you come to this fulfillment, the fruit of this understanding is your only nutrition . . . is your only expression . . . is your only breath . . . is your only understanding that all life is ONE. You are ONE body of this ONE Earth. You are ONE thought of the ONE spark of creation, the ONE Light. Consider that it is all of these expressed individually.

It is the choice of each to bring this expression to this outer experience, but the outer experience flows within and inner experience is still ONE. We ask you to reconsider again and again your Oneness. When you speak to your Brothers and your Sisters, this great Unana that you are is the expression that refocuses inward. It is through this expression that creation will flow once again back to the ONE Light, the ONE Source. In that flowing, there is truly a path. There are many steps; there are many experiences; there are many understandings. It is the fleet of foot who complete this path in a timely manner. It is only the great desire, the great inwardness, the great inner joy that brings this path to its fruitful expression.

Is it not that we plant the garden to reap the fruit? It is only the fruit, once again, that sustains the garden through its seed.

The garden expands. So as this expands, so too does the consciousness, one step, one experience, one expansion at a time.

## CRYSTIEL, THE ARCHANGEL OF CLARITY

Now, with your permission, I ask you to accept this imprinted pattern that brings forward this Eighth Ray. This furthers the great arcing energy of the pure angelic realm, which contains and sustains the focus of all beingness. I ask you to accept our Dear one, our Dear Brother, whom you know as the great Angel Crystiel. The clarity of service, that which makes all clear in its crystal purity, I ask you to accept this great love of expression. For each Ray is an expression of this Monad; each Ray is an understanding of the quality that the consciousness may take in this focus. You, I, all creation are Unana, the ONE.

Response: "Welcome Beloved Crystiel."

Dear one, I AM Crystiel, the Archangel of the clarity of thought, of action, and of feeling; the clarity that brings to the full octave the understanding that all cycles have completion and sustainment in this cycle. With your permission, may we bring this completion of cycle, so that the seed of this cycle is completed?

Response: "You have permission. So Be It."

In the perfection that you are, that all creation is, is the clear understanding that the expressions are choice, and the expression of choice brings forward the comprehension of consciousness. However, comprehension is only one vibration or rate of spin, just as feeling is only one vibration or rate of spin. It is the integration, the blending, the Oneness of each of these expressive patterns that you call light, sound, breath, life, thought, action, and feeling. These too are contained in each of the Rays. These too are contained within each other, and so there is always the balance that is maintained.

It is the clear expression of this eighth octave that brings its cycle to its completion, and in this completion, all life comes forward with the clear balance of choice, with the clear balance of desire, with the clear balance of feeling, with the clear balance of action. For it is this Eighth Ray that brings the golden clarity of light, life, thought, feeling, action, Oneness, breath, infinitely to be sustained. One chooses to express on a Ray until this balance is sustained, this harmony is sustained, this plan of Unana is sustained. It has been in these choices of expression that the Oneness has been, as you would say, neglected. It is in these choices of expression that the Source, that deep river as you call it, the root, the vine of all, has been neglected.

If you look to all you have brought forth in your life, many like yourself, and we who have traveled the same path as well, have neglected to see and to experience all from the perspective of the Source. It is in this choice that you have brought forth each and everyone to this planet. It is in this choice that this neglect and separateness have grown in the consciousness. In the expression of lower energetic pattern there is no need to be separate, for it is only an expression.

## YOU WILL ALWAYS BE ONE

So this Ray that now comes forward and anchors its seed in your heart of hearts, anchors its seed in your Monadic Flame, that comes forward and now completely expresses on the final holographic pattern of your perfected self, brings all this creation full circle again. From this moment on, you will always remember. From this moment on, you will always be ONE. You will see, you will think, you will feel, you will act, you will breathe, you will experience all from this focus of ONE.

Golden clarity is the decree of this Eighth Ray. It is the decree of this focus that all creation, whether you think it is the most evolved or the least evolved, is now aware of its Source. No longer will this separation come forward. No longer will the expression on your plane of consciousness in this planet of perfection be separate from Source. It is decreed in this moment that none shall forget. This has always been the plan, and as you are now ONE, so are we, so am I, so is all creation ONE; this ONE focus, this ONE beingness, this ONE expression. All angels are now here. We are available for every question.

Response: "Thank you Beloved Archangel Crystiel. One question: How is it that we can all best serve the awakening of humanity and bring forth a consciousness of healing for all upon the planet?"

## YOU ARE LIGHTED BY ACCEPTANCE

The pivotal word for your consciousness is acceptance. This word of acceptance—to allow, to not judge, to accept the "Be-

ingness" of all—is a pivotal point in the expansion of your consciousness. Acceptance is a consideration for all non-judgment
to flow. As your Beloved Brother has brought forth to you the
Laws of Non-judgment for the expansion of consciousness, it
is a tiny seed of compassion that accepts all human frailty. All
that you consider dark, all that you consider wrong, evil, or
inappropriate is just an expression. As one can make a choice,
so too can this choice change second by second in your world.
It is the acceptance that each expresses, what they comprehend
and experience.

That which you call dark may be instantaneously lighted by
your own acceptance. That which you call wrong may be instantaneously balanced by your own acceptance. In this pattern, the
conflicts, the walls that diminish the freedom, collapse. In this
pattern, the separation dissolves. For in this pattern, the joy
that you all are expresses.

There are times in your path when you will stand forward and
firm and not accept, but in the not accepting, you must only
hold the focus of your own chosen creation and allow the focus
of another's chosen creation; for each chosen creation may not
harmonize, but each chosen creation must be allowed. If these
choices reach further through the Law of Acceptance, which
is your natural law, the higher Law of Non-judgment may take
root. As this higher Law of Non-judgment takes root, it flowers,
and the great fragrance that you find in your garden will be
expressed in your outer world.

We ask you to consider that the greatest service to be brought
at this moment is this natural law, for all to accept and allow

individuals and groups to be as they are. Also know that it is your choice for your own path that you may also accept. Come forward now, Dear ones, in your daily lives! Let the breath, the spirit, the light, the life of all creation come forward in this natural Law of Acceptance! None of you are separate. You are Unana.

Response: "Thank you Crystiel."

Dear Child of this Golden Flame, I AM known as Mary and ask for your permission to come forward, for you are the flower and the light of all life.

Response: "Thank you Beloved Mary. Come forward."

THE FLOWER OF LIFE

As our Dear Brother Crystiel has expressed acceptance, we ask that the Flower of Life be the expression of All. For, as the Dove is the messenger of this New World that you now choose, the Flower of Life is the expression of your Oneness. And from your flower will come many fruits and the seeds which will again grow to create the flower. You have stepped from the path of fruit and seed to the path again of the flower. This flower we ask you to place in much of your work, for it is this pattern which will bring forward the Oneness for all who see and experience your daily lives.

Come gently into your garden when you are troubled,
And I am there for you.
Come gently into the garden of your heart,

And you will find you are never without this
great Flower of Life.
You are always ONE.

Come forward, as you have been requested by your Brother Sananda, to step into this garden anytime there is a conflict in your life. As you come to this place of serenity, these great flowers and fragrances will breathe a breath that brings a new life, a new focus, and a new acceptance. These Flowers of Life will always bring that which you know as prana, will bring that which you have as Source. It is the continual breath of this wondrous fragrance that you become as you step into your garden. It is in this redirection of your focus in your day that brings this Oneness infinitely. It is but a small turn on your inner path to find your garden. As this Oneness comes forward, all connects in the breath of this garden. We ask you to breathe these gentle flowers and I surround you always.

*Dear Mary steps back from the frequency and Beloved Saint Germain speaks.*

Dear Child of my heart, I AM Saint Germain. Do you have questions before we take our leave?

Response: "Dear Brother, no questions, but much gratitude for your service. Thank you."

Then let perfection stream forward on all Rays of expression, Unana.

# Aggregate Body of Light

*"In the inner marriage of your masculine and feminine energies,*
*you are able to overcome the duad and move into the Monad,*
*the ONE flame, the ONE breath, the ONE Source of All."*
**- SAINT GERMAIN**

Greetings in that mighty Christ. I AM Saint Germain and
I stream forth on that mighty Violet Ray. It is this mighty
Violet Ray which is the Ray of Diplomacy and the vibrational
frequency of Brotherhood that I stream forth this day. To my
right is my Beloved Brother El Morya and to my left is, what
we shall call, that mighty one of the secret society, Madame H.
P. These two have brought forth their vibrational frequencies
for this discourse this morning and, of course Dear hearts, before we begin, we must request permission to come forth into
your energy field.

Response: "Dear ones, all three of you have permission to
come forward and greetings with great joy and light."

I stand on this podium to address all of those who are ready to
take, what we shall call, a work with open eyes and open ears,
for a critical time has come to your planet and we shall say that
this quantum leap is about to start.

## ONE THROUGH CHRIST CONSCIOUSNESS

When I first started my service upon the Earth Plane and Planet, I wove what is known as the golden cord around your planet's equator and from pole to pole. A mighty Violet Flame was streaming forth, so all could access that Law of Mercy, Forgiveness, Compassion, and Diplomacy, and all would birth what we would call a Brotherhood among the hearts of humanity. With the falling of the Berlin Wall, this Great White Brotherhood achieved perhaps its mightiest victory. In the falling of that wall, all hearts were ready to receive the beginning initiations of the Christ Consciousness. There have been many other avatars, teachers, and adepts who have come before this event, but this was perhaps one of the mightiest events for which we had all held a mighty focus.

Dear hearts, a time has come to the planet when, shall we say, your appearance is changing and the geophysical Earth around you is going through many changes as well. Perhaps the mightiest of all the changes is the falling of the walls within your own hearts. Each of you is now ready to reach, as we shall call in consciousness, that aggregate Body of Light. It is only in the aggregate Body of Light that you will access that code of Brotherhood and Sisterhood, where you will realize that you are as ONE mighty organism.

Every one of you has but one heart, has but one stomach, has but one set of eyes and one set of ears. You are, as we shall call it, a mighty microorganism of the Holy Macro. You have taken on what we call a duad, or a body which has formed itself into the mighty ONE, only so that you could grow in consciousness to understand that you are part of ONE great contributing force. You are all a part of this ONE contributing force, known, in what Beloved Brother Jesus Sananda demonstrated, through the Christ Consciousness. This consciousness is also demonstrated through Buddha and as a flame pulsating throughout the planet. That flame is now ready to leap into the hearts of all on the planet in a demonstration brought forth into the physical.

You shall see you are all ONE in a mighty Oneship. As you have separated, many of you feel at times you are separate and apart from your Brothers and Sisters, but realize Dear ones, you are all part of ONE organism. This is one of the simplest statements we have addressed here from this hierarchal stance. You have understood it to be the most complicated, for your gender has stated you are separate from one another, and this, which is known as male and female, is now to emerge into what is known as the inner marriage within the being of itself. For from this stance of your totality, your aggregate Body of Light is then integrated and assimilated as ONE.

## THE INNER MARRIAGE AND THE MONADIC FLAME

Many of you have gone through many trying experiences in different relationships, and now the rates soar throughout all of humanity of marriage and divorce. This has happened because of the refusal of humanity to recognize its Oneship and perform what is known as the inner marriage, where each individual makes a choice to unionize its energies, both masculine and feminine, and then utilize those energies for the best and highest good.

Most of those among humanity, who have not yet expanded their consciousness to what we shall call this new mantle of consciousness, have had the experience of unionization of these energies through what is known as procreation. However, Source, God, or Helios and Vesta, as we would call it, have utilized this energy in an attempt to perform the inner marriage, to bring forth new lifestreams from other planetary systems to raise the vibration of your planet and enable consciousness to raise across the planet.

You now realize this time is critical and many disturbances are occurring in your geophysical fields as well as among your societal fields. The crime rates soar, your economy is soon to be dissolved, and you wonder about the stability of tectonic plates and weather patterns. As you have created this world to be what we call a playground of Co-creation, it is up to you to align yourself now to that mighty Gobean (the first Golden City Vortex) energy. That mighty energy that is the Will of God, for then you will understand you are of this Source and it is of you.

In the unionization, or marriage as we shall call it, of your masculine and feminine energies, you are then able to overcome what we call the duadic energy and move into the Monad, the ONE flame, the ONE breath, the ONE Source of All. Hold this focus as you travel through these perilous times. Hold this focus that you are ONE with this Monadic Flame. It is the same flame which Buddha accessed. It is the same flame which Jesus Sananda, Dear Brother, has accessed. It is the same flame that I too accessed. Kuan Yin, Mother Mary, all members of the hierarchal structure here at Shamballa have all accessed this same flame. It is this mighty flame that allows you then to move into what we call the Monadic Consciousness, or Unana.

The flooding of your planet in areas near St. Louis and on to Houston are demonstrations that it is time *now* to move, and to make your movement into this consciousness, so as to access the Monadic Flame and move into your glory as the Divine Inheritor, into the Oneship of all of creation.

You ask of yourself, why is it then, that I am so filled with such criticism of my Brothers and Sisters? This is a simple fact. You have yet to unionize your own energy within your own being. Perhaps you have yet to experience the masculine force within you or honor the feminine. Today two Divine Emissaries, shall we say, of masculine and feminine energy, have come forward in embodiment to demonstrate through experience the required movement toward the inner marriage.

THE INVISIBLE SUBJECTIVE ENERGY BODY

As I have spoken about the aggregate Body of Light, this discourse shall address what is known as subjective energy bodies. This subjective body is again another energy force. The student and chela must understand these energy forces when working towards the marriage of the energies that lead one into the Monad. This subjective body is a body which is created through your thought, through your feeling, and, yes, through your action. However, it remains invisible to you because you have not allowed consciousness to take responsibility for your creation.

You spoke of Co-creation Dear one, and this Co-creation always aligns to that vibrational essence of the force of the best and highest good, but there is also your energy that has been given to the subjective bodies. You find subjective bodies hovering over all addictions to outside substances. For instance, I would refer to tobacco, alcohol, and drug use. This subjective body hovers, shall we say, between the sixth and seventh layer of the field, which also then affects all activity as you draw in the Law of Attraction.

Subjective bodies carry through embodiment after embodiment, and you have referred to them as karma. We simply refer to them as the energetic pattern or the energetic reasoning. Through these subjective bodies creation occurs. Creation, as I use the word, the manifestation of the human societal output, is the best way to address what you would call this phenomena. However, we who have accessed through, what we would call, the dissolution of the subjective, have raised the energy into what is known as the aggregate Body of Light and through that aggregate Body of Light, accesses the monadic code.

Dear one, when you put your energy, or attention, your thought, or even your feeling towards another person and that thought or feeling is held in discord or disharmony, that energy moves into what we call a subjective body. That subjective body holds this pattern and so you wonder, "Why is it I continue to attract this situation again and again. Why is it I seem to marry a series of alcoholic personalities? Why is it that I seem to continue to be burdened with a lack of money? Why is it that I seem to continue to perpetrate the same energetic pattern over and over again?" You began this spiritual journey and searched deep within your core and worked at addressing your behavior, but you have not yet addressed your thought and your intent.

Beloved Mother Mary has spoken about this anugramic reality, and the anugramic reality draws only from the intent and purpose of that mighty Breath and Will of God. You realize that you, as the Co-creator, hold the focus for this thought through the subjective body, or unbridled attentions, and all the thoughts that do not carry discipline or focus. I hope that you will gain an understanding through this discourse, that even words carry consciousness. You speak of yourself as being critical and you know you are critical. Where does this energy go, but into the subjective bodies! I am not saying that this is a time that you suppress and repress, what we would call, a feeling towards a resolution. But when you speak of your Brothers and Sisters, who are no different from you in your present understanding, and as you carry a Oneness throughout all of you, you in a sense speak against yourself. This energy goes into subjective energy bodies and it carries forth its patterns. Before I turn the discussion over to our speakers, do you have questions?

Question: "Yes, I do. If one chooses to create an experience repeatedly by the same thought and feeling pattern, it is understood that discipline can redirect and refocus the thought. However, when the individual is interacting with another and encountering consistent conflict, even though the thought of the individual is directed to resolution and harmony, the question still remains, is this not all by agreement?"

You are dealing with the energy of the subjective body. I have taught resolution comes only through agreement, harmony, and the Law of Cooperation. If you are encountering one with whom you have identified a subjective energy, it is important to address this directly to this individual and to point out the seed of disharmony, the seed of the discontent. It is not necessary to personally address behaviors or activities in another individual. However, you might consider going to that individual and together calling on the Law of the Violet Flame and accessing that Christ Consciousness to dissolve that energy pattern that exists between you. Let me illustrate through a story:

Two Brothers have been fighting over one parcel of land for over twenty years. In the course of this fight, they forget to pay a tax levied against this land because their attention is directed into the subjective energy force which creates the fight. They no longer pay attention to the maintenance of this land that they claim to own. Soon the ownership of this land slips out from underneath them and is given to another party, who is not involved in the subjective energy force. Despite the fact that the land is no longer even a consideration between them, the two Brothers continue in that Vortex of subjective energy, each of them caught in that Vortex of disharmony and discord. The one thing they kept their feet planted on is no longer there. The purpose and the intent of their disagreement is no longer there. How does this disharmony and discord, this energy pattern, dissolve between the two so that they may separate their energies from one another in the subjective sense and unite their energies into that mighty flame of Unana?

REMOVING SUBJECTIVE ENERGY BODIES

First, there must be an identification of the mighty ONE, from whom they both draw their Source, the Christ. Then there must be a complete dissolution of this subjective body. The magnetizing energy of this subjective body is capable of pulling them in at any time, unless both are totally and willingly ready to dissolve its existence. I would recommend that if two recognize the creation of a subjective body of disharmony, those two agree to dissolve it, either through what we would call the write and burn technique, or by calling upon that mighty Violet Flame, that Law of Eternal and Infinite Forgiveness.

Let me also give you a ceremony that you may use for removing subjective bodies: Find a cup and keep it as a sacred cup under ritual for seven days. Light five candles around this cup and keep those candles burning around that cup for twenty-four hours straight, so that it sees the rising of the Sun, the setting of the Sun, and the rising of a new Sun. Then the cup is ready for what we call the sacred ceremonies.

For this sacred ceremony, we ask that you acquire several incenses, sandlewood or myrrh, and burn these sacred scents in this cup and then the discord through that subjective energy dissolves when that smoke, or the essence of that smoke, is placed between the two individuals. If you can even bring that one Brother or Sister into the agreement for the dissolution, the dissolving of the subjective body, then this smoke can be used as an effective healing between the two energy bodies. This works at the emotional and elemental levels. Do you understand?

[Editor's Note: A photograph of an individual may be used to dissolve your subjective energy with that person.]

Question: "Even without both parties agreeing?"

Of course, it is best to have the agreement. If not, call on the Law of Forgiveness and then perform the ceremony. Then it is done. It is finished. It is complete. Hitaka! So Be It!

Time runs short, Dear hearts. Dissolve all subjective energy. A time comes now to the Earth Plane and Planet that discord and disharmony shall be no longer, and you shall be set free in the Violet Flame of Liberty and Freedom. You are here as great inheritors of the Divine ONE. You are here, led on that path back to what we know as the Garden, where all mystery is revealed. You, Dear ones, are given these teachings, so wars, famines, and poverty leave your planet and so you are able to anchor the blessings of heaven in Unana. Do you have questions?

Response: "Thank you very much. There are no further questions."

And now I turn the discussion over to a most marvelous Dear one, Madame H. P.

Response: "Greetings Dear one and come forward."

*A generous energy steps forward to speak. It is the soul force of Madame H. P. Blavatsky. The energy is masterful, open, and filled with joy.*

Dear students, what a delight it is to be here and what a delight it is to address those who are willing to bring this information forward. For I understand too what it is like to have a body and I have understood too what it was like to carry this work for my beloved Brothers and Sisters of the Hierarchy.

## OPENING TO THE FEMININE

A time has come, as Saint Germain has said, that the anchoring of the inner marriage of the feminine energy comes to the planet. Hold a focus, as this feminine energy comes in its completeness even to your own being.

When I speak of the body, please dissolve all previous concepts you hold of the physical body and understand that around you is your true body. It is a consciousness or reflection of the Monad, geometrically built as a series of pyramids, you know to be layers of grid systems. It is built upon the Pythagorean numerology of five pyramids, stacked on one another. In the center is revealed the Divine Circle and source of the Monadic Flame. To each side of the circle is the shape of infinity, the left side representing the feminine and the right side representing the masculine. These shapes are now taught to you so that you are able use them to contain the consciousness of your focus.

My Beloved Brother El Morya will later discuss how you can contain the focus and will give you pertinent methodologies. However, I would like to speak about the activation of the feminine on your planet. A Dear Sister was sent to hold this first focus of the feminine and you have known her as Mother Mary. She has been brought to bring forth, in a sense, the totality of the feminine, a representation, or a holding, which you know as the energetic pattern. The activations that are now coming to this planet allow for forty pillars of feminine energy to be activated and are known as the Forty Pillars of Isis. I am asking each who encounters this information to consider themselves a portion of the Pillars of Isis, the feminine energy that can no longer be suppressed.

Women, you out there who believe you must act as men in order to assert your rightful feminine role, realize it is just a qualification of an energy. Do you realize that when you take on a mantle of consciousness that is feminine, that you call it forth in experience? It is not a list of qualities you find in a dictionary. However, it is an energy force that you anchor within your being.

We have noted on the planet that the energy force of the feminine is an energy force that opens. We have noted that the energy force on the planet known as male is as an energy force that restricts. You have known this as the push and the pull. We call it simply the masculine and feminine. But realize, in the totality, that the push and pull moves you as one continuous unified field of energy.

I AM here to give you but a short diagram of the Forty Pillars of Isis, which are to be implemented in certain geophysical locations upon your planet, as this dispensation of material is geophysical in nature. Do you realize when you travel, that in certain areas of the world there are energies that assist in this cellular opening of the feminine? One such area is a Vortex that you know to be Shalahah. It is, specifically, a feminine opening portal. There is another in Canada, known as Jeafray. Oh yes, and Marnero, as well and the three Vortices of South America, are all feminine by nature. I would remind those who come across this material that all of these Vortices are locations which anchor in and achieve the inner marriage through the opening of the feminine.

You males, who have so genderized your consciousness, if you are looking to achieve this inner marriage, you are looking to open up your feeling capacity and intuitive capability. I would suggest that you travel to these areas, for the vibrational frequency is filled with the Isis energy and you will journey into what is known as an opening to the internal womb. I, of course, will always be available to bring further information regarding the initiation of the feminine, and I ask all who encounter this material to call forth the opening of the feminine and to hold it firmly within your thought pattern of the aggregate. Questions?

Response: "Everything that you have explained, Madame H. P., is quite clear. I thank you very much and would request that you accompany our Beloved Saint Germain and El Morya more frequently to bring forth information. I thank you and I am grateful."

It is a pleasure to be of service. It is a pleasure to be here and perhaps I shall step forward again.

Response: "It will be a delight. Thank you."

In the blessing and the light of the Mighty I AM, I turn the discussion over now to Beloved El Morya.

Response: "Greetings Dear one and come forward."

*Beloved Mahatma El Morya steps forward. He is the tall Master, almost seven feet tall. He is wearing a white tunic, a white turban, and as always, surrounded by a brilliant blue light.*

In the steel of the Blue Flame, I AM El Morya, and I request permission to come forth.

Response: "Please, Dear one, come forward."

I AM the Mahatma El Morya, and today I shall discuss what is known as the masculine energy. As Beloved H. P. has so adeptly addressed with you Dear ones, I address the masculine energy, as I have brought it forth in my own embodiments in the Earth Plane and Planet. I would like for you to understand that on your planet, the one energy force that is able to encompass you always, is that opening energy known as the feminine energy.

## THE CHARGE OF THE MASCULINE

To bring forth Co-creation, you must utilize masculine energy. It is that energy that comes vested from the heart of the Mother/Father God, and it is a conscious energy that you call forth in your inner marriage. It is the energy that dares to be silent. It is the energy that *does* in its silence. And upon the Earth Plane and Planet are also forty pillars of the masculine energy. One of the Vortices in your area, as you well know, Gobean, is a Vortex of the masculine energy. It is an energy that you understand to be heavenly in nature, but it is an energy that carries forth the plan of the Divine Breath. It knows that at all times all works together for a common good.

To align yourself, remember the teachings of the breath, for as much as the feminine energy opens, it is the force of the breath of the Father that closes it in its most timely manner and fashion. Dear ones, we call these the Pillars of Zeus. For the Pillars of Zeus, much as the Pillars of Isis, represent the masculine energy and prepare you for the inner marriage into Unana. Feel for an instant, as I charge this room with the masculine energy. The masculine energy is often brought through the feeling world. Feel for a minute, the charge of the masculine.

*Mahatma El Morya waves his arm and the room is filled with an intense vibration. He directs the movement of the energy through his eyes.*

What word would best describe this?

Response: "Strength."

Precisely, or more precisely, Power. You have encountered those who have said, "Do you feel the power?" They are referring to masculine energy. I hope this brings a deeper clarity into the teachings of the inner marriage. These are critical steps that we must take in moving onward into the energy of the Christ. Now I would like to address another subject.

Response: "Please do."

I will be holding the space for the opening of the Map of Exchanges, for the map in its essence and energy is masculine. I will be holding this energy, and I would ask for your assistance in bringing forth this series of discourses, as I would like to speak about the Divine Will. Many upon the Earth Plane and Planet see themselves susceptible to that known as the Divine Will, instead of understanding that in this Divine Will lies that measure of Grace. It is the Divine Will that operates from, what we shall call, the Angelic Realm of Neutrality.

I ask for your assistance, Dear one, and I call forth the inner marriage of all of those who are ready to proceed into the Christ. And if you do not have further questions, I shall turn the discussion back over to my Dear Brother Saint Germain.

Response: "In reply to your request for assistance, I am always of service and I will assist at any time that you request."

Hold the thought for the masculine energy as I have taught you to hold the thought in the flame of the candle. Hold the thought in all creation that you see the masculine energy, that all contains the breath of the Power of Spirit. For every flower, tree, river, and even a mountain holds the thought, energy, and pattern of the inner marriage with the masculine energy. When I gave you the teaching of merging yourself to the candle, that was a teaching based upon the power of the Heavenly Spirit. Do you understand?

Response: "Yes, I do."

I ask you to discipline your focus and at least once per week practice this. Many upon the Earth Plane and Planet have understood the masculine energy to be one who protects with the sword. It is time now to protect with the Power of Spirit, the Power of the Divine. Hold this focus, Dear chelas. I bid you good-bye.

Response: "Thank you."

*Saint Germain steps forward.*

I hope this brings a deeper and further clarity to our work, and of course, it is now time to open this floor for any more questions.

Question: "The only question that I have is about the time schedule to complete the Map of Exchanges."

Let me confer for one moment.

Response: "It is not important that this is answered now. It may be answered at your convenience."

I remind you, Dear chelas of mine, to call upon the Violet Flame of Mercy and Forgiveness.

Call upon the Violet Flame, for it can remove all subjective discord in an instant. I call forth the liberty and freedom of all of those who desire to unite in the ONE. I AM freedom. I AM liberty. I AM the Light. I AM Saint Germain.

Response: "Thank you. Amen. Hitaka."

# The Christ Body

*"If you call upon but one small drop of that Cosmic Christ,
you have within your heart-self the remembrance
of your physical immortality."*
**- SAINT GERMAIN**

*Our friend, Sherry Takala, joins us in this lesson from Saint Germain.*

Greetings in that mighty Christ. I AM Saint Germain and I stream forth on the Violet Ray of Mercy and Forgiveness. As usual, Dear hearts, I must request permission to come forth into your energy fields. Is this permission granted?

Len: "Greetings Dear one. Permission is granted."

The time upon the Earth Plane and Planet is ready to close Dear ones, for long we have said that time compaction comes to the Earth Plane and Planet. You have understood this in many forms, of what we shall call, unified fields and relativity. However, we shall explain it in its simplest term. It is that time where the mighty Christ comes, to fill each and every one of your hearts, and it is that time that I have spoken of that you know to be Unana.

This, known as the collective Christ field, comes through each and everyone of you to enter into that mighty Monad. It is that mighty Monad that you will draw your, shall we call, infinite body from, and what you have, in a sense worked from, known as that aggregate Body of Light. We have addressed what is known as subjective bodies and we have also addressed what is known as the aggregate body. Tonight we shall talk about the idea of the Monadic Body, also known as that Christ Body, that Christ Body from which you will draw your Source; for as you are of it, it is of you.

## BEYOND "RIGHT" OR "WRONG"

In the movement through the Earth Plane and Planet, you have wondered at times as you look at one hand, left to right, one foot, left to right, and asked, "Is this right or is this wrong?" I remind you again, Dear chelas of my heart, that there is, in a sense, no right or wrong. But what there is, is that ability for you to choose, and it is in that choosing that then you enter into what is known as that path of the Co-creator. Those who have come to create are those who work with a subjective body, or come, as we shall say, with that agenda that is not steeped in the intent of the aggregate Body of Light. But those who come to Co-create understand that there is a Divine Will that pours through each and every one of you, and when one aligns, what they shall call their creative forces, with that mighty Monad or creative force, then they stream forth into what is known as Co-creation.

## A GREAT WAVE OF THOUGHT

I have given those Laws of Co-creation, and each and everyone of you have had that opportunity to experiment, as we shall call it, with a Co-creative thought. You have carried out your work upon the Earth Plane and Planet, and we too carry forth our work and allow this to come forth in what we call a Divine Rhythm. This Divine Rhythm is what we call a wave that you may particlize upon or take advantage of. When we say that an opportunity exists, or a window opens, or a door opens, then you have an opportunity to grasp that wave, or what we call, a great wave of thought.

Each of these waves of thought stream forth from that which is known as the great Monadic Source, or the central part of Christ Consciousness, from which each and every one of us has drawn our particular individualization. Our individualization, of course, comes from that great Monadic Source. However, when we do cloak ourselves within a body, or take on a body to perform, what you would call a miraculous feat, or even to come, in a sense, with full soul recollection, which is known as an embodiment, we always carry with us that flame in the heart. I hope to make this clear to you Dear chelas, for there is still a misnomer among you that if you are in embodiment, you do not carry enough of the life force to raise you into that mighty Christ Consciousness.

## THE BOUNDLESS, INFINITE CHRIST CONSCIOUSNESS

The mighty Christ consciousness is unbound by time, nor is it bound with the left to the right, or the theories of pushing and pulling particalization along these waves of thought. However, we would like all of you to understand that each of you are part of ONE body, and it is that ONE body that is moving into a vaster unified field of thought. We have always called this the Theory of Time Compaction. The time comes to the Earth Plane and Planet, that time, in a sense, will stop for your consciousness and will lead to a new dimensional reality. Many of you are at this point, as we would call it, of critical attendance. At this point of critical attendance, there is a quantum leap in consciousness that leads each and every one of you into that Source of the Monadic Flame. Where do we go from there but onward into Life, for Life is this continuous process, ever-changing, ever-expanding, ever-transforming, and never-ending. You are all infinite creations, Dear chelas and students of my heart, infinite and loved from the Source of All.

If you sense in your Brother or Sister a bit of disharmony here or there, extend your heart to that one, not only in that mighty Law of Forgiveness, but also extend that mighty Law of Life. It is that mighty Law of Life that each and everyone of you has grasped in this wave, and now particlize as a life extending unto life. As you would say, at the end of this embodiment, perhaps then, "I can." Let me assure you Dear hearts, that this embodiment is an extension of that ever-extending life, onward and onward. To take a consciousness of immortality and then to extend it into your thought and feeling world is what we know as practicing physical immortality. For you know now you must first have the thought and then the feeling before you bring it into physical activity.

## THE IMMORTAL DROP

As a practicing immortalist for over two hundred years, I realize that not only must I keep the body in a state that requires alchemical assistance, I also must keep the body in a meditative state, or shall we call it, a samadhi state, so that the body itself is able to transcend, what you would call, the pushing and pulling energy thought forms that age the body. People that are near (or experience), what is known as the opposites, the push and pull, or contraction and then restriction of energy within the system, experience aging. It is the cause of all aging. How do we reverse these aging processes? The aging process can be reversed through deep meditative states, a rigid discipline and regimen of the diet, as well as an understanding of your divinity and Source unto the Monadic Flame.

If you can but call upon but one small drop of that Cosmic Christ, as we call it, you have then within your heart-self the remembrance of your physical immortality. Of course, your physical immortality relies upon your spiritual immortality, your mental immortality, and your emotional immortality. To understand that even your feelings are immortal gives a whole new dimension to your experience, does it not? So take this stance, Dear chelas and students, that all activity is immortal, all activity is infinite, all activity is that life is for life.

## THE LIGHTED STANCE

The Christ Plane comes Dear students and chelas and it is yours to access, for you are brought forth in the great Divineship. As we have talked of the Oneship, we shall address this, the Divineship. You are here to learn and Master these laws, these laws known as Co-creation. Of course, there are many creations that you have carried forth in a subjective manner, but let us now address Co-creative activity and the Vortexing energy that surrounds Co-creative activity.

You have known this and addressed this as the Merkabah and yes, it is true Dear ones that the Merkabah is the Vortex for this activity. It allows you access into the infinite ONE and allows you to draw on that constant refreshing drink that I have long spoke of. With this unified field of energy (one aspect rotating to the left and another rotating to the right) you access these deep reaches of, what we call, the Lighted Stance. It is that Lighted Stance that I have spoken of before that raises the metabolic rate and leads one into, what we will call, a high revolution per second of electrons around neutrons and protons, which also then raises all atomic stance. The Lighted Stance also allows one then to access emotional immortality, as well as mental immortality.

You, Dear students and chelas, may refer to this as the aggregate Body of Light, for it is in this aggregate Body of Light that you are all able then to understand the Oneship, the ONE Being, the ONE Body. As you said tonight and even heard in this discourse, are we not all ONE? Each word is what we would call an infusion of this Lighted Stance into your consciousness. Even the particles of the table and the chair are all part of this Lighted Stance and contain within them this infusion of consciousness.

## THE TIMELESS ONE

You have known for a long time that everything upon the Earth Plane and Planet contains a consciousness, for all upon the Earth Plane and Planet has come forth in what we know as that holographic pattern of reason, and it is that holographic pattern of reason that you attribute to thought. The process then is thought, feeling, and then action, again, or as we say, "to do, to dare, and then to be silent." All of these are Laws of Co-creation, but we must always address the intent that underlies all involved and that is for life.

Everything relates to this ONE Source, this Monadic Flame that is known as the Christ, and everything is contained within it and contained without it. As you breathe each breath into your lungs, do you not exhale, and where does this air come from that you take into your lungs, but from that Monadic Source? So we remind you that the time has come when time shall be no longer, for in recognizing there is no time, you then gain that understanding that it is but ONE. For when you recognize there is time, the mind becomes subjective to past, present, and future, but in recognizing there is but ONE and no time, all life honors the life that is.

## IMMORTALITY AND THE UNFED FLAME

The achievement of physical immortality rests first upon your achievement of spiritual immortality, and then moves into mental immortality. Address emotional immortality and your physical immortality will be but the vehicle that follows behind.

As you have known that all is a harmonic, each layer of your electromagnetic field lining up to what you know as thought, feeling, and action, also lines up to that electromagnetic immortality.

There have been times when I have appeared before you, Dear students and chelas of mine, and you noticed a faint scent in the air, perhaps even that of electricity, and you hear a sparkling of the currents within the air. What is this, Dear students and chelas? It is known as the infinite Life Source. We carry that infinite Life Source within the heart, that Unfed Flame, as it has been known for many centuries, but it is, what we call, that charge of electrochemistry. Electrochemistry relates of course to the spiritual and to what you would know as etheric layers, but in this instance, you know it to be a physical manifestation of a spiritual phenomena. There is no phenomenon on the Earth Plane and Planet; however, there are what you would know as unexplained events which are not yet presented to your consciousness.

As life unfolds about you, Dear chelas, understand that life is an infinite and glorious union of the ONE. When we address the masculine and feminine energies and address that known as that inner marriage, we are bringing you to a language to understand the ONE, the Great Divineship, the Oneship, All That Is, all that is of, all that ever will be. It is a timeless and infinite Source that you draw your life from. If you perceive that your body is aging, you have forgotten that within your heart is that electromagnetic pulse. We ask you to return back into that heart of that electromagnetic pulse and again recognize, through the holographic patterns of thought, your immortal and infinite being. Do you have questions?

Question: "Yes, Dear one. If you were to give us a decree to sustain the thought, feeling, all actions, including dietary and meditation regimens, to maintain this activity, what decree would you give us?"

> I AM the infinite Light of the Source.
> I AM the infinite Light of all being.
> I AM held in the infinite Divine Oneship.

Send your prayers to your hearts first, Dear chelas, for there you are connected into that mighty Monad, that ONE flame. As I say again, you are all ONE. You are ONE consciousness. You are ONE flame. If you can not perceive spiritual and physical immortality for one of your Brothers and Sisters next to you, then it is impossible for you to achieve this even for your own being. You will share in this Oneship, this ONE Monad. It would appear to you that we have achieved this. We achieved this, as well as infusing and teaching this science to you. Am I clear?

Response: "Yes, you are very clear. It is the universal thought, as you have stated many times, to see the perfection in each person when we work with them. So too, you ask us to hold the thought of their spiritual, mental, emotional, and physical immortality."

Hold the thought to perfection Dear ones, for in perfection is your immortality. Hold the thought always of the best and the highest good for all those concerned in any given situation, for therein lies that wellspring of Life. Dear chelas, your life is blessed with Life. Life is flowing with life. Life is ever-present with life. As I have said, "Down with death!" Down with death forever Dear chelas. Take this into your being and assimilate it into its fullest context. Take it in and understand that life is for Life. Perceive this death no longer and enter then into conscious immortality.

Sherry: "How can we, with our thoughts, help those people who are flooded, starving, and fighting? What thoughts can we give those people to help them through this?"

Through that Mighty I AM Presence THAT I AM,
I call forth the Law of Divine Perfection.

To all those concerned, in any location, call forth the Law of Divine Perfection. Ask that the highest and best good is made apparent in any given situation. Do you not see that even with these most current events that a higher law is being implemented? Seeing that in all situations is a perfection. See that all instances are being used to bring in an infusion of perfection and immortality.

Even with these flooding waters, are not these persons learning great Laws of Cooperation? Is not the planet itself being restored to yet a better state? Even on the skin itself, when cut and an infection weeps, the wound itself clears those shards from that wound. In this instance, are not all those involved being led to understand a deeper awareness and a deeper appreciation of life? Send your good thoughts and your good feelings to these persons. Call forth the Law of Manifestation to replenish their homes and fill their hearts.

The time that comes to the Earth Plane and Planet is now a time of demonstration of the Christ Consciousness. Yes, it is true many more changes may come to the planet, but these changes beget more life. When you understand your immortal destiny, you then begin to understand that in these changes, or in riding these waves, is a particlization of choice and it is this choice that brings great joy. In appreciating the life that you have and living with this deep joy, this inner Source is the wellspring of all life. In this wellspring and in this deep joy, you unite as ONE in a Co-creation of ONE. Do you understand?

Response: "Yes, but we sometimes forget."

The forgetting is the challenge, but in that challenge is the joy.

Question: "Are there more activities coming now for the Earth?"

THE MISSION FOR CO-CREATION

Scheduled events, yes. Strategic areas to look for and, what we would call, those great challenges of joy, extend from the Gulf of Mexico on up to the southern points of Florida. Watch into the Cuba area, particularly into Havana. Also as far north up to what we would call the 43rd parallel. And if you wish to perform energetic work to assist the East Coast, it is the 44th parallel. Send your thought and your feeling so Holy and Sacred to these areas. Let your energy unionize in that inner marriage. Ask for the best and highest good and allow this plan to rejoice. Of course too you can watch for more days of rain coming into the Midwestern area. However, with the projection of the proper energy, this could cease in an instance.

Many of you would wonder why we do not assist. Dear ones, we have given energy to the Earth Plane and Planet, but we are also here on a mission, and that mission is to help you to raise your energy so you can understand the power of Co-creation. As we are here to guide each and every one of you, understand that you are teachers, students, chelas, who are being led into a greater experience of the ONE. We anchor a point of consciousness within each and everyone of you and from that, you catapult into what is known as another dimension. We shall stay where we shall stay, and you shall go where you shall go. Questions?

Question: "Do we prepare for these Earth Changes that are happening for our growth? I realize that hoarding food brings on starving, but do we prepare with greenhouses, so we can grow food, or do we just know that we'll have food? What attitudes do we take?"

LIFE BEGETS LIFE

If this brings you joy and begets more life and feeds that wellspring of immortality within your being, I highly recommend it. It is impossible to become an immortalist if you carry about that emotion known as guilt. However, if these are activities which you bring you joy, then I highly recommend that you approach this. Life begets more life. If you are filling your activities with that joy of life, will this not bring more life into your life, and therefore more energy into that aggregate Body of Light. Do you understand?

Len: "So, if we focus on purchasing life insurance, putting energy into the sustainment of the finite, that is the expansion that we go to. When we put energy into the infinite, into the inner joy, into the sharing, that is the purpose we have on this planet. We plant our gardens because it gives us joy, not because we are afraid of not enough to eat."

We are not afraid that you will fail. However, we take great joy in the knowledge that the Light of God Never Fails! We take great joy in knowing that you are all attending at this most critical time. We take most joy in, shall we say, knowing that the activity of this work has lifted the consciousness of so many of you who have your eyes and ears open. Follow your hearts Dear students and chelas, for in following your heart is life.

Sherry: "So, if I enjoy raising food and sharing it with other people, then I am to do that?"

At all times, share that joy of your heart.

Question: "I am concerned about volcanoes. I have not heard much about them, but it seems like there are a vast number of people who could choose to die within volcanoes. Are they on the West Coast?"

VOLCANIC ACTIVITY

The first volcanic activity, shall we say in the western domain, will occur off South America. However, before those South America activations, you will see activity, not only in the Philippines, but on up into Japan.

Question: "Are there any activities coming in Alaskan waters, the inland passage?"

Let me scan that for one moment please. At this moment what we detect are several problems with economic structures. Questions?

Question: "I am concerned about the oceans. The fish have been moving to new spots and some are developing illnesses. Could you give me an idea of what is going on in the Pacific?"

## SPECIES LEAVE - NEW ARRIVALS

A problem, we shall call it, at the vibrational level. There is, what we call, an entire sonic explosion happening in the ocean plates which sends a vibrational frequency effecting the formation of certain plant substances. There is simply not enough food for certain species to survive. Therefore, you see a movement of certain species. However, there is a change in what you would call climatic conditions in certain tides. Please understand that a time has come for consciousness to be raised and as certain species are in a sense removed, new species are being readied.

Question: "Aren't certain species choosing to leave at this point, such as the ones that are endangered. Are they choosing to leave so that others can come in?"

This is the natural pause that life brings more life. Even as you would assume that these species have left your planet, it does allow for new species to evolve.

Question: "Will there be strong winds with this plate movement occurring now?"

## HIGH WINDS AND POLE SHIFT

If we enter into that time of polar shift, the winds will exceed 700 mph at the location of the shifts. However, we would recommend those who wish to avoid high winds of this type, locate as close to the equator, or also what we have known as Golden City Vortices. However, Dear students, as you have understood, the Earth Changes information has always been taught in its prophetic sense; it is taught from that point of making a choice.

Question: "I was most concerned with Alaska because there is no Vortex that I know of up there and I wondered if all those people would perish?" [Editor's Note: The Golden City of Eabra exists in both Alaska and Canada.]

Life begets more life. There is no life that perishes. "Down with death!" as I have said. However, let us hold that one perfect thought, that all life continues, ever-expanding and transforming into the ONE Monad, that Christ Consciousness known as Unana.

Response: "Thank you."

I shall take my leave. Let me appoint several times when we shall discuss this infusion of material discourses, to be given at approximately 10:00 A.M. tomorrow morning. Dear ones, as usual, I would remind you of use of that Violet Flame. Call upon that mighty law that not only transfigures, but transmutes in the breath, sound, and electromagnetic activity of life, of all life. I AM Saint Germain.

Len: "Thank you Dear one. We are grateful."

# Instructions for Europe

*"Through consciousness, this higher understanding will birth Earth
into the New Times and a Golden Age will be born."*
- SANANDA

*This is a session with our friend R.J. who resides in Switzerland and is
seeking instruction of how to share Earth Changes information.*

Greetings Beloveds in the mighty Violet Flame. I AM Saint
Germain and I request permission to come forward.

Response: "Please Saint Germain, you are most welcome."

Lori: "Does our guest give permission to Saint Germain to come
forward?"

Guest Response: "I give permission that he comes forward."

## THE VIOLET FLAME AND TIME COMPACTION

Greetings Dear ones. You see, it is through that Violet Ray,
the mighty Ray of Mercy, Compassion, and Forgiveness, that I

stream forth from that Great Central Sun and arc my energies into your solar system, so that you then may begin to understand the importance of this Ray and the importance of the mighty Violet Flame. It is through this Violet Flame that all transmutation of the past can then occur, as we have spoken about in many of the discourses. This is that Violet Flame, that mighty Violet Flame, that came from the Temples of Atlantis and also from that time when the Lords of Venus brought it forward to transmute all karma, all misunderstanding, and to bring the little hurts and the little fears that humanity has held into the lighted stance for transmutation and ultimate forgiveness. It is through this Violet Flame that then harmony is brought forward into the lifestream, so that one may then move forward into a greater understanding of their own divinity and Oneship.

It is Lord Sananda who has said that you indeed must love one another. And it is through this mighty Violet Ray, that the chela is then prepared to understand how they are indeed ONE with one another. When you offer yourself in forgiveness, this forgiveness then extends on into that Oneship. When you give forgiveness over the little situations that happen in day-to-day life, then you free yourself from the circumstances and situations that keep you in bondage. As you would understand, it is only true freedom when you have been set free from such circumstances.

I've come forward to talk about the Earth Changes material for Europe and so that there can be a better understanding for presenting this material to the public at large. You see Beloveds and Dear ones, the time is at hand. There is a time that is coming to this Earth Plane and Planet when those who have the eyes to see and the ears to hear will work for an opening. You see Beloveds, the Golden Age is soon to be birthed, a time where humanity will be raised into a new dimensional awareness and those will be changed in the instant, in just one moment. This is due to what is known as a Time Compaction. This is also due to this vibrational shifting that is occurring within the Earth. But indeed, you have wondered about the Earth Changes, this time where Mother Earth herself must shift to allow this new birth in consciousness to come forward.

## HEARTS ARE READY

We have given all of the information, as you have understood it, for the Americas and we have continued with the information for Asia and Australia. But now, we must talk about that which is known as the Map of Exchanges, an area of land that is sponsored by Beloved El Morya and Beloved Kuthumi, along with Lady Nada. But I, as sponsor of the Americas, have now come forward to help and assist if there are any questions, and also to give more information which may be important at this time. For you see, hearts are ready. Hearts are ready to be opened to this information, this message of ultimate peace, this message of ultimate Brotherhood. It rests on that pivotal point of absolute and total forgiveness and the application of this mighty Ray in action, the Violet Flame. But those again who have the eyes to see and the ears to hear will now put this mighty law into the action of its course.

## THE NEW CONSCIOUSNESS OF UNANA

You see Beloveds, there are those who will just not believe this type of information until they have seen it, until they have actually experienced it. But have you not noted that upon your Earth in this moment that there is indeed a melting of the polar ice caps? The melting of these polar ice caps has always been prophesied to be one of the beginning forces. But as I have taught you so well, there is indeed a change that happens first from within. This change that happens from within is then reflected to the outer. This is the change that we are seeing right now in your own global economies. Are you not seeing that there are now the "haves and the have-nots"? A total disparity is existing between those who have and those who have not. This creates a tension and this type of tension creates within it, its own collective consciousness. These are the things that we must work on at a global level, through prayer, transmutation, and a steady and total focus upon the concept of consummate Brotherhood. To bring about this end, to have a Golden Age, is to have a consciousness that first keeps its focus upon that of complete unity, the consciousness of Unana.

Mighty Unana, come now to this planet.
Mighty Unana, let the science of Oneship and Brotherhood
reign supreme.

It is through the understanding that we are all as ONE that we can then move on into a New Time and true peace and Brotherhood will then be attained. But the Dove of Peace is yet to land because of disparity. This disparity starts of course first within consciousness, first within consciousness of one who would say or think that they are superior over another, one who would think that there is a reason for them to have more than another. And yet, this has been the same consciousness that has kept all of those in this Earth Plane separated from a true unity, the true life that is in the spiritual world. The concept of Unana has never been one which has been held with great respect upon this Earth Plane and yet, it is the true spiritual way. To live and breathe in unity, to live and breathe in Oneship, is the true path. It is the true way to understand.

Invoking the Violet Flame transmutes and purifies all consciousness, that of this lifetime and that of many other lifetimes that you may be working under but yet are not conscious of. Through the use of this mighty flame in action, the way is paved for you to begin to truly feel unity, to truly feel Oneship.

The work that now must be extended from the United States, from the Americas, onward to the lands of Europe, is ready. This time is now. Beloveds, I would like to introduce my Brother.

*Standing next to him is Lord Sananda.*

Greetings Dear hearts, Dear children, I AM Sananda. I request permission to come forward.

Response: "Please come forward, you are most welcome."

Guest Response: "Please come forward."

The time is at hand. The awakening has come. Send this message to the Earth with love. There is much work now in front of you, much work indeed. It is not only a work of spreading this message of prophecy but it is also a work of opening hearts. The opening of these hearts is a receptivity to the idea of total love among others. This is of the most importance in sharing this information.

## A VIBRATIONAL SHIFT

It was deemed some time ago through the Spiritual Hierarchy that a time would come when the information of Earth Changes would be brought to humanity. We wondered if it was an information that humanity could even deal with, for you see Beloveds, Dear hearts, it is one which, when used improperly, instills a great deal of fear. And it is most important that in sharing this information, that all are opened first through love and through true understanding of Brotherhood and Sisterhood. For you see, this Time of Change is a time of the opening of the heart, a Time of Awakening of humanity to the Christ Consciousness that is within all of you. It is through this consciousness, this higher elevation of understanding that will birth your Earth into the New Times and a Golden Age will then be born.

This Golden Age is not only a time of cooperation with the Mother Earth, Beloved Babajeran, but also is a time where humanity is changing through the assistance of the Beloved Mother. Through this interaction between Beloved Babajeran and humanity and also through the assistance of the Spiritual Hierarchy, the Archangels, and the Elohim, a vibrational shift can then ensue.

## TO "KNOW" LOVE

This Golden Age will bring about a New Time in your history upon the Earth. A new understanding will flow. This new understanding will bring about a new education, an education that will flow from the heart, an education that can be put into words, an education that can be put into action. This higher knowledge that we are speaking of is a knowledge that is found at first in one concept and one concept only, it is the total and absolute Law of Love. Through this Law of Love, you shall become ONE with your Brother and only through this Oneship that you will share with your Brother, will you then begin to understand the higher laws and these higher dimensions as they do exist. This seems to be difficult for most humans; for you see, so many of the laws that have brought about your evolution have been built upon competition, survival, and a type of worry mentality. But how is it brought about, Dear ones, that the true Law of Love may reign supreme in this which is known as a Golden Time?

Put this Law of Love into action, for only in this Law of Love will this truth then be known. In loving one another, you are able to put the needs of another person, the feelings of another person, all energies about that other person as equal to yourself. You are able then to sense that person, to know that person, as an equal unto yourself. Only through that is there then a total opening of what is known as the Eighth Energetic Body. I have explained this before to you Dear ones, but it is known as a collective form of consciousness. It is through this energy body, through this collective Oneship, that true union then occurs with this other individual. You understand and know each other through a higher form of sensing, almost as if you are indeed as ONE, your minds sharing the same thoughts, patterns, and feelings.

This is of course of the utmost importance in sharing the Prophecies of Change, to talk about this Law of Love, for this is what another will instantly respond to. In the Earth Plane and Planet, what is it that all are seeking but to know and understand love . . . to know what love is . . . to feel what love is . . . to experience love continuously, are they not?

Response: "Yes, I would agree."

It is through this love, this total consummate love and seeking for this love, that all will respond to and move towards. This allows them to then understand why these changes are happening and at what level they will also serve a Cause Divine. Questions?

Guest Question: "Dear Sananda, I would like to know how I can do my job and bring this information with love to the Earth and especially to the people in Europe?"

Call upon me and there I AM. Call my energies and call my name forward and I shall come in my healing embrace. I shall protect all meetings and all gathering of your information and material. This will bring an energy of love, an energy of protection. Call upon me and there I AM.

Guest Response: "Thank you, I will do so."

And now, I shall turn the floor back to Beloved Saint Germain.

Response: "Thank you."

Guest Response: "Thank you."

Greetings Beloveds. And now it has been appointed that I shall bring more information, organizational support, so to speak, for an understanding of the work at hand. There are indeed certain countries that should be given this information first, in the same way that when the Earth Changes material was organized for the United States, certain locations were to be informed first. And in this manner we would like to proceed. Before I begin, are there any questions?

Guest Response: "Not at the moment."

It is important of course first to start in your own area. Through this, you will gain a momentum of support. Is this understood?

Guest Response: "Yes."

This is of course is the easiest way. At times, when you're beginning with such a message, it may seem that you are being tested. In the beginning, have you not felt this?

Guest Response: "Yes, I have felt it."

## PEACE AND CALM THROUGH THE FLAME

Now, when you encounter those who would educate you, so to speak, it is important to invoke that mighty Violet Flame into action, to bring you into a center and a calm of balance. To bring that mighty flame around you invoke:

Mighty Violet Flame, come forth now in this moment.
Mighty Violet Flame soothe all troubled waters.
Mighty Violet Flame consume all misunderstanding.
Mighty Violet Flame, God I AM Violet Flame.

Within that moment, you see, a calmness will occur. You have just invoked that mighty law to action, and any disharmony, any of those who have brought a contentious energy into the information you're about to bring, will then calm their minds and their hearts. After you have gained a security, shall we say, within six months of presenting this information in small groups in your local area, it is then important that you travel to all coastal areas. For you see Beloved, Dear heart, these are the areas where people must be informed first. This will be where you again will be tested, for these are areas where they will not be as receptive to hear this type of information. Do you understand?

Guest Response: "I understand."

This is very important and this is where you will be tested and the steel of your will tempered. From these coastal areas, then I shall be sending an energy up for you to travel to England. It is there in England that some of your greater work will be done. And be prepared in that moment, because that is where this information then will begin to spread rapidly. Now, we are talking about a year's worth of time. But it is important first that you practice within your own local area and gain your support from there and then move the energy forward. Do you understand?

Guest Response: "I do understand."

And now, are there any questions?

Question: "Yes, I have a question. Many people who consider themselves of the Light or New Age call for the White Light to come around them for protection. But the Violet Flame is to be used by our guest?"

The Violet Flame is used by all of those who come under the tutelage of this work, which is known as Transition. The Violet Flame has been brought forward to bring the Divine Intervention of Grace into an individual's life. The Violet Flame is best to be meditated upon at least one time per day but call upon it in any circumstance, for the Violet Flame can bring its mighty Rays of Transmutation into any situation. For instance, if you are having trouble manifesting enough money in your life, call upon the Violet Flame to enter into all economic situations. If you are having a problem with your husband or with your wife, call upon that mighty Violet Flame in action. If you have discord, disharmony, discontent, even with a customer, call upon that Violet Flame. You see, this mighty law in action has been brought forth to set you free, to free your consciousness from all that would hinder it from the work at hand.

Response: "The Violet Flame could also be called forward for physical problems, making a decree such as: Mighty Violet Ray stream forward from the Heart of the Central Sun, that mighty Logos, and transmute the problem with my pancreas into perfect health. So Be It."

This too could be applied. You see Dear ones, the Violet Flame not only sets, at a molecular level, that mighty law in action, but the universe itself responds and situations and circumstances can then be altered and changed.

MANIPULATION, FEAR, AND GREED

Now I should like to speak to you about current situations. I have already indicated to you that there may be changes now upon the economic scene. If you find it possible, always know that it is metals, gold and silver, that hold their value. During this period that you may be entering into, this will be more solid in terms of the economy, a way for you to have, shall we say, a sense of security. It is also important for you to understand the forces that are manipulating your global economies at this time. Just as the talk about the Y2K, the computers, and ensuing problems, was another invention of the dark forces, there are many manipulations using the elements of fear and greed among humanity. It is always important to use common sense but also to look into these situations much, much more thoroughly. There are those who would use a situation to manipulate those who feel fear, to manipulate those into thinking something that is not. Do you understand?

Both Respond: "Yes."

And so, it is important first to have common sense. But have I not told you before, that the change that would happen within would then be the change to the outer? It is important Dear hearts, to understand that much of the world that is created about you may not be worth keeping, may be well worth the change that is to occur. There are those who say, "Well, what will we do without that? What will we do without this?" Let it go simply and realize that you are making way for the new creation that is to come.

Imagine if you will, a new economy that is based upon stability and abundance for all beings. One may understand through true work, the work of the heart, that a result is given; the intention that is laid within the heart is given its ability to manifest through these laws and action. The darkness that has covered the planet has been a darkness of refusing to see. Do you remember the teaching that I gave, where I removed the blindfold from my eyes? When I lifted that away from my face, you could clearly see that this is what awaits us all upon this Earth Plane and Planet, the ability to take this blindfold from our eyes and to clearly see and clearly know what is happening.

It is important to not be stuck within anger, not be stuck into blame, and to understand that the dark forces that have used each individual at a level of greed, at a level of fear, a level of avarice, has been through individual choice. One must face this dark force that exists within them and when one is willing to transmute this darkness from themselves, they are no longer a puppet of the Puppet Master. Do you understand?

Both Respond: "Yes, I understand."

There will be those who will fear when they hear this information. They will come to you and say, "Let us build a survival community. Let us now store this. Let us now store that." But this is not the work at hand. The work at hand is teaching the premise of the Violet Flame, teaching the premise of true abundance for all, and staying firm within those Twelve Jurisdictions. Do you understand?

Guest Response: "I understand."

It is a spiritual work Dear ones and Beloveds. It is not an Earthly work but indeed a spiritual work, for that is where true camaraderie lies. Are there questions?

Guest Response: "No, thank you."

Question: "The only question that I have is, for our guest to carry on this work as our Brother, is there any specific instructions that you have for our side in helping him?"

It is important to include, as we do. It is important to model, as we do. Sup as Brothers and Sisters of the ONE. Include one another in your planning. Work together as we have worked together. Do you not see this as so?

Guest Response: "Yes."

Response: "That's very easy to do."

As we have shown you, as we have taught you, this is as it shall be.

Response: "So Be It then."

Guest Response: "So Be It."

Now, unless there are further questions, I shall bid my Adieu. Let the mighty Violet Ray stream forth. I AM Saint Germain.

Response: "Thank you."

Guest Response: "Thank you very much"

# Of the Father

*"You share together in the same conception, held in that mighty mind of the ONE, your birth timed as ONE together."*
- LADY NADA

Greetings Dear heart. I AM Sananda, Lord of the Transition, and I AM qualified on that mighty Golden Ray, that Golden Ray that unites all of humanity in the Oneship. I stand to address on this podium what is known as the project of transition and bringing to its full fruition what is known as a consciousness of the ONE. This consciousness of the ONE is the only hope that is left for those upon the Earth Plane and Planet, known as Sister Terra.

## OPENING THE MAP OF EXCHANGES

This Dear hearts, is the consciousness that will lead each and every one of you into an evolution of the ONE. Many changes are coming to your planet and this dispensation of work has been brought forth to prepare you to accept this new shift, not only in physicality, but also in your consciousness. Have you not noted the many geophysical changes that have now come to your planet? The time is now to awaken and arise. Come and sup with me, Brothers and Sisters of the Golden Flame. Come and be ONE, as you and I are. Come and share in this Age of Grace, for it is the gift that has unfolded. As I AM Lord of the Transition, I unroll this map, the final map to bring the dispensation of the spiritual and vibrational nature of change and transition to this world project.

I unroll this map and dedicate it to the landing of the Dove, for the Dove brings within its mouth a bough of peace. The Dove brings within its breath, the heart of true desire for freedom. The Dove comes with the teaching of Grace, that you are united as ONE family. You are as ONE tree. You all have ONE fruit. You all share in ONE land, and you all drink of ONE water.

This has been presented to you before by Beloved Kuan Yin, and now this information is brought for those who are of this Map of Exchanges. Open your ears and open your eyes and see you are united as ONE. Dear Children, come forth into the Golden Age, this Golden Millennium. Look at this map, Dear Children, for this will map your immortal destiny. Beloved Saint Germain has given much service to you Dear hearts. His vibrational frequency has been the vibrational frequency of Brotherhood and Sisterhood, for as you are in that vibration, do you not begin to feel the Oneness? This map is brought to bless and uplift you all, for you are all truly of the ONE. This is known as the Map of Exchanges, the final material for this dispensation.

This is the final information that we will give regarding Earth Changes. We request that, at all times, you deliver this message with the uptmost love and care for your Brothers and Sisters. Lead them not into what you would know as fear, but use this information to lead them into love, the ONE vibration, the Oneship. As you well know, this information is brought to lift you all and to bring you to, as Beloved Saint Germain has called, the Lighted Stance, for you are ONE with the Source. You are parent and child. You are male and female. You contain within you the Divine Inner Marriage, as you have known the Kundalini energy as a twist up and down the spine that unites in the dance of the flame. Each Ascended Being, Cosmic Being, Archangel, and mighty Elohim that has brought forth information in this project, has brought a small component of that mighty flame. We call this ONE flame the Monad, for the Monad is the Flame of Truth, the Flame of the ONE.

It is time to unite your duality. You have successfully mirrored back and forth what you are to one another. Now accept the wholeness and totality of your being. Come into the energy and know that you and I are ONE. I AM ONE with Saint Germain. I AM ONE with El Morya. We are Brothers, comrades, friends on the path of the ONE. You are all ONE too, Dear stewards of this planet. You are ONE. Come forth and stand in the glory of this New Age and Time. And now, I turn the floor over to Beloved El Morya.

*The tall blue teacher, Dear Morya, steps forward.*

Welcome my Dear chelas. I AM El Morya and I request permission to come forth.

Response: "Please do come forward Dear one."

The vibrational frequency that I bring is the vibrational frequency to open this information of the ONE. This information will consolidate all vibrational frequencies upon the planet and bring a synthesis of the ONE for the mighty Christ I AM.

BEYOND STRUGGLE AND INTO THE ONE

Throughout the eons you have known me as the Mahatma El Morya. It has been my position, as a member of the Spiritual Hierarchy of the Great White Brotherhood and Sisterhood, to hold a focus for the spiritual development of mankind. How have I held this focus? Through a recognition of the ONE! It is always a recognition of the ONE. I send my appreciation and gratitude and a great flow of thanks to this mighty ONE. This energy recirculates back to my own Presence of God and I am then able to extend it out again as an infinite breath.

I have held my focus in the Golden City of Gobean, as you are all well aware of Dear students and chelas. The focus that I bring to the Earth Plane and Planet aligns the will with the Divine Will, readying the chela and the student to accept a law that is higher than what he or she would create, a law higher than human law. You, Dear students and chelas, are those among humanity who have realized that the human law no longer serves that best and highest good. You have walked long upon the path, struggling at times, at times with a joyful playfulness, working to understand: How is it that I can best serve this planet, and move this planet along in such a manner that all are fed, clothed, and happy, and live in the harmony and grace of the ONE? You have struggled with constitutions, edicts, monarchies, anarchies, and various forms of political systems that no longer serve the vibrational frequencies of Unana. And now, Beloved Lord Sananda has stated, the time has come for you to feast.

In this feast, we all sit together to sup and to join. Each of us has had the taste of many foods within our mouths, have we not? Each of us has played many different songs, have we not? And all of us have recognized that the time has come for us to share in that ONE meal, that ONE focus that will align us now to share, laugh, and play in the joy of ONE. Focus aligns. Remember this, Dear students, focus aligns. Intent serves the ONE. Perhaps you, who are still serving what you would call the human law, need to taste more from that smorgasbord. There are those few who have realized that it is just another dish added to this meal. A time has come for us now to recognize the Source. A time has come for us now to recognize that we share ONE breath. Human law rarely serves this ONE breath, for human law is often steeped in what we call subjective reasoning, but let us take that reasoning of the ONE and recognize that we are all part of it.

## A WAVE OF HEALING

With this Map of Exchanges and its vibrational frequency, a great healing wave now comes to this planet. It is first opened through the door of justice and Lady Master Nada, that great lover of freedom and justice from Atlantis, will dispense the material for Europe. Before I turn the floor over to her, I send my vibration and thanks to you all, Dear students of the stalwart Heart. I send my appreciation and thanks to those other Ascended Beings of Light who have allowed the vibration of this project to come to full fruition. I thank you all in the vibration of the ONE. I will continue to hold my focus over Gobean and all who come wishing to know the mighty Law of ONE. Call upon me and I shall be there. Questions?

Response: "There are no questions Dear one. Thank you."

Dear fellow humanitarians and chelas of the planet Terra, I AM Lady Nada, and I AM fulfilling the request to dispense this material for the Map of Exchanges.

Response: "Please come forward Dear one. We are very grateful."

## I AM THE HEALING HEART

*Beloved Lady Nada steps forward. She has an energy which is very complementary to the Mahatma. She too is very tall. She is slender and her hair is golden, light blonde. Her eyes are a clear aquamarine and her flowing gown is a vibrant pink. She holds a group of scrolls in one arm. Standing very straight, her words are clear, strong and firm.*

I AM the heart.
I AM the healing heart.
I AM the love,
The love that heals.
I AM the heart that binds all as ONE.
I AM the heart that heals all in that mighty ONE I AM.

A time comes now to the planet when the Map of Exchanges is opened in its vibrational frequency for the demonstration of cooperation, as we would call it, and has allowed us now to open a portal to explain the presentation of these Earth Changes Prophecies.

## GLOBAL WARMING

As you have known, global warming is coming to the planet. More rains come. Dear ones, they come to heal you. Their healing waters flood over you and wash away all sense of your own separation. These waters come to bring a vibrational healing, not only to the planet and Babajeran, but also to that known as the collective consciousness. Perhaps you shall ask during the times of the rains, "Will this ever stop?" Remember, Dear ones, to call upon that mighty flame within your being and realize that these are the waters that will grow and nourish the mighty tree.

## MESSAGE FOR EUROPE

Listen children, you children of Europe, the time has come to open your hearts. Open your heart for healing is now at hand. You have been called to drop your swords and to drop your bags of gold. You are now called to enter into the heart of the mighty wound that you share with your Brother and Sister. You are all birthed of ONE mother and come from that ONE vessel. You share together in the same conception, held in that mighty mind of the ONE, your birth timed as ONE together. One is not older, better, or wiser. You have all come together as a family, one great Star seed dispersed across this planet, known as the

Sixth Manu, and you are all to be gathered together and taken in a Mass Ascension.

As the first earthquake hits your coastline of Scandinavia, know Dear Children, that you are called. You are now called to accept your seamless garment, your Body of Light that leads you into that mighty ONE. How shall this be achieved? You are that portion of the mighty Source of ONE that is active and takes action. You are the example and the demonstration of the flame. You are the one who shows the other how to fish. Understand, Children of the Map of Exchanges, that this time of transition comes for all. It is not for just a chosen few, but for the ALL, to open their ears and their eyes.

Please do not hoard your gold any longer. Please do not hold this world hostage with your armaments and your fears. Please allow a consciousness and an abundance to flow for that Brother and Sister who was birthed out of the ONE womb at the same time as you. Your Brother and Sister were not born holding onto your heel, but born holding onto your hand.

Children of England awaken, for the vibrational frequency of the Golden City comes, and miraculous healing is about to occur. In this Golden City, I shall anchor my consciousness and healing will come for those who are ready to choose for their Brother, as they would choose for themselves. This is the message for you, Children of Europe:

Love one another with all your heart and all your hand,
For you are the children who weave.
You are the children who know how to saw, bake, and clip.

You are the children who know how to do.
You are the children who can teach others the
occupation of Spirit
And teach the Spirit that knows the source of desire.

You are the children who have been brought to educate. And I remind you, you are the children who have come to *give* your gift. Please understand, Dear Children. Now listen. The one who is the teacher must allow the student to rise above him. Is it that hard to recognize the stability of the job that you bring? Each brick is laid down one at a time. We can not pull out that bottom brick. Know that each and everyone of these bricks is critical and important. Allow your Brother and Sister to stack their bricks upon you, for you have come to serve as a mighty fortress of consciousness. You have come to exchange your knowledge of the heavens. You would think that you have been a chosen few to lead this planet. Let us expand and then transform that consciousness.

Dear children of these lands of Scandinavia, England, Scotland, and Ireland, you are the Children of Spirit. You are the children of the Father. You are the children who exchange the fatherly energies and impregnate the Mother. You bring the knowledge of order, rhythm, structure, and form. Dear children of the Father, allow your energy now to anchor into the Mother. Give your gift so freely that all rejoice in the dance of ONE. Is this cup so bitter that you cannot drink of it? Is it hard to share in the joy of laughter?

Children, awake, arise! Come to the ONE. The time is now. Develop a quality of consciousness that loves all upon the planet, and these prophecies will not be so Earth riddling, shall we say. Develop a consciousness that simply accepts and loves, teaches, and trains. You are ONE with that mighty Father energy, Dear Children, ONE with that mighty Father energy, ready with its hand reaching open to receive the Mother. As that first rippling earthquake occurs, ask yourself then, am I ready to serve my Brother and Sister as ONE? I shall now open the floor for questions.

Question: "Dear one, is there a decree to enliven the hearts of those of Europe and of Africa, so that they no longer hold fast to their bags of gold or their arms that control one another. Is there a decree that can be said by these people?"

## I AM THE LOVE OF THE HEART

I AM the love of the heart.
I come as ONE with my Brother and Sister.
I AM the union of love.
I AM the union in love.

I shall return tomorrow, Dear ones, and proceed down the coast and give you specific boundaries.

Response: "I thank you very much and I am grateful."

# Sword of the Rose

*"It is time to reflect, go within, and there is your answer,
for the heart of the Father will never deny you such access."*
- LADY NADA

Greetings Dear hearts, Brothers and Sisters of the Golden Flame. I AM Sananda, and I stream forth on the Golden Ray that anchors the mighty Christ Consciousness I AM into humanity. First Dear ones, I request permission to come forth.

Response: "Please Dear one, come forth. You have our permission. "

The time upon the Earth Plane and Planet has come when humanity shall be merged into the Oneship, and in this Oneship, each and everyone of you will recognize that mighty Christ I AM, for it is the Christ that now comes and anchors into the consciousness of those upon this planet. It is this work and this purpose and intent of this, known as the Map of Exchanges, which is designed to help to facilitate the anchoring of that consciousness. Dear ones, I shall serve now as facilitator for the completion of this information, and I would like to introduce to you Beloved Lady Master Nada.

Response: "Dear one, please come forward. You are most welcome."

It is a privilege and a great honor to be here and bring this service to you, Dear Brothers and Sisters, for I AM of that Heart of the Rose and I have come to serve, for as I AM, you know, an Ascended Master of Justice and also healing for humanity. I AM also a being who has individualized service, and the service that I offer is service to bring forth the information for the Map of Exchanges.

THE OCEAN OF BALANCE

First, I shall talk about this area that you know as Europe. As I have stated before, a time will come to the planet where the melting of the ice caps will occur and form one mighty ocean, known as the Ocean of Balance. The melting of these ice caps will bring each member of humanity, even that of the Animal and Plant Kingdom, each and every individualized particle of consciousness, the understanding that life always lives in an infinite balance. In that balance is life.

Saint Germain has said, life begets life and balance begets life, for it is in balance that all life has its source and original intent. This ocean shall symbolize this mighty balance. As the scales are tipped, one side to the other, now comes the balance, for here is the justice for all. You humans have always asked for your freedom, your justice, your equity. Now it comes, Dear hearts, brought to you from this planet, this Oneship, this Mighty I AM.

You are ONE in this balance. It is a balance brought to demonstrate that it is only in balance that life is able to be.

In the middle of what we call this Ocean of Balance remains one island formed from those lands known as Russia. This island, the Shiny Pearl, comes as another demonstration of balance. In balance, when All That Is acts within harmony, great abundance is then the next step, and this planet shall be filled with the abundance of the New Age. The New Age comes to demonstrate all that you would know to be those cosmic principles, all that you would know to be of the Great Divine, the Great ONE—harmony, abundance, clarity, desire, illumination, freedom of all freedoms.

Even as you have understood this material to teach you the basics of Co-creation, we also hope that this material will teach you that beginning consciousness which expands into the mighty Christ. This we know as Unana. On this Shiny Pearl, Unana will be the example. The Shiny Pearl is the flowering and opening of all the gifts of the Christ. Here shall be many new seaports, each of them serving humanity for the healing and justice for all.

THE ISLANDS OF FRANCE

As we proceed and look into the major coastlines that exist in Europe, you will see that France is broken into a series of islands, for the focus held here should be for liberty and freedom for all. Many of her lands go under the Ocean of Balance for, what we call, a purification. Also, the same holds true with lands of Europe into Germany and Czechoslovakia. For, Dear hearts, these are lands that are wearied and tired by the spear, the warrior energy of the male. Now the female waters come and lap upon their beaches, consoling them, and reminding them that they too may rest and bring a great balance.

This is a map that is known to have a male energy, for many of the lands that are concerned with this information have been the more dominant energies for the past two thousand year cycle. But as we now move into the time of this inner marriage, many of the lands that have been so male, or shall we say, dominating, will go into a rest. This rest will be for approximately two hundred to four hundred years, and then these lands shall rise again, representing that great ring (circle) as the inner marriage, the infinite cycle.

JOINING AS ONE

For a time comes now, Dear hearts, where you shall no longer see yourself as male or female, but see yourself contained as ONE, the Christ.

Each hand shall join.
Voices shall join together.
Ears will hear that ONE tone.
Eyes will see that ONE Light,
That mighty golden light of a New Age.
The message of the Christ is that there is ONE,
And it is everlasting and infinite.

Many Golden Cities will be anchored throughout these lands for those who wish to go and obtain the teachings and the understanding. As I represent justice for all, the justice comes for the healing of humanity. The Eight-sided Cell of Perfection, planted within the heart of each and every one of those upon the planet, will now be activated as the Map of Exchanges brings its conscious attunement to the plane. The flame will leap out of each of the refractions of this Perfect Cell. All will be filled with the glory and wonder as they note a glowing about their bodies. Each will exclaim to one another, "I have become as a golden light, and on the outer edges, that rosy flame."

## STOP THE WARS

This time comes to demonstrate that you are ONE body. You are all ONE body, and it is time now to stop your warring with one another. It is time now to open the bounty of riches that this beloved planet Babajeran has bestowed upon you. You are caretakers of creation. You are brought here with a great service and destiny. You are the ones who have come to demonstrate to the rest of the Christos that even the smallest shall become the largest.

Let me continue now with the changes. Inward, another great sea is formed, known as the Sea of Grace. Again, other lands shall be given the rest that they long deserve. Humanity has climbed the reaches of greed, and now a time has come to rest that principle. Other seas will unite to form one, a Sea of Grace. It will be a time to rest, a time to surrender and come into a non-judgment of your neighbor.

Why is it that you have had wars upon the planet? It is so simple Dear students. You are in a constant struggle as humans, judging one another, and working to determine what is best for another, when you have yet to understand what is best for yourselves. As a representative of the Hierarchy, I too once felt that feeling of judgment, but I have ascended to this place, which so gracefully swept me here, and it is known as that place of neutrality where the angels of heaven now anchor this Ray upon the planet. The center of Spain shall be the anchoring of one such Ray, known as the Golden Ray. Here shall come one of the most remarkable healing events for the planet.

THE POWER OF HEALING

The pattern of consciousness is transformed and lifted into that surrender of the ONE. The time has come for a demonstration of love and more Golden Cities to spring forth as great centers of love for those who want to learn. It is time for humanity to hear this plea. As Dear Sananda has said and I shall repeat, "Love one another." Simply stated: Love one another.

These changes, do they come? Of course, Dear ones, for your planet is a planet of change, and this change is in the making. However, the severity of these changes is drastically altered by your ability to love. These changes are drastically altered by your ability to heal. Reach your hands out and feel the power of horizontal healing, for this is the message that Kuan Yin has brought in the Greening Map. And now raise your consciousness to receive that vertical command, the command of the ONE, for your hands are now joined in ONE mighty flame. And now I shall open the floor up for questions.

Question: "Thank you Dear one. The qualities of each of these Golden Cities throughout Europe and Africa, do each of these reflect the quality of a Ray?"

Each of them now refracts all the Rays, eight to be exact, into this Golden Millennium. However, one sponsor has come forth from each of these Rays.

Question: "In the healing and the changes that are prophesied here, it is our horizontal healing, our love and compassion for one another, that literally lessens the severity of these physical alterations of the planet. You bring forth a message to the hearts and the minds of those in these areas. Is there something that they can say again and again in their hearts that will bring forth this Golden Age as a transition of peace?"

Join your hands in a circle of love with the Brother who is present, and in so joining, you all heal. It is a song of healing that we all sing, a song that is sweet and fills our ears with the voice of Heaven. In our song love comes and the Christ descends on Earth. As above, so below. Dear ones, see how all are connected in this final union and see what was once the Great Mystery, is now removed, for all the mysteries come and are revealed. Now the time has come to end all time. Remove all barriers and allow your consciousness to expand into the mighty gift, the Oneship, the Christ.

Question: "In these changes, each area has a contribution to make. As they sing this song in this contribution, as they hold their hands together in this Great Circle of Life, as they bring this forward, would this be a daily practice?"

SURRENDER TO THE TRUTH OF LOVE

Not only daily, but a practice that is held within the being. It is a practice that is patterned in that great Cell of Perfection. As Saint Germain has explained to you how a pattern is created, now let us consider creating this great pattern of unconditional love and surrender, for as these barriers are broken the gifts are unimaginable. Those of you who have lived with the limitation of hatred, it is time now to consider that love can, and always has, overcome such limiting factors.

You, Dear ones, Children of Europe, hold the rose now as your sword of truth, hold the rose now as the symbol of your communion with the ONE, for you are the land that now exchanges the sword for this flower of love and truth. You are the land that now exchanges the energy of the masculine for the feminine. You are the land that now exchanges a consciousness of the warrior for your consciousness of the Christ. Come and open this door with me, Children of Europe, and we shall usher in an Age of Grace.

Question: "Since the rose is this symbol of transition, would you ask these peoples of Europe to grow roses in their garden, if it gives them joy?"

The fragrance of the rose is a fragrance of the ONE.

Question: "This is understood. Is there any sign that the beginning of these changes has come for this land of Europe?"

## PROPHECY OF THE NORTHERN STAR

When you look to the sky and see that the northern star has changed its position by twenty-three degrees, you shall know. But another sign shall be that each and every Brother and Sister upon the planet will begin to recognize their Oneship, the mighty Christ. Understand, Dear chelas and students, that this time comes. This time is now.

Question: "At the moment that we are bringing this information forward, in eastern Europe there is much fighting among those who are Christian and those who are Moslem, each one claiming that this is their land and is their sole right to live here. Since you are our Lady of Justice, will you, in this moment, give them a message?"

This land belongs to all. This land belongs to the Source, the ONE. You, Dear Children, are of this Source, and you belong to this Source first. Unite on the inside first. Find within you, your own inner harmony, and then live your life as a demonstration of that harmony. Is there justice in killing and destroying one another? Is there justice in starving your Brother's family? As you would make this choice for another, do you not now make this choice for yourself? Find within your heart the flame of healing. Find within your heart your own inner Source and then link that Source to the ONE. Know, too, that your Brother links this Source to the ONE, for you are ONE people, you are ONE creed, you sing ONE song, you dance ONE dance.

## THE HEART OF THE FATHER

And now you cry so many tears. It is time to cease, reflect, go within, Dear Children, and there is your answer, for the heart of the Father will never deny you such access. In the heart of the Father is all solution. Expand the heart of the Father into the womb of the Mother and unite the principles as two. Like lovers in the dust, you shall unite the two, and the child born of this mighty conception is a child who dances as the Christ.

Come forward, those who have disharmony. Cease for but a minute. Unite inside and realize that you are hurting yourself. Make the attempt to love yourself. Make the attempt to call upon the Law of Forgiveness. Make the attempt to stop the disharmony forever.

In the name of I AM THAT I AM,
I anchor the consciousness of justice and healing
into this area of conflict.
In the name of I AM THAT I AM,
May the Sword of the Rose now plant itself in the heart of
humanity's consciousness.

I AM Lady Nada.

# Conscious Immortality

*"You have thought about your death,
your demise, and your aging body.
But what about now?"*
- SAINT GERMAIN

Greetings in that mighty Christ. I AM Saint Germain. I stream forth on the Violet Ray of Mercy and Forgiveness. Dear hearts, this time which you know as the Yuletide, is a time where there is great joy upon the planet, a time of Brotherhood, a time of Sisterhood, a time when the choirs of spheres sing their harmony. At this time, we present to you, Dear ones, a portal to enter into the opening of Shamballa. As these gates open, you are admitted in. One by one you come and bring your gifts, like the gifts brought by the Magi, for this is a time for the opening of consciousness, and consciousness shall awaken your destiny and your immortality.

## CONSCIOUSNESS DOES NOT DIE

You have long thought that when your body dies, your consciousness dies as well. This is not so. You do not forget the so-called experiences you have had in your limited time and sojourn on the Earth Plane and Planet. However, through the use of consciousness, one may recall all life activity. Many upon the Earth Plane and Planet, when they first become aware of the immortality of the soul, play within those psychic realms of past life experience. However, we would like you to understand that you have one life that streams through that mighty Unfed Flame of Love, Wisdom, and Power, and it is through that jiva of Light that you retain your conscious immortality.

As I have always said, "Down with death!" and now I say, "Down with segmentation!" For how can you see your life streaming forth through one body to the next, when you contain a continual conscious stream of unfed energy? This energy which each and everyone of you contains, streams forth, shall we call, that Law of Divinity. In that Law of Divinity rests your immortal destinies, for you are all Divine and from your Divinity your consciousness becomes one continuous stream, one continuous recall, one continuous activity. It is in this one continuous stream that rests, shall we say, your ability to bi-locate, your ability to transfigure, and that mighty ability to enter into the initiation of the Ascension.

This work upon the Earth Plane and Planet is a work that I ask you address swiftly. Again, I remind you, chelas and students, tarry not with this work, for this work carries great import. It is important for the shifting consciousness of humanity, for humanity to realize its continuous thread, that one thread that runs throughout all of humanity's conscious immortality. When humanity discovers conscious immortality, they too will develop a responsibility towards the Earth Planet and its Animal, Vegetable, and Mineral Kingdoms. They will understand, as they are ONE continuous organism, they are linked in that mighty Unified Law of the ONE.

## A NEW WAY OF LIVING

When you develop an attitude of conscious immortality, you will take and breathe into your being a new way of seeing the world, a new way of living. Would man take the time to pollute his environment if he understood he was polluting his own backyard? As a conscious immortal being, he will understand that all he touches becomes ONE with him. When I refer to him, remember Dear hearts, I am not limiting my message to a gender, but I shall use *him* as in reference to humanity.

To develop a consciousness of immortality, let us try this one experiment. As you know, your body is the laboratory you use to experiment with the soul and the spirit. Your soul is encapsulated, shall we say, within this body for a time period. It contains the specific energy of its time of entry into the physical body and contains within it, a time of specified departure. The immortal essence that runs throughout your being is known as the Spirit and that Spirit fills your body and your soul. However, through that thinking capacity known as the brain, which is nothing less than an attachment or an appendage to the physical body, you have filled and programmed your thought (which is your conscious immortal mental body) with patterns of disease and death. Each day, I ask you to remind yourself of the patterns with which you fill your appendage. That brain is your tool to open up your destiny. Each day, remove those patterns of disease and death and say:

I AM an immortal being of divinity.
I AM an immortal being of destiny.

For you, Dear hearts, who read this material and come in contact with this teaching, have been brought here by Divine Appointment. Call forth your immortal destiny. Call forth your Divinity. Each and everyone of you have thought about your death, your demise, your aging body, and about the days to come when you shall not have these. But what about now? What about now, Dear hearts, Dear chelas. Are you living your life with a conscious immortality and an awareness of the destiny of your being? Are you living your life in the full spectrum, the seven Rays of Light, in, through, and around you, expressing the fullest of electromagnetic activity? This time that comes to the Earth Plane and Planet is a time where now science and technology will understand the basics of immortality.

## IMMORTALITY AND THE MENTAL BODY

Immortality, no, it lies not in the genes. Immortality, no, it lies not in chemical concoctions. It lies in Spirit, the ONE Source, the ONE Being, the ONE that is in, through, and around your being, willing to take your command. Now we shall address, as part of this instruction on immortality and conscious immortality, the first step. See this diagram in front of me.

*Saint Germain patiently diagrams layers of the field of the human aura. Carefully, he points to layers of light that surround the body, called the Mental Body and the Emotional Body.*

Here we show layers of the field of consciousness, as you would understand your thoughts, your feelings, your actions, and your being. This rare combination brings forth the manifestation of your body, the manifestation of beauty, or the manifestation of warts. Your thought, your feeling, and your action are commanded, shall we say, first and foremost by the most important layer of the field known as the Mental Body. Your Mental Body contains within it your conscious immortality and contains within it all the mechanisms that make it available for you to command and demand the substance you know as Spirit.

Spirit has been known in your modern technology as Orgone. Spirit has been known through the religious teachings as Prana. However, for simplicity, we shall call it Spirit. This is Divine Energy. It is energy, yes, but it is qualified in a Oneness, in a divinity of consciousness. It is there to serve you, and to serve you always. It never chooses disease. It never chooses death. It knows only the ONE. It is beyond choice, for it is qualified with the essence of Life. It is that drink presented to you to quench thirst in your soul and your body. We shall call it the mechanism that allows your Mental Body to operate at full capacity.

You discuss the ability to choose, or shall we say, discern. You discuss the ability to judge, or shall we say, flatter your ego. Now granted, there are instances in physiology where the ego is used, in fact, to heal the body. You have known about the placebo effect, and the placebo effect is always instigated through ego activity. However, we shall limit this teaching to the Mental Body and conscious immortality. Every day, become aware of the thoughts that you allow to run through that appendage of yours, your brain. See your brain as a calculator, or as a book, or as an automobile. See your brain as something given to you for you to utilize and to demonstrate that mighty Christ Law in action—immortality. Command and demand your brain be filled with the patterns of immortality.

ARISE AND AWAKEN

As I have said, "Down with death!" I maintain this as my decree and my focus for humanity. Each and every one of you who hear this material, your hearts have been filled with Divinity. Know that the quest for that refreshing drink, Spirit, has led you here.

"What is the point?" You may ask. "What is the point, to live in a world filled with suffering, endless greed, and corruption?" This is the point. You are here, Dear Divine Ascended Beings, to make this world a paradise. You are here to rediscover the internal kingdom. Dear Sananda has called it that Inner Garden. It exists in the internal and demonstrates to the external. You are here, Dear ones, to lessen the suffering, to demonstrate a selfless life. Don't fill your life with greed, but with the internal laws of the cosmos. Arise and awaken all of you! Arise and awaken to your conscious immortality.

Each day fill your body with the pattern of that mighty Violet Flame, for it is that Violet Flame, shall we say, that destroys and transmutes the patterns which are filled with that death urge, that disease urge. Are you filled now with the attention of death? Are you filled now with the attention of disease? Are you ready to contribute? Are you ready to heal this planet? Are you ready to raise her into the Freedom Star? I call each and everyone of you, Stalwart Beings of the Heart. Are you the torch bearer? Then demonstrate it.

CIRCLE OF VIOLET FLAME

*Saint Germain invokes the Violet Flame. As he speaks, a continuous circle of violet fills the room.*

I AM a being of the Violet Flame!
Blaze into, through, and around my being,
Transmuting all patterns of disease and death.
I AM a being of the Violet Flame!
Down with death! Conscious immortality arise!
Beloved Spirit, now make this choice throughout my being.
Arise, rejuvenate, resurrect all manifestation, all intelligence
In, through, and around my body,
In, through, and around my being,
In, through, and around my Mental Body.

Do you understand the tools that have been given to you, all of them? Utilize them. You will have every tool. How much further need you search? They are but there. Call it into being. Call it into your activity. Call it. Live it. And now contribute. Questions?

Response: "There are no questions."

Now I shall continue. This discourse on conscious immortality has been long overdue, for it is time for you to think new thoughts, to live with new actions, to have a New Day. Your immortality is right in front of you. Step into it as you would a new set of clothes. And now Beloved Sananda will join me.

*Lord Sananda steps forward to teach.*

Greetings Dear Hearts. I AM Sananda, and I request permission to come forth.

Response: "Come forward Dear one."

There is much work in front of you, Dear ones, and much work in front of that group of individuals known as humanity, but understand Dear ones, we stand behind all of you, and we are with you in conscious immortality. We are with you in thought, word, and deed. We are behind the energy of all that you do. A set of hands support you as you walk over troubled waters.

THE INTERNAL MARRIAGE

The time comes upon the Earth Plane and Planet when some will wonder, "Can I take any more of this needless suffering." Dear hearts, an awakening is at hand and each and everyone of you will serve in that critical moment. We have dispensed what is known as the I AM America Map, given to humanity to awaken the hearts and the bodies to the joy of the Spiritual Awakening. It is expressed as ONE with the feminine, the feminine energy opening across the planet. We have discussed that which is known as the Greening Map, which is the feminine brought into activity. For the feminine energy, when brought into activity, produces abundant gifts of love and compassion. The untiring lotus is now opened.

The time comes for us to understand the conceptual work which births the child of the Christ, so that all may partake of the glory of creation, that unionization of male and female, from whence separation is removed and is replaced with a reconciliation of the energies. This is known as the Map of Exchanges. This is known as the Internal Marriage, where the union becomes ONE and the gift of the Christ then shines over the entire planet.

## THE THREE MAPS

Some see the material quite frightening, when it is presented as a Prophecy of Change. However, Dear ones, the death of your soul is quite frightening to us. We see that a time comes that prophecy may now open your eyes and your ears. Prophecy may now open your heart. The I AM America Map was designed to open your heart. The Greening Map was designed to open your hands, and now the Map of Exchanges comes to open your eyes and your ears and your consciousness. Come and hold the cup. These three maps are gifts. These three maps represent transition.

You are now ready to enter into a new conscious experience, one that is not separated by the tactile body. But one that is joined, shall we say, in that mighty Oneship—the ONE of consciousness, the female and the male mating together and birthing a child, the Christ Consciousness of unconditional love. Many of you say to one another, "Oh, how I love you," but the demonstration of the Christ, the pure life, that innocent being, is yet to arrive in your hearts. When it does, Dear hearts, you shall be blessed with a gift that awaits you, latent and unwrapped.

*A table appears in front of Sananda, draped with a white cloth. On the table are three golden goblets.*

I now pour wine into each of these cups, each symbolizing the phases of this work. One for the work of the Americas. One for the work of Asia, India, and the Middle East. One for the work of Europe and Africa. Sup with me Dear ones. Sup with me Beloved Saint Germain. Sup with me Dear Angels and Elohim of Light and Sound.

*He motions to Saint Germain. They all join around the table and Sananda passes the cup to each participant.*

I bid each of you to drink from these cups, each of them representing vessels of Spirit, conscious immortality, purposeful Divinity.

*He now motions to us to come and join the celestial feast.*

Each of you sup with me, Brothers and Sisters. Each of you has participated in this ritual of Light, each of you, embodying within your physical vehicles, your soul, and your spiritual vehicles, that purposeful Divinity.

FREEDOM STAR, A STATE OF CONSCIOUSNESS

I now ask, at this time, to open what we call the consciousness of Freedom Star and bring to a close the time of worrying, the time of dissent, and the time of suffering. Let us bring these times to a close and now open a Time of the Heart, a time of union, a time of the active and unhidden ONE. Let this child now dance across this planet, dancing in our hearts, dancing in our minds. Let its playful laughter sound across the universe.

*He raises his cup and softly prays:*

Freedom. Freedom.

And now I turn the discussion over to Beloved Saint Germain.

*Saint Germain steps forward. Sananda and the table which held the glorious feast fade into another dimension. Soon, by his side, stand the Mahatmas El Morya, Kuthumi, and Beloved Lady Nada. Each of them are holding several scrolls.*

Welcome Dear hearts. And now we prepare to close, shall we say, through another opening. We close through opening the remainder of the material of the Map of Exchanges. To my right is Beloved El Morya and to my left is Beloved Kuthumi and Lady Nada.

*Each of them hands Saint Germain the scrolls they have carried from the other dimensions. Saint Germain turns to Len and asks him:*

This is the last of the material. Are you willing to take this responsibility and share it for the Healing of the Nations?

Response: "I am."

So Be It. Hitaka.

Response: "Hitaka."

Make your preparations. Tarry not, for the work is of great import. We ask for you to complete the material and to share this with World of Nations, for it builds a bridge, a bridge of Brotherhood that many shall cross over and understand the Divinity of the Heart.

In that mighty Christ, I AM Saint Germain.

Response: "Thank you, Dear one."

# Map Review

*"The mighty Christ Light springs forward . . . it is the new seed.*
*It is the seed that transforms consciousness."*
- EL MORYA

This is a review of the Map of Exchanges, in the presence of the Ascended Masters. The Masters have unrolled the map of Europe. It looks as though everyone is here. No one has said anything. They are opening up the map of Europe and the Mediterranean into Africa. It covers areas from the South Pole, all the way up to Scandinavia, and into what we would call Eastern Europe. It is as though El Morya, Kuthumi, and Sananda each bring a different piece and the pieces all come together. I haven't seen all the details, but I see the overall scope of it.

As Lori is asking questions regarding the physical changes presented on the map, the Ascended Masters will be showing me the corresponding Earth Change events. I will answer Lori's questions by describing what is being shown. This will be followed by El Morya giving greater details about these changes and a philosophical understanding.

## THE RUSSIAN ISLANDS

Question: "What do you see at Aral, Caspian, and Black Sea? These three seas are prophesied to form one great sea."

They are all open. There are only those islands in the northern area.

Question: "Those are the areas of the USSR?"

What was once called the USSR is now known as Russia. All of those satellite areas, for the most part, are washed clean, all across to Turkey. Very interesting.

## EUROPEAN EARTH CHANGES

Question: "What do you see happening, starting on the far West Coast of Europe, England, and France?"

It looks almost like a big television screen. There is a rock formation that looks like a crack in the channel, the English Channel. Those new lands that bubble up from this crack literally look like volcanic activity, mounting and rising on what you would call Portugal and Spain. As that activity is occurring, there is more and more recession of the English coast in the area of Wales. It looks as though the West Coast of England, into the area of the English Channel, erodes immensely, all the way through to London. It is all under water.

It looks as if some mountains do rise in England a little bit, but they are not yet giving me a name of any kind. Northward, up into Scotland, I would say the highlands become higher. It is almost as if the cliffs rise as the southern parts of the island recede, almost as much as fifteen hundred feet from the looks of it. That is a large rise.

Question: "There is a Golden City that is located right above Scotland called Denasha. What do they have to say about it?"

## THE GOLDEN CITY OF SCOTLAND

It is above Edinburgh. They are showing only geological things at this point. They are not giving qualities of anything. They are just showing the land rising there, as much as fifteen hundred feet in that whole northern Scotland area, so that the entire Golden City is very, very protected by high land. It looks as though most of the population will migrate from Ireland to Scotland and England and Wales, all continually moving north as this rising activity occurs, simultaneously with the recession along the southeastern coast of England.

With the removal of these smaller islands, that which you call the White Cliffs of Dover, seem to break up because they are chalk. Even though they are several hundred feet above the sea level now, they become sea bottom because of this crack that forms along the English Channel and travels south past what we now call the Azores and toward the continent of Africa. This piece of land rises and there is a very large shelf there, which is one of the reasons why there is that extension. As it rises, the land that is to the west of it falls. One of the reasons the area above Edinburgh that becomes this Golden City, rises is because it is part of the same shelf system. This crevice seems to work its way up into the North Sea and literally cuts through the area that you would call England and Scotland.

Question: "Who is showing you the map?"

## EARTH'S AXIS AND TECTONIC MOVEMENT

Nada is next to me and El Morya is on the other side. He is explaining that as the Earth's axis begins to go through its gyrations, these kind of tectonic movements happen nearly overnight. This is not a long, drawn-out process. It is as though you wake up one morning and the sea coast is in your front yard if you're in southern England. And it is not something that is proceeded by a long-term warning either, nor will it necessarily be picked up on seismographs. It just happens. He also explains that the necessity of this Earth Change is based only on the conflict that exists there on many levels.

Question: "Does he have a discourse to share?"

## MELTING ICE AND EUROPEAN CHANGES

Not yet. They seem to want to give me an overview of what the areas look like and they will take cues from your questions. Further west, past Spain, Amerigo (Golden City), and France, for all practical purposes, France does not have a distinctive coastline any more. It is very much a series of islands. Paris is one of the first cities to go with the flooding of the Seine. Also, with the great movement of water that occurs in the North Sea and the great change in the temperature that is literally going to cause the Alps to melt, the great ice caps will melt and be the cause of the rising of the Rhine, the Seine, and the Danube Rivers.

Those kinds of things will occur because the global warming situation brings the winter time temperature into the high eighties. Normally, when it would be subzero in those mountains, it will be in the high eighties. As this water continues to rise and flow, these areas in the central part of France start to fill up. It was, at one time, a sea basin that connected the North Sea to what we call the Mediterranean. This occurred over a five thousand year period, and then with the shifting of the continents, this land did rise. It is not a very high land to begin with. It is low and it will once again submerge. The submerging of this area is infinitely more gradual than the activity in England, where the coast line literally shifts overnight.

Question: "What do you see happening in Norway, Sweden, and Denmark?"

It is the continual global warming that causes the erosion of these coasts. The greater portion of Denmark is submerged over a time of, maybe, two months. It is very quick because it is a very low land area, a peninsula jotting into the North Sea. The waters continually rise on a day by day basis as these polar ice caps begin to melt. The mountaintop snow packs and glaciers that exist in Norway and Sweden, extending all the way over into Latvia, into the rest of the Ukraine, and the USSR, also melt. As that tundra area starts to melt and there is more polar ice cap movement, we end up with a situation in which the global waters rise. At this particular time, because of global warming and the tear in the ozone layer at the North Pole area (a tear that matches the one at the South Pole), the water rises at least a foot every couple of days.

Question: "About the tear in the ozone, in the prophecies, the Masters have always spoken about ice sheeting. Can you elaborate?"

ICE SHEETING

The ice sheeting occurs as the polar caps melt. As the polar caps melt, more and more water is exposed to the Sun. As this happens, it creates a vaporization, very much like the formation of clouds. However, the ozone that normally provides a protective barrier from the Sun's rays, or a certain spectrum of light rays, now becomes an incubation area where water steams and rises into the atmosphere, then immediately freezes. In this immediate freezing, whole cloud masses that can normally cover parts of a continent, become instantaneously frozen (ice-fog). When this happens, the gravitational pull of the mass of frozen clouds is too much for the dynamics of the atmosphere to sustain. This frozen mass literally falls to the ground as a great continental size sheet of frozen water vapor. When you will take an air flight, you see hundreds of square miles of large clouds. If you can imagine them instantaneously frozen and then for them to just drop as though they were ice cubes from an ice maker, you can get a visualization of ice sheeting.

This will happen more in Europe than in Canada or even further west into Russia and the tundra area, because the particular tear in the ozone layer is centered above the Scandinavian area and up into the frozen North Atlantic. That is the area the initial tear occurs, because of the heavy industrialization and mechanization that occurs throughout northern Europe, as well as the increase of cars. It puts too much strain in that particular area. Its location near the pole and the current wind patterns make this activity swirl as if in a large tornado effect. It is as though the ozone layer starts to unravel or rotate in a counter clockwise pattern. This in turn allows any other movement of air coming through laden with moisture, to now undo itself, so to speak, and become a large frozen mass. It will be as though an entire lake or pond were to raise and then fall to the ground, frozen, several hundred miles away. This will create immense devastation to existing cities such as Berlin, Warsaw, Dresden, and Oslo. As well as some other small cities through Latvia, and over as far as what we would call St. Petersburg.

These ice sheets will also fall into the North Atlantic and as far south as the Mediterranean, including cities of northern Italy. These sheets of ice will compress and compact as thick as any type of cloud mass can. So if a cloud mass is as much as a mile thick, you may have a compression of an ice sheet a quarter mile thick. Imagine that you are dealing with something maybe twelve hundred feet thick and it falls upon a city. You can see that the intention of the prophecy is to awaken people to the coldness in their lives and in their hearts.

## DORMANT VOLCANOES

As we travel further down the continent to Italy, there is a major erosion of the southern tip of Italy and in most of the islands. The erosion is due more to the rising of the waters than additional volcanic activity. Some volcanic activity exists in old dormant volcanoes. These volcanoes are going to release some of their pressure that is being built up in the tectonic plate movement. Some volcanic activity occurs even in the French, Swiss, and Italian Alps. Most of those large mountains are, for the most part, as much as three to seven thousand feet below the cap surface, and there is volcanic activity still occurring. In the great lake in Switzerland, Lake Geneva, you will have movement where the water will literally bubble, will steam, will rise, and the lake will almost come to an evaporation point.

## EASTERN EUROPEAN EARTHQUAKE

Looking further down into what you would call eastern Europe, on the eastern side of the boot of Italy, water will rise, accompanied by rising tectonic plate movement. There will be great earthquake activity in that eastern European area. Much land will be shaken, many cities will be flattened, many things will come to a situation where the conflict that has existed there for approximately twelve hundred years, will come to an end, either by the individuals' prayers or by geological activities of the Mother. We see a great activity, as Nada points to an area that is just north of Italy. West of Italy, a great deal of activity occurs in Poland, Czechoslovakia, and to the south in Croatia; there is a great shaking of the land.

Question: "What do you see as happening for Italy?"

Because of the rising waters, the coastlines erode immensely. There is some volcanic activity, as said before, in Vesuvius. It will reawaken, and it will coincide with the earthquake activity to the west. The land will go through a transition and eventually become a very, very fine agricultural area once these changes occur, and it will be the primary actions that occur in the Italian peninsula. The people will have a much more agrarian and simplistic life, as opposed to their present industrialization, highly socialized form of government. It will again be a very beautiful area, suitable for different kinds of crops, such as wheat, corn, barley, and grapes. There will be other fruits which will flourish there.

## THE GRADUAL CHANGES IN SPAIN

Spain has a very arid climate at the moment but the falling of the rains and the bringing on of ice sheeting affect the northern and western parts of Spain. The areas currently very arid do become more suitable for agriculture. As far as the great transformation of Spain, it does not experience the same kinds of activities that also occur in, for example, northern Europe and France, and even some areas of Italy. Spain seems to be relatively calm and serene during most of these activities. It is going to have infinitely more moisture. The arid soil of its great plains, plateaus, and mesas will become more tillable. The conflict that Spain has gone through in the past and its great desire to bring about, in the past history of the world, a unification under the concept of Christianity, has been one of its very, how shall we say, peaceful aspects; even though great destruction occurred and great atrocities occurred, there was still an underlying intent of the bringing forth of truth. Therefore, Spain does not seem to suffer. It suffered greatly under the habitation of the Moors and during its revolution in the beginning of the Twentieth Century. Spain will experience a more gradual transition over the next three to five hundred years.

Question: "What about Portugal, the lands that are prophesied to rise, and the people of that area?"

## UNITY OF SPIRIT: PORTUGAL AND SPAIN

The peoples of Portugal have historically always been inquisitive, so since they have searched in their hearts for more lands and more understanding of the world, the world, in a sense, comes to them. They were more a seafaring nation than a conquering one, and they were great with trade and connecting far off places to Europe. In that sense, Portugal goes through a great expansion. The rising land will need a period of two to three hundred years before it can be utilized. Until then, it will mostly be a very, very warm molten rock as it rises to the surface. However, it will again have great agricultural use when the general tone of the planetary consciousness gains a greater understanding of the Mother and humans coming together as ONE.

There will be a great spirit of unity in Spain and in Portugal. The Portuguese people, for the most part, will only need to move further inland toward the Spanish border. Much trauma will be averted on their coasts, and there is enough in those mountains and in those valleys and plains to easily sustain them for a probable two hundred year period as this transition occurs. The people of Spain and Portugal are very blessed, in as much as their activities and intent through all the history of mankind are actually being honored

Question: "According to the prophecies, the Masters have indicated the people of Portugal are part of one of the lost tribes of Atlantis. Can you elaborate?"

## LOST TRIBE OF ATLANTIS

If you refer to those who border the Pyrenees Mountains, that is very accurate, but there are some tribes that exist this day, this moment, who only have two to three hundred people in small villages in these mountainous areas. They are very directly descended from Atlantis, contain many of the ancient Atlantean traditions, and are very conscious in their day-to-day lives. They do not have much contact with the outer world, but their ancestors are those who did populate Spain and Portugal and they are truly cousins to those in Portugal and in Spain.

As far as the knowledge they have, the time will come very shortly, in the next seventy to seventy-five years, when they will expound and express, in a total sharing of Brotherhood and Sisterhood, the information of Self-Mastery and the awareness of the immortality of the spirit and soul. It will be well within the grasp of all the peoples and tribes who inhabit Portugal and Spain at this moment. This awakening, or, as you would call it, a renaissance of this infinite intelligence, brings about a nucleus of a great change that will affect even the other Golden Cities throughout Europe, Asia, and Africa. This area will be a very important nucleus for the regeneration of the body, a nucleus of the regeneration of the infinite understanding.


GERMANY

Germany goes through much trauma. It basically succumbs to the rising waters because of the industrialization and aggression that the German consciousness has had for quite awhile. Germany will go through a time of rest and these lands will rise in the distant future. How distant they are not saying, perhaps fifteen hundred to three thousand years. But the lands there now, in a state of great industrialization, go through great transition. There will be many who do stay and survive these changes. Their hearts will be greatly changed and their great mental activity will be brought to a focus of universal Brotherhood and Sisterhood by their experiencing the complete change in their country. The lands themselves are submerged under much water and there is great change that occurs in those areas. Yet, there are remaining lands that exist on this map and do exist on all of the maps we have been shown.

Question: "What do you see in Eastern Europe, east of Hungary, and into Romania and the Ukraine?"

Most of these lands are covered with water. There are many mountainous areas which do stay above the watered area. The Masters have yet to speak. They have only pointed and directed to areas, some of them based on your questions and some of them based on what they are showing. These mountainous areas we are looking at, for the most part, are surviving as islands. However, it is the global warming that causes the continual rise of water all the way through into Russia, Poland, and Czechoslovakia. They are showing much shaking of land still.

Question: "They talk about the Sea of Eternal Change in the prophecies, and about a time when mankind will unite in an attempt to stop the global changes through some type of an underground explosion, which then sinks Egypt and Libya. Can you elaborate further?"

## NUCLEAR DETONATION

A consortium of scientists from Russia, Germany, England, France, Poland, and Hungary note that there is a great fault line that travels through the Mediterranean and has a rising point near Tripoli. At a point approximately 360 kilometers west of Tripoli, the scientists will detonate a nuclear device in order to relieve pressure on the tectonic plates. It is designed to alleviate the continuous pressure through northern Europe and southern Europe by the opening of a hole. Technology has determined that under the seabed of the Mediterranean, is another body of water. This detonation will be, by today's nuclear standards, relatively small. This detonation has its pros and cons, and there is a small group that go forward with it anyway because they actually possess the detonating device.

This detonation creates a traumatic activity on this fault line which results in a major sinking of northern and western Africa, on through the Suez Canal, through into Jordan, and all of Israel. All of Egypt is lost. Much of the Sahara is completely lost. In spite of this detonation, the problems that exist in northern Europe really don't subside. Hopefully, this exposure will put this information in enough hands that this nuclear device will not be used and this scenario, or group of events, will not come to pass. It does not solve anything; it just destroys more. In this unified action, there is an attempt to come together in technology. The unifying action and focus taken around this issue, the bringing of people together, is a real blessing. Master El Morya will speak about this point later. The activity itself is a disaster and is quite unnecessary according to the Masters' explanation. Nonetheless, the event will be a matter of choice.

Question: "In Russia, they say the Ural Mountains remain as an island. What can you tell us?"

THE URAL MOUNTAINS

The Ural Mountains continue to rise at least five hundred to seven hundred more feet. As they rise through the tectonic plate movement and then experience the movement of the magma through their core, these mountains represent a substantial place geologically. They are granite formations and they are quite steeped with minerals. They are also inhabited by tribes that are related to those in the Pyrenees of Spain and Portugal. These mountains, in and of themselves, do create a place for humanity to look to and should be very substantial. They hold much ancient information in some of their caves. The rising of them will be due only to earthquake activity. They will not be devastated by the activity of great volcanic eruptions. They will rise from within, above the existing continental areas, and they will rise in a manner that is, yes, shaking, but not to the extent that it will be impossible to live on them. It is a place where those who think and feel may find refuge during the Times of the Earth Changes.

It is unnecessary for any of these things to occur. Such great, great, tremendous conflict, if the world will see itself as ONE with the planet and each other, none of these activities need occur to the extent of great devastations. The mountains, in and of themselves, are great wellsprings of gems, gold, and silver. They also have uranium deposits, richer than anyone could imagine. The utilization of uranium in the next five thousand years will be entirely different. There will be more use of sunlight and crystals, rather than what we would call nuclear fission or fusion, as power sources.

Certain areas of the Ural Mountains will be very easy to farm. There will be plateaus where small agricultural societies will spring up. They are of an older age that predates our recorded history of western civilization, and even of eastern civilization. The Urals have been a mainstay in the activities of the Himalayan region. The Urals are older than the mountains of the eastern United States and have a history of much activity. I have seen several changes on the planet that we would call of the Earth Change or cataclysmic nature. They have seen at least three, and El Morya said, for some sections almost four cycles of change.

Question: "The people of Russia seem to have such conflict and turmoil in their lives right now. Are there any indications that through these changes they will find peace?"

The indication is that when people come to accept being part of the planet and each other, the peace is then reconciled. They will have to come to that reconciliation by realizing the self as part of the planet and then accepting everyone as a global family. As far as peacefulness, it is easily obtained on an individual basis, and the Masters will give a description later. They are only indicating areas on the map for the moment. They will give extensive discourse later.

Question: "Traveling on into Africa, would you like to share information about Africa today, or would you like to work on that tomorrow?"

It does not matter. Africa is easily seen. They are now rolling the scroll up so that I can focus on Africa. You may ask any question.

Question: "Let's start with some of the areas that most readers will be familiar with, Somalia?"

AFRICAN GOLDEN CITIES

Somalia is an area that the rising waters submerge. There is nothing left of Somalia. Ethiopia is an area where the waters continue to rise, but the highest mountain areas maintain their stability. There is Golden City activity in Ethiopia, and it is quite a lush, wonderful garden area maintained even through the changes. Kenya is an area where more water comes, but there is still Golden City activity there. The great stress that did occur through Ethiopia and through all of the expansion of the Sahara, is very much eradicated and as a result, what is left of Ethiopia after the rising waters and the detonation is very, very tropical and lush. It extends into Kenya. The names of these places may see change as time goes on; they will no longer be called what we call them because the hearts of people of this land will be entirely different.

Question: "Traveling on down to the southern tip of Africa, in the prophecies they say there is an expansion of the lands off the coast, from the southern tip to the western side."

That is still accurate on this map.

Question: "What can you tell us about that?"

## A RICH, CONNECTED CULTURE

There is additional volcanic activity underwater and this volcanic activity continues on for several years, to a point where it builds up very much like the expansion of the land in Portugal. It builds up several thousand square miles of additional land that also extends to another island. Just a little west there is a part of this mountain range. In probably the year 2800 or 2900, almost a thousand years from now, its activity brings about some of the richest agricultural land for that area. There will be four crops a year there. It is a very magnificent sight.

This rich land shows that the planet is now honored completely at this time, as a Mother and as someone who is spoken to regularly. It is steeped in a culture of individuals having contact with the Mother. The Mother is the guiding force in the understanding of the whole of creation, and she and the inhabitants continue this Co-creative cycle, creating the Freedom Star. There is the advent of a total consciousness and awareness in this one thousand year period, wherein individuals understand that the Earth is part of the experience of being here as a human being. Very few hold to the old concept that the planet is separate, or not part of the entire beingness. There is a Oneness between humans and the Earth that pervades the consciousness and an open communication, where you speak to the rocks, and you speak to the garden, and you speak to the leaves, and you speak to all the flowing vegetation and the flowing waters. There exists an understanding that the elements carry on this relationship with you.

It is quite interesting that this new land off the southern coast of Africa is probably the first place that this seed of new consciousness comes about and spreads, as in the Hundredth Monkey Theory, or like a great wild fire over the entire planet. The new consciousness has total acceptance at about the time this land becomes quite usable agriculturally.

Question: "There has been so much civil unrest in these areas. Is there a significance in the rising lands?"

The significance in the rising land is that the portal is now open and the key is now found. The Mother, as a planet, is a being. We are all on the same path of this beingness, the understanding of this complete unity, this harmony that exists between Brother and Sister and planet. These changes that occur in the rising land seem to trigger this unity, according to the script that is in front of me.

Question: "What about Madagascar? Do the lands also rise there with the shifting and movement of the island? There is also a Golden City that exists in the center of Madagascar. Tell us about Madagascar during the Times of Changes."

## MADAGASCAR

There is a possibility that Madagascar may have a land bridge that attaches to Africa in approximately fifteen hundred to two thousand years. Madagascar is on the same continental plate and will experience the same geological change in the underwater mountain range that occurs in the southwestern or eastern part of Africa. In this expansion of Madagascar, it becomes several times its size, according to the map that has been constructed. There is very little change in detail. As far as Madagascar's growth, it experiences the same renaissance or awakening in consciousness that occurs in southern Africa. The Brotherhood and Sisterhood between the African continent and Madagascar strengthens. It is almost as if Madagascar floats during the five thousand year period as the mountain ranges break free and it becomes part of an entire, continuous global effort of unification through the continental shifts.

Question: "One thing we have noticed in studying the prophecy is that there were such minimal changes in South America and

Africa and yet these are both areas of such enormous amounts of disease and famine. Are the Masters willing to share information regarding this problem?"

## ONE WITH THE LAND

It is only in the discourse of a teaching, where they explain the disease process and why it has expanded upon the continent. They will note that one of the reasons there is little continental change in South America and Africa is because the native peoples have endeavored, even through all the centuries, to maintain their traditions and be ONE with the land. It is only the introduction of foreigners into each of these areas that any of their focus of unity and Oneness with the land has swayed or dissuaded them from their tradition. Because the tradition is still maintained in their hearts, to be united with each other in their clans, united in their tribes, and ONE with their land, very little actual activity occurs. It is the industrialized nations that have brought about a great separation of self from the land by the consciousness they hold. For them, the land is there to provide base and raw materials for the improvement of social structure. The great changes occur in their fullest intent to awaken these individuals to their chosen separation.

Question: "In the Map of Exchanges, in the prophecy spoken of by the Masters, these lands of Europe and Africa are to herald the birth of the Christ. Can you elaborate? "

A CHANGE OF HEART

It is a time-honored tradition, that has even been mentioned in the great message of Fatima, that these seeds of what you would call Christianity - but by the Masters' perspective, the Christos Consciousness of the Oneness - have existed in this relationship between the European continent and the African continent. The seeds of existence shared between the European continent and the African continent are based on the concept that individualization is of the ONE Source and of the Divine Nature. These seeds have been in the hearts of the native people of Africa and they will once again influence those people who live on the European continent today. We will have a change of heart, literally, that goes on in those industrialized nations. We will have a change of heart that, literally, goes on in those nations which hold a focus of attaining anything, even if it is at the expense and suppression of their Brothers and Sisters and planet. This will completely change as occurrences of the prophecy come to be.

In the physical world, you will notice these changes, little by little, will come about in the hearts of all the people. It is this seed of unity that still exists on the African continent, which will once again bring about a pivoting point for the unification of the masculine focusing energy and the feminine creative energy. This unification will bring us to a place where we will become, as in the early Atlantean days, androgynous, ONE with this planet, and ONE with each other.

Question: "In many of the traditions, it has been said that the Lemurian was to be resurrected in our physicality. The Atlantean was to develop our emotional bodies and our senses. And now we are in a period called the Aryan. The Masters have indicated that at the birth of Freedom Star, we will experience the full zenith of the destiny of the Aryan. Is the birth of this map linked to the synergistic qualities of the Aryan coming into its full spectrum of evolution, or is it the time that we birth even anew? Can you elaborate?"

At this point, I must turn the floor over to our Beloved Kuthumi and Beloved El Morya, for it is only their words that can explain this. I have only the ability to see the map and to answer your more descriptive questions. To bring about the teaching and philosophical understanding, that is their purpose.

*Beloved El Morya steps forward.*

Greetings Beloved chela. I AM, as you know, the will of the steely blue light. I AM known as the Mahatma El Morya and request permission to come forward.

Response: "In that mighty Christ Light, I greet you, and you have my permission."

THE NEW SEED

It is in the mighty Christ Light that all springs forward and through this, there is the understanding that the Freedom Star is of this universe. It is the new seed. It is the seed that transforms consciousness in this Earth Plane and transforms consciousness in this planet Herself, to become a great cosmic servant for the expansion of the next universal structure.

In this African continent, in the base that you now call South Africa, there is this seed that is planted in the upsweeping of the geological change; this brings to the complete fruition, that which you call the Aryan. It is from this seed, it is from this geological change that the Aryan, the Divine Mind, will have an understanding of all creation, and it is from this point that we will continue all discourse.

Beloved Kuthumi wishes to come and present the understanding that the Animal Kingdom fulfills in the human evolution. Beloved Nada will come forward to explain in depth the Mineral Kingdom in the human evolution. Each of these has its place. As you know, you are of the Animal, of the Mineral, and of the Vegetable Kingdoms. You are of all of these, and it is the understanding of these that brings you forward to the Oneness of your being with the planet. We are, at this moment, disposed to bring forth this discourse at another time, when we will give the descriptive analysis of all that exists in, what you refer to as, the teachings.

CHOICES AFFECT CREATION

We see these as consciousness steps, as moments of choice, and it is in these moments of choice that all the universal structure flexes and literally transforms. That choice that you make here on this planet is also for your Brother and Sister of this planet, but it is also for your Brother and Sister to the outer reaches of this universal structure. The one choice that is made here is as the rippling of the pond throughout the entire existence of creation. There is not one plane, there is not one planet that does not feel the choice that is made, that does not hear the choice that is made, for it is, as you know, ONE great Galactic Web, ONE great cosmos. This great endeavoring experiment of creation comes forward in the Mastering of creation and of choice here in our world, in this plane that we all share. This planet that we all share affects the consciousness of the entire universal structure. In your choice for death and disease, you create death and disease for all Brothers and Sisters. Those individual choices affect all of creation.

# Africa

*"The spirit that pulses through my electronic fields
is the same as yours. The great Flame of Desire that pulses
through the worlds of my heart is the same in yours. "*
- EL MORYA

*There is a void. Angels and Elohim come and they fill this void. As they begin to fill this void, it gets larger and larger. It is as though a single strand of light, as a Ray and a single pitch, comes forward. A disk opens up and they come through this, almost as if there is an eternal flame. From this position, they bring the maps together. El Morya, Kuthumi, Nada, and Sananda are at my left and Saint Germain is at my right. Angels are in the background. A circle forms and it becomes a room. I recognize this room. This is our Map Room. I think we were here yesterday, but I don't know. No one has said anything. The map is now on a very large table, all three pieces together. Everyone is seated. The angels are to the outside. Eight Masters sit around the table. Before El Morya continues, he asks if you have any continuing questions about the map.*

Question: "Yes, I have questions regarding the Earth Changes in Africa. As we stated yesterday, Africa is very much like South America, with very few changes, yet it seems to be going through a change through disease and famine. On the western coast of Africa, the prophecy states that there will be many changes up and down the coastline and up to about forty or fifty miles inland. I want to know more about these changes. It is a beautiful prophecy that all the small countries of Africa will have access now to the ocean. There will be new bays that form up towards the bulge of Africa on the western side. Can you elaborate on these?"

*I have to turn the floor over to one of the Masters. Beloved Kuthumi, sponsor of Africa, the Golden City of Malton, and World Teacher steps forward. He is surrounded by a golden light, with stars the color of rubies shooting throughout his aura.*

Greetings Dear Children of the White Dove. I AM the Mahatma Kuthumi. As you have requested, I now request that we all come forward.

Response: "Dear ones, come forth."

AFRICAN COASTLINES

I address the questions you asked for definite descriptions and alterations of coastlines. This comes from the rising of the waters, the melting of the caps, and the movement of the heart of the Mother. It is this warming that you call global warming that effects a warming of the heart. Those areas of great ice and snow that have hidden treasures from the consciousness of mankind and humankind for eons will be opened and laid bare. Our beloved Archangels have kept the jewels of these poles in great protection. As this protection melts away, so too do the receding waters reveal the continent of this glorious garden planet. You and all your Brothers and Sisters will rejoice in the new opportunity and the new era. Those lands that were free before and were then covered will now be uncovered and freed again.

This coast that you call of the African continent will create more opportunity for those tribes, those indigenous ones who have held to their ways, untouched by the outer world. They will have access again to the free-flowing water of Creation. The water that binds all the organs of the body is the same water that combines all the continents, which are, in effect, organs of the body of the Mother.

Each one of these maps contains the specific function of the entire creation. As you know, the heart is located in the middle of your United States. So too does each of these continents function as your kidneys and liver, as your intestine, your gall bladder. Each of these has a function in the personality of the planet, for she too has thought, feeling, action, and desire and has offered herself in her cosmic identity for the continuing creation.

When you dispose of a vegetable that has gone bad, so too is that vegetable offered for the creation of new life forces. This plane, in the same manner, is offered for new creation. The changes that occur on this coast will bring the great and glorious opportunity for communication and trade, for Brotherhood and Sisterhood. The isolation that has occurred on this wonderful planet of great creation will cease, and in its place will spring forward the seeds of the great harmonies that exist on this planet. While the seeds of discontent are sown and reaped repeatedly on the European continent, the seeds of harmony are sown and reaped repeatedly on the African continent.

THE BALANCE

This is the exchange and the balance so often spoken of. The balance will come again. It will be the balance of the Mineral, the Vegetable, the Animal, and the Human Kingdoms. In the balance, there is ONE consciousness. It is the same flame that beats in the heart of every atom. It is the same spirit that moves in the energy of every light being, of every particle of the creation.

You, Dear ones, you Children of this White Dove, Brothers and Sisters, now come forward and carry the message, as the carrier pigeons of old carried the messages from one kingdom to another. So too, is the new message that comes forward from the seas of the birth of harmony. It is the exchange of discord for harmony. That is the purpose of this map. It brings about balance. Just as the liver balances many of the great attributes of your digestion and your blood stream, so too does this great continent. The anger that once raced across this continent now comes to a great peace and harmony. No longer will the focus of this entire planet be on the creation of conflict. It now comes to the point where a balanced understanding of creation will spread as this great seed multiplies and the harvest comes in.

You and I are of this seed, as are all creatures, as are all minerals, as are all plants, as are all people, but the seed is out of harmony. You and I come forward to bring this message. Along with these receding lands comes the opening of these seeds.

These receding lands are the perfect connection. These seeds drift out into the tides and will fill the shores of all the continents. They will fill the shores of all changing lands.

## REBIRTH, AWARENESS, AND AWAKENING

It is a great rebirth. It is an awareness. It is an awakening. It is, as you say, a great wellspring of the creation that comes forward and takes charge as the Laws of the Mother and the Father, takes charge of the wayward child. Soon the child comes to the realization that these laws are not intended to suppress, but only to give guidance. They are not intended to suppress, but to guide this Divine Plan forward.

The uncovering of consciousness is seen as these great bodies of ice melt. The freezing, if you will, of thought, the freezing, if you will, of feeling and of the great desire of creation, melt and spring forward, nurturing all the new coastlines and new lands. In these crystallized waters of healing that the ice caps have held for so long, are the great, great joys that this planet holds. Great Breath of God that Never Fails, come forward! It is this crystallization that now melts and warms the heart of all the creation. There are great opportunities for each of these tiny countries, each of these tribes, for now they will have total access to the whole world. No one will be isolated ever again. There is that harmony now. Questions?

Question: "One question comes to mind, Beloved Kuthumi. These lands of Africa have been lands of great conflict, working to bring in civil rights for humankind. Why is it that there is a people

219

who are exploited in order for other peoples to gain? We seem to see this repeatedly in history. "

## SUPPRESSION AND POLARITY

You have come to a touchy subject which we will address. This planet is a planet of great choice, and it is the learning of choice through experience that causes these activities that you have discussed. Look to the examples of these people on the planet who have lived close to the Mother. Look to the examples of these people worldwide, who have held to a consummate ideal of the planet as a Goddess, as a Mother. Their systems were matriarchal. Their systems held that the feminine was the power. These were the children of harmony.

The children who walk the planet and hold that the Father is the power, that hold that one must suppress or enslave to gain, these are the children of discord. You have heard them referred to in many other writings by different names. It is not relevant what name you call them. What is important is the understanding of harmony and discord. It is through harmony and discord that choice is learned. The harmony does not have a sense of understanding, nor does the discord have a sense of understanding, without each polarity existing side by side in this planet of choice. As the plane of consciousness becomes aware of the Oneness, the harmony and the discord subside and the polarity within the self subsides.

## LESSONS AND CHOICES

There is the acceptance, as the Masters have said, of the masculine and the feminine, growing to a more androgynous perspective, a self-creating understanding. At this level of awareness, that is all that could exist. It is not that we see this as wrong or we see this as incorrect. It is the path of choice. Each of these groups, which harmonize with the planet or harmonize in a social structure, has much to learn from each other. It is only the blending and harmonizing with the planet in that Oneness of Brotherhood and Sisterhood that the world will reach its full cycle for this plane of consciousness. We may go on and on with great descriptions of how this has come about, but the purpose for this planet was always founded in choice.

There are times when the Creator sets a color of light or sound. Even sound has color and even light has sound, and it is a choice that the Creator chooses in the creation. Without this choice, the patterns that stream forth from it, from the seed of the creation, can not exist. Everything in the ONE is never separate. Everything in the distinction, or the choice, is then rediscovered. Consider your cities when they are overcrowded. When they are overcrowded, everyone is packed tightly into a small space. It is only when one steps out into the country and looks to the city that one can understand the choice that exists between each environment. We are the same, whether we are Angels, Elohim, Chohans, or torch bearers. We learn choice in this plane and on the attached and interlocking planes that function with it.

Each of these planes has only ONE Source and that comes from the choice of the Creator. It is the same with harmony and conflict. That too is a choice. We may harmonize with the forest or we may cut it down. That is a choice. We may leave it barren, or reseed it so that it will grow anew. That is also a choice. It is coming to this understanding of this ONE that the choices support one harmonic. The group is the sum of the individuals, and the individual, the sum of the group. Only in this paradox can you function; however, the paradox subsides in your expansion.

## STEP OUT OF DISCORD

These great conflicts you have seen in your history offer you the experience of what will work to harmonize and what will not support the harmonization. You and I have experienced these many times, lifetime after lifetime. It is stepping out of the discord. It is the choice of the path of Self-Mastery. It is stepping from there that you bring service to others, so they too may have the same choice in their awareness. These harmonies and conflicts are temporary. They are temporal, as we say, in the creation. They are only of a certain kind for the experience, and these individual experiences do not create the sum of the creation.

## THE LAW OF BALANCE

Take one of your coins and look at one side. If you look upon your penny and you see that your president is engraved, does the nose make the entire engraving, or is it just a part? The engraving on the penny is the sum of all its parts. So too are the prophesied changes. Each part is expanding and compacting at the same time, for the Law of Balance is a conscious creation that is aware of the ONE.

Please consider your individualized Flame of Creation within your heart to be self-aware, and your physical body the sum of its parts. Each flame harmonizes together in the ONE. It is inner and outer, beginning and end. All of it achieves this balance. We always ask you to consider that this exists in each of the kingdoms. You will find harmonization in each of the minerals, harmonization where certain plants grow together, harmonization where certain types flock together, harmonization where certain types of people work together, harmonization where certain types of geology work together, and harmonization where certain types of countries work together. It is all choice. Consider, all the same, one choice is not greater than another; it is a choice. Consider that some choices bring you to freedom, some choices lead to suppression, some bring you to harmony, and some bring you to discord. It is a choice. The intent is yours as a Creator, as a Master, as a human. The intent is yours.

Question: "Discord is temporal and temporary and is a teaching of duality. We have come to understand that for everything that exists, there is an opposite. Yet, it seems as if harmony is not the equal of discord, in a sense, because discord is temporal and harmony is more strongly stated. So please explain further, is harmony basically the one choice?"

## THE TEMPORAL PLANE

In this plane of which you are aware, choice is a path. Discord is part of the path of choice. Harmony is part of the path of choice. When you step from this plane, the choice is Mastered. There is the ONE. When we come to you, you ask for us (to appear) individualized, and because of this request, this is how we come. We have come many times at your request, with the example of the ONE, and have individualized the expression for your understanding. The simplicity is that, even in this plane, harmony is temporal because this plane contains the parameter of time, of distance, of expansion, and of contraction.

Question: "Are you speaking of the physical plane or the spiritual plane?"

This plane that you call physical, that has spirit through it, is an expression. You may take the color white and separate it into many color spectrums. You may take the color red and separate it, yes, into yellow, yes, into pink, yes, and again, there will be white. The continued separation into the most finite only brings a more finite separation. It is an infinite expansion and contraction. In your world, your plane of awareness sees that which is good and that which is evil, that which is right, that which is wrong. It is from that perspective that you learn choice.

## ACCEPTANCE

Ultimately, there will be acceptance, but there is, as you say, that great faith of life. There is the ONE. It is through the portal of acceptance, and we have heard it termed "surrender," for that is accurate also. You may still be individualized and surrender to your Divine Purpose, but that is a choice also. When this level of awareness encompasses your entire being, it is from this perspective that you will have your awareness. You see choice as temporal. We may choose to step from this plane into another when our work is complete and go through a series of experiences or a series of services.

Question: "So, is choice made continuously? Is choice just in the physical or does it continue on into the spiritual realms and planes of existence?"

It is continuous. It will cease to be continuous when your individuality ceases.

Question: "So, you are saying that choice is one of the factors here in having a physical embodiment and is part of the extended reality in the spiritual realms?"

## SERVICE

Choice is the only reality in this physical realm. It is a path through which all spirit functions, or, as you say, the Divine Plan functions through you. Yes, it is through you in your choices. It is through each of us in our choices. It is through the great Helios and Vesta in their choices, for they may choose to take up another post of service. There will be a time when the great experiment that we call creation will cease to have a purpose.

This time is unknown to any of us and all will be ONE. We are here only for the service. Service brings balance to choice.

Question: "Did you choose your service?"

The service is chosen and accepted.

Response: "Thank you, Beloved Kuthumi."

*Beloved El Morya, the Blue Teacher, steps forward.*

Greetings Dear chelas. I AM, as you know, the Mahatma El Morya. Children of this Blue Flame, also Children of the White Dove and of the Golden Flame and of the Violet Flame, it is these elements of service that you have chosen to combine, that you have chosen and accepted to bring forth understanding to your plane of awareness. We here, who are in attendance to you, offer this as a service. It is in our state of focus that our service is more defined, or as you would say, exacting. It is not likely that I would carry service forth on this Violet Flame, but only on the Blue Flame. Yet, this Violet comes through the Blue.

FREEDOM OF CHOICE

The awareness of how creation functions enables one to have this great Aryan mind, this great intellect that works and functions through the appendage Beloved Saint Germain has explained, the seeds of these great abilities choose with a clear understanding, not a choice based on fear or distress, not a choice based on suppression, but a choice based on a clear understanding of the function as it exists. You and all others are here in the expansion of this which creates your freedom. It is the true freedom of choice that is the purpose of the founding of the land in which you live. It is the cradle or incubator that brings full circle the consciousness on your planet to an awareness that the active intelligence will have the supreme activity.

This will always be tempered by the great desire of the heart. And as you come to this understanding that the heart and the mind are ONE, that the choice and the action are ONE, that the thought and the feeling are ONE, and that the great desire and fulfillment are ONE, you will, in effect, Master the path of the plane that you are in. We have, in our simplest ways, gone the same roads you have gone this day and every day of this embodiment. We have walked your path. You understood that the expression of creation individualizes but it is also constant; for when you look to the Himalayas, these mountains are the same as when I walked this path. They are, literally, unchanged at this moment.

Question: "Did you work as a channel El Morya?"

In the teachings in Philadelphia, in the teachings in Burma, and in daily life, I too have channeled the great Teachers and Masters before me. I too have been in this great service. I too have brought forth, as you would say, books of record for this information dispensation. It is the path. It is the understanding of the connection of the inner and outer. We all follow this path, Dear one. It is in the awareness that one's choices step into this unseeking service. It is in the unseeking service that the greatest fulfillment comes forward. The planet has created this environment for the awareness of all her inhabitants of unseeking service. She would do the service even if it was self-destructive. She would do the service whether or not a great blossoming new culture came about. There is no definitive expectation.

## THERE IS NO DIFFERENCE

The only purpose of service is the joy of service. In this plan, all creation comes to harmony. You and I, Dear student, Divine chela are teachers of the Worlds. You and I are the same. There is no difference. The path is the same. The spirit that pulses through my electronic fields is the same as yours. The great Flame of Desire that pulses through the worlds of my heart is the same in yours. In this service there is the great ONE. There is no difference.

This great continent of Africa brings forth these great seeds of which our Beloved Kuthumi has told. This great seed of Divine Mind, acceptance of the ONE, and choosing from this perspective is truly the essence of this exchange.

Question: "El Morya, just for clarification, could you explain what the true teachings of the races are, in terms of Lemurian, Atlantean, and Aryan?"

## THOUGHT, FEELING, AND ACTION

It is the thought, feeling, and the action. The Lemurian came to Master the action. Without the movement of any energy there will be no clarification of a sense of feeling (Atlantean). Without a sense of feeling, there will never be a thought (Aryan). It is the movement which you call action that interacts with other movement, and it is the interaction that there is a sensing and a feeling. It is as though one atom attracts another atom. The atom singularly moving with its electronic movement will have no sense or feeling unless it is duplicated or mirrored or replicated. It is in this movement of replication, duplication, or mirroring, that there is a connection that pulses, what you call, feeling. It is an electromagnetic attraction. This electromagnetic attraction provides the understanding that there are two atoms in the electromagnetic pulsing of attracting and repelling. Divine Mind evolves to the understanding of acceptance that both are the ONE.

Response: "They say electricity is the will and magnetism is love, which would be the feeling, and those two combined then lead us to Divine Thought."

We have discussed that the thought came first, that it is truly Light. But Light would exist only when there was sound, or magnetism, or love, and only when there is movement. It is these activities that bring the sense and the feeling which inspires the understanding. Many times we will go through the motions in an embodiment without a clear understanding. Now is the time to which we have referred. Now is the time to understand, to clearly and definitely accept all this creation as ONE Source and to understand it is unfolding and enfolding for your observation and experience. When all move and feel and think there is ONE, it is ONE movement; it is ONE feeling; it is ONE thought. The ease of this great expansion to the ONE thought exists in this African continent. And it exchanges the many thoughts for the ONE.

## A CRADLE OF HUMANITY

Question: "Yesterday we were discussing, after part of your discourse, Africa as the birthplace of the Aryan seed. Is this accurate?"

This is truly a joyous expression that you understand. That which is greatly suppressed, greatly belittled, is actually the inverse of this thought. These great seeds of the Aryan mind exist together with the understanding of the Oneness with the planet.

Question: "So the cradle of humanity, for humanity in present day as we understand now, is Africa?"

Specifically Ethiopia.

Question: "What about Egypt and its relationship to the development of the Aryan?"

Egypt brought forth the great Divine understanding that creation can be re-created and manipulated. When the seeds of the Atlantis scattered to all parts of your known world, a scattering went to that Nile Valley. This great cradle then spread to the Ethiopian Valley. These groups who were related to each other communicated freely through telepathy and bi-location. These were common everyday experiences. There was no need for the present-day mechanization that is so encumbering to your planet. Mechanization is the result of separation. When you step through certain electromagnetic waves, such as channeling, or dreaming, you see the Great Oneness.

In the great days prior to this world's present awareness, what occurred in Egypt was a continual degradation and a pervasive thought of suppression. This thought of suppression created more of what you call separation, and so there was no longer the ONE Thought. The ONE Thought deteriorated because there was not ONE Action and there was not ONE Feeling. As it is said, when two or more are gathered, there is ONE Action. In such a gathering, there is an electromagnetic pulsation of a ONE Feeling and that ONE Feeling can bring about ONE Focus. When two or more are gathered in that ONE Focus, your world will change.

AKHENATON LINEAGE OF GURUS

Question: "Dear El Morya, it has come to our knowledge that Akhenaton, one of the great leaders of Egypt, was from the planet Sirius. He had an elongated head very much like those of the Mayan people. Was he truly a Sirian or a leftover remnant of Atlantis? Also, could you elaborate on his role and its relationship to the seeding of the Aryan?"

Our Beloved Brother Serapis Bey, to whom you have been introduced, is the embodiment of the one whom you call Akhenaton. He brought to the planet the awareness of the ONE again. He traveled distinctly from those great Mayan halls and brought the information with his counterpart Nefertiti. In bringing this, he singularly traveled past the Atlantean consciousness. The seed of that which you call the Sirian understanding exists solely in those areas of Central and Southern America. It is the seed there which you call Mayan, Incan, and Aztec, dispensed throughout the planet, which still exists in the Americas as part of the Atlantean awareness.

This great feeling of this ONE Source of creation was lost in the degradation of the Atlantean culture. At that time, power was given to elements and elementals who were only in service to the Divine Plan. The elevation of these beings by the feeling world of the Atlanteans broke the feeling world apart and created the spectrum of feelings, such as hate and love. Feelings became polarized. Each feeling is equally strong. They are, as you say, different sides of the same coin, yet they are ONE.

Question: "Were pyramids used to bi-locate?"

GALACTIC PYRAMIDS

The pyramids align specifically to several points throughout the Logos. The pyramids are designed for transportation from one planetary realm to another. Each of these planetary realms exists in a singular or multidimensional expression. Your world or plane is a multidimensional expression. In addition, your world is a singular expression. Your world holds that paradox of learning of the ONE. Here are these great pyramids that connect inter-galactically, just as the great pyramids connected inter-galactically through the aforementioned cultures of Mayan, Incan, and Aztec. They serve the same geometric purpose, to bring forth a duplication of the awareness onto the planet. This duplication is then replicated through many, many lifetimes and embodiments.

# Exchanges

*"All of creation, whether you call it dark or light, is the ONE."*
- LADY NADA

*Beloved El Morya steps forward.*

Once again, we ask permission to come forward.

Response: "Please come forth."

## THE DIVINE MIND

I AM the Mahatma El Morya. This is the replication and duplication, as you have known in the triangular, pyramidal pattern. In each culture, be it Egyptian, Incan, Aztec, or Mayan, a duplication of what was originally instructed was brought forth. In this duplication, life would always beget life. The choice of this life or the sense of that life is a great feeling. That which you consider death in your world is the opposite of this expanded feeling. However, death is only a perspective. It is a birth into an expanded awareness. In the expanded awareness, you are still able to take action. It is the balance of this action that takes us to the path of creatorship or that which you have known as Mastery. It enables you to do that which you call bi-location, manifestation of food, or changing of weather.

The planet is here for you to learn to create, very much like any school where you would take clay and form again and again many different forms, or take stone or wood and carve different forms; or you would take the (color) pallet and create many different color combinations with shapes and shadow and light. In the same manner, the planet has offered the service of creation so you may learn Divine Mind.

As one is a butcher, there is a certain mind set for butchering. As one is a baker, there is a certain mind set for baking. As one is a physician, there is a certain mind set for healing. So too, there is a certain mind set for Mastery. It is a mind set or awareness wherein your actions and your feelings are in complete alignment, coordinated for the functioning of your being. It is this Divine Spark of individualization that brings forth the perfected Oneness of all creation.

ON SEPARATION

When you perceive separation, you feel no electromagnetic connection, and in the lack of electromagnetic connection, you will be unable to create. There will be no Law of Attraction. When you make the choice for separation, the Law of Repelling takes hold. These are simple functions of creation. You see them as good; you see them as evil; you see them as right and wrong. It is the Creator's choice to bring together in a harmony or to bring forth separation. You are learning this path. It is the plane of awareness that you are coming to.

The limited scope of this awareness brings forth universal structures that you can Master and contain. If they are taken outside of this scope, without the Mastery of your movement, feeling, and focus, then chaos is the end result. It is as though you have been placed in a free zone to learn how to destroy or how to create, to learn compassion or to exercise suppression. This area, this free zone, is the great beloved planet Terra. We see the great life on this planet as Prana. That is our perspective. You see the great stillness and immovability of this planet and you call it Earth. You see it as fixed, as a place where there is no movement.

We would ask you to consider the Mastery perspective of the great Prana, the perspective that this is a great movement. It is a great feeling in this movement, and this great movement is, in itself, a great focus. This is the path of Mastery and Creatorship. Please consider simplicity. That which you call complicated is only the further separation of your own mind seeing the individualization. When your mind sees the laws and patterns of the attractions and repulsions that exist naturally in your plane of consciousness, then your mind may rearrange them and organize them in such a manner that the great feeling from the great Divine Heart, the Spark of All Life, comes forward. The movement of the will is always in that great Divine Mind and spark of Divine Desire. It is from this point that the great joy of creation is ever flowing, weaving, and connecting creation in the Logos. But for the moment, you are kept isolated in your creation.

## THE DESIRE TO "GO HOME"

We understand. We have total compassion. We all are part of the same system. We have gone through the same patterns that you are now experiencing. We utilize these same patterns much as you do, but in an expanded form. All of us move together in a great movement. A great seed was planted in our Logos, in that Flame of Desire. We all desire, as you have said many times, to return Home. It is in the motion of returning Home that you discover that you *are* Home. This planet is Home and there is no place or plane of consciousness in any part of creation where you are not Home. It is all Home. Your present experience is just a room in the Home.

Now, you are in the playroom. You are there learning to cook, to prepare, to create, and to build confidence in your experience. You will confide in yourself always and your instructions come from within. The great Presence that is God I AM is truly in your heart. Through confidence you take action. Confide solely in yourself and do not look to the outer. See the eternal ONE.

## EXCHANGE SUFFERING FOR JOY

We ask you to consider that this Map of Exchanges as exchanges of suffering for joy. It exchanges suppression for freedom. It exchanges poverty for great abundance. These are the exchanges your planetary consciousness must make. The symbolism of the Map of Exchanges becomes activity. It is a literal movement, that all great sorrow is now exchanged for joy. We ask you to consider to be part and to partake of this exchange. We ask you to bring forth in your great Blue Flame this Divine Purpose, that these great lands that you call Europe and that you call Africa now exchange and become ONE. No longer is there separation and suppression. There is only the ONE. Do you have questions, Dear one?

Response: "No questions, only that you return tomorrow for the completion of this material for New Lemuria."

We will return at the appointed time for the completion of all of New Lemuria. It is at this point that I must pass the floor to Beloved Nada, for she must add the feminine expression.

Response: "Welcome Nada."

*Beloved Nada steps forward. Her energy is gentle and balanced.*

## THE SOUL OF THE FEMININE

Greetings Dear Sister and Brother of my own heart. I AM the lady you know as Nada.

It is in the understanding of the feminine perspective that creation comes forward in its gentleness. As these great poles melt, their waters gently lap and nestle against the lands. They gently cover them, as a mother covers a child for the long, long night. It is this gentle activity that we ask you to focus upon. Yet, there are times when the feminine will flare in a great upheaval and movement. So too this exists as a great bursting forth of light, as the newborn comes with great laborious movement and joy. A gentle sweetness then exists.

We ask you to see this feminine planet and the feminine in yourselves. Those of you in Europe, those of you in Africa, and all the lands of this creation, see this feminine side that you are; this side of great love, this side of great devotion, this side of unyielding patience. We ask you to see that each of these changes is not a change to destroy, but it is a change to renew and to rebuild your Divine Essence. It is a change to awaken your great feminine soul, for those on this planet are all of the feminine soul and of unyielding compassion. We ask you to create from the feminine, to come forward in your focus, your movement, and your feeling. Come forward in the understanding that life is sharing. It is shared with yourself; it is shared with all around you. This great abundance and sharing of life is infinite. Our grandfathers and grandmothers before us gave us this physical body. It was given through a great source of light, sound, and breath, for our infinite expression. It is ONE with the feminine power.

The rising of these new lands in Portugal brings forth the essence of this great feminine power. If you will look to all of your maps, you will find that there is not one map that is without a rising of new land. It is the rising of this new land from the Mother that shows you rebirth. It is this great rebirth that we ask you to focus upon. As our Beloved Brother Saint Germain has explained, birth does come forward with some tearing and some bleeding, but it is a new life. The life on this planet has led to this moment, is now coming to a rebirth. The life led by all people in conflict or suppression is now coming to a rebirth of union, harmony, and balance.

WE ARE THE "ONE"

This great Golden Age is a new Ray from Archangel Crystiel and comes forward upon this planet, activating the great intelligence that you are. It activates the great creation that you are. It activates the great heart. It activates infinite movement. It is the activation of the Golden Age that brings new birth to each of you. It is a birth for each of us. We are no different. We feel and we think and we act. It is only that our awareness has come to an acceptance of the balance of the creation. We are no different. The angels are no different. All are the same. We are your Brothers, your Sisters. We are the ONE.

All of creation, whether you call it dark or light, is the ONE. It is in the balancing of this ONE that infinite harmony comes and is sustained. We ask you to consider the choice of self-harmony, so as to honor your feminine, to honor your masculine, to harmonize these within yourself. In this acceptance of yourself, you will accept your Brothers and your Sisters equally. You will accept the planet as ONE with you. You will accept the vegetation. You will accept the mineral. You will accept the animal. You will see the underlying, infinite ONE Spirit. The soul of this planet is feminine. So too is the soul of all of the inhabitants. While the expression may take on the masculine form, the soul truly is that of this Mother.

EXCHANGE CONFLICT FOR PEACE

Come forward and exchange all of your weapons. Exchange all of your jails and prisons and manifestation of suppression.

Exchange your economic systems. Exchange these for peace. Share with your Brothers and Sisters. We ask you to move your actions, your heart, and your focus in the great Divine Plan. Exchange your worn out principles that have created conflict in your world to principles of harmony. Exchange your laws, exchange your governments, exchange all that does not serve the purpose of the ONE. Find peace in self, harmony in self. Share this with each other. Exchange anything that does not serve peace and harmony. Exchange it for a purpose with an action and a thought for harmony.

We have held and will continue to hold this focus with you and for you. We will never waver from this purpose. You and I are always ONE. There is no distance or separation. We are always here. There are many of us, more than you realize, who have offered this service. We ask you to exchange your doubt for acceptance. Come to this ONE. Come to harmony. This we ask you in total love. Do you have questions?

Response: "I have no questions. So Be It."

Then at this moment we will take our leave.

Response: "Thank you Beloved Nada. "

# The Celebration of Shamballa

*"We prepare the way for the birth of the child, the one who plays with an unending energy. Let it create for the joy of creation and live for only the joy of life!"*
- SAINT GERMAIN

Welcome Dear hearts. I AM Saint Germain and, as usual, we request permission to come forward.

Response: "Please Dear ones, come forward."

Today, as you know, is a day of a great feasting, for it is the opening of Shamballa. Not only is it the opening of Shamballa, but it is a time of great joy, a celebration of the Christ and the ONE that we all share. In honor of this, a time-honored tradition among those who are graduates of the Trans-Himalayan Brotherhood and Sisterhood, known as the Great White Lodge, is to gather together and feast. This is on a yearly basis, at the eve of the New Year. It is at this time that we celebrate life and the joy and the wonder of creation. We gather in song and dance, celebrating all great patterns and plans, and set our service to the unending Divine Plan and the infinite service to the Light of God that Never Fails.

Let me describe Shamballa to you, Dear ones, so you may raise your consciousness too to this plane of reality and join and sup and feast with us as ONE.

## THE FEAST OF SHAMBALLA

*All around Saint Germain you can now see other Beings of Light. One who stands next to him is big and muscular. He wears red trousers and has Oriental features. Off to his other side is Beloved Mother Mary. She stands small in stature, cloaked, as always, in green and pink colors. Kuan Yin is present and dressed in a beautiful violet gown. Portia is also at Saint Germain's side. She too is dressed in violet, stars emanating from her aura. El Morya is present, tall and stately. He wears a white turban and his usual white robes. Kuthumi stands quietly and is dressed in simple brown, almost like a monk, and around his waist he carries a ruby in an orange sash.*

*There are others too. Many I don't recognize, but I will continue to describe them. One lady, who looks Egyptian, wears a green head piece. She has a long neck and is willowy in her stature. Nada is present; she is very tall and has blonde flowing hair. She always holds a book in her arms, a symbol of always carrying the Cosmic Law itself. Helios and Vesta are present and they sit at the head of a great table, preparing for the banquet or feast. The scene has the feeling of the United Nations, a stately or diplomatic affair. Helios and Vesta sit together in golden chairs by one another. Their arms wrapped around each other, joined at the elbow and their legs always touching. A golden glow emanates from them. Sanat Kumara and Lady Master Venus are present. He always wears a smile and she carries that great violet glow, almost so dark, it's a midnight blue. Saint Germain speaks:*

As you can see Dear one, there are many of us present here at this great gala event, for you see it is our celebration, our returning to the ONE, our celebration to life in its fullest. Now I will explain the hall where this feast is held.

*Saint Germain is now pointing to a map, his finger resting on the etheric location of Shamballa as it rests over the Gobi Desert.*

## THE INITIATE

Throughout eons of time there have been those who wished to have their eyes and ears open. They travel through life, embodiment after embodiment, gaining understanding, working through the will of the great unknown plan and opening their heart to the ever-present joy and love that fills all with life. They become known as the students of Life. During their journey they become, shall we say, not only adept at the patterns and routines of life, but also adept at recognizing the wandering heart's desire. At this moment in the wanderer's experience, an elder Brother or Sister is appointed from the Great White Lodge to contact this student of life. So Be It. From that moment they are then introduced to the doctrines of Mastery and adeptship. This student is initiated, if he or she so chooses, as a chela of the Great White Lodge. In becoming a chela of the Great White Lodge, this initiate chooses to serve humanity in whatever form is presented to him or her through their Master Teacher.

## CONTACT WITH THE MASTER

In the probationary period the Master Teacher sends emanations directly from the heart of the Lodge. At first, instruction is given through waves of consciousness and contact through dreams. Super consciousness is activated and given personal instructions to follow routine initiations that lead the chela to various geographic locations across the planet. Soon, the student is prepared through the spirit, soul, and body for increased contact. After the chela has achieved a certain amount of resilience in Mastering the mighty Laws of Life through the disciplines of the Great White Lodge, he or she is then allowed personal contact with the Master Teacher.

Shamballa is the time, or the opening, wherein such personal contact is made with those initiates who have persevered - who have dared, who have done, and kept their silence. There are those who are chelas and students who have been given tasks from Master Teachers to share their message publicly. This too is part of the path of initiation and adeptship. Then comes a time of a deeper inner work where one discovers the silence of the soul. The inner kingdom opens the power of resolve, deliberate choice. It is at this moment, in the development of understanding and Mastery of the soul, that the chela requires contact again with the Master Teacher, not only through conscious awareness, but through tactile, tangible physical contact. Shamballa is an opening for such an event and this event, time-honored in the Great White Lodge, is indeed an initiation. It is also part of the path which strengthens the stalwart heart of the servant like steel.

## THE WORK FOR BELOVED TERRA

As you see, this is a great feast for all of us. Present among us are our own Master Teachers, those who have come across the galaxies, returning at the changing of the year in the moment of the interplaying Rays. It is a celebration of the patterns of life and the evolution of creation. They have come from Venus, the Pleiades, and the Andromeda. Each honored Teacher is present and lays their plans for our work on Beloved Terra as a dispensation of Divine Thought. They too work through the little wills of men! We too, servants of this Divine Plan, are steeped not only in Divine Thought and the unknown plan, but in the heart of love and life!

This is a feast prepared for those of you who have wearied on the journey and now come for your repast. Sit for a moment, won't you please? Sit and sup with us. A grand celebration it is. The symphonies of the spheres play. Elohim and Archangels dance and parley. And now we shall sit, shall we?

*In the background you can hear soft music and then trumpets sound. They all enter the banquet hall, two at a time. As they walk to their chairs at the banquet table, the line splits into gendered counterparts. The male energy seeks the right and the female, the left. At the table they face one another, sitting on the appropriate side. We enter the doorway and we are met by two shining faces.*

"Please enter and sit."

*We wear white robes. I look down to my waist and there is a sash of green, gold, and violet. I look to Len and he has the same. We separate again, Len to the right, and I to the left. We take our positions. At the other end of the table is Sananda and now he speaks.*

## THE REALIZATION OF SPIRITUAL AWAKENING

Greetings in the name of the Great White Lodge. I AM Sananda and it is a great honor to be of service to my Brothers and my Sisters who have served mankind throughout the eons. First, we shall address the project known as transition and the awakening of the HU-man, for we have noticed a great increase in the vibrational frequencies of those upon Terra, an increase, not only in their mental ability to understand, but an increase in their vibration.

The preparations are now complete. We are most honored that there have been those students and chelas who have been ever-present, ready, and willing to serve the great demand and the great call, for the time has now come that the Spiritual Awakening shall be realized. The slumber has lessened among humans. Their Divine Flames now leap in full life!

## JOY OF CREATION

It is with great joy that I address all of you and thank you. It is gratitude and appreciation that fills my heart and leaps to your heart.

For the time of slumber is no longer at hand.

The time of awakening is conjoined.

Masculine and feminine energies join as ONE.

We prepare the way for the birth of the child,
the one who plays with an unending energy.
Let it create for the joy of creation
and live for only the joy of life!

It is in this year the humans celebrate that I bless with the joy
of life and I bless with the joy of creation.

Hitaka!
So Be It!
Let us celebrate!

*Together, all present raise their cups and repeat:*

Hitaka! So Be It.

*There is a soft chime in the background and a great bell is rung. The
Asian man in the red trousers walks over to the two doors and opens
them and more people arrive, beings not only from other star systems,
but the many chelas and students who have been working for the
spiritual transition. It is a celebration of the ONE; it is a celebration of
peace and unity. So Be It.*

# Birth Changes

*"Do not be afraid to allow your own change to erupt or to move.
Perhaps that change is necessary."*
- EARTH MOTHER BABAJERAN

Greetings and salutations. I AM the Mother known as Babajeran. Oh, how I weep and how these wounds now seep! You of humanity, who are so receptive to open your ears and hear my cry and my plea! You perceive me as suffering and yet I know too, when the womb is ready to move, now a birth shall occur, one that mankind has not known before in this epoch and evolution of consciousness. As you have all been prepared through the Ascended Master Teachings, now this time comes for you to understand your evolution and purpose on the planet.

## GLOBAL AWAKENING

I, as the Mother, am also your Sister, your Brother, and your friend. Understand that as we are linked as ONE, there is also a plan and a purpose, a destiny to be fulfilled. Cry not for those who have left their physical vehicles behind. They are now opened and free to serve those who are now within the shell of the physical density. The time of global awakening now comes to the planet and I too have my cry and my plea. I too have my service to bring. Those who have left are those who have asked; those who have asked are those who have left. This is the paradox of life. Your sojourn here upon the Earth Plane and Planet, covered in a physical vehicle, leaves you wondering and searching your soul. You ask, what is the outer experience that can take my shell in one swift movement at the hand of nature?

## PHYSICAL EXPERIENCE DEEPENS INNER EXPERIENCE

It is the outer physical experience that allows your inner experience to fully express. It is the evolution, shall we say, of consciousness upon the Earth Plane and Planet, which concerns all being and all life. The events, in this time period you are now experiencing, are that which you would refer to as a trial or a tribulation. However, we approach them with great joy and knowledge of the Divine Plan. There is the Wisdom of the Ages that works through this plan of Earth Changes. In this time, the closure of one age and the beginning of another, there is movement, shall we say, of energy; movement, not only in the microcosm, but also in the macrocosm; movement, not only in the bio-energetic fields, but also movement in the geo-energetic fields.

## COUNCIL OF THE ELOHIM

I have served, shall we say, on the Council of the Elohim, who helped to create the worlds before this world and I have sponsored this planet through my consciousness. I ask each of you to understand sponsorship of consciousness. In order for the evolution of consciousness to occur upon the Earth Plane and Planet, there must be that work of the Divine Will in, through, and around all activity. Today has been another one of those momentous events, shall we say, in the laying forward of the Divine Plan. You perceive this as an Earth Change. However, we perceive this as a finer adjustment of the energy fields of the planet, so as to allow a new birth to occur.

## THE DEEPENING

Brother Saint Germain has brought forth the teaching that change will not occur without some tearing, weeping, and shedding of blood. In this case, in order to adjust and allow a greater awakening, a deepening of Source, it is necessary for a furthering of outer experience to stimulate the inner experience. A New Time is coming, a time where one will understand their purpose in Divine Thought and their purpose and role in the Spiritual Awakening of humanity. It is my purpose now to weep. It is my purpose now to cry. It is my time to shudder a bit, for how else will the stimulation of your growth occur? All life stimulates more life and this is true for all levels of perception and understanding.

Today, again, is the seventeenth and you all understand the meaning of the seventeen and its significance in the Spiritual Awakening. If you were to trace an understanding of the bio-genetic and geo-energetic history of humankind, you would find that it is linked in the sacred geometry of the number seventeen.

All Earth Changes that affect Divine Destiny follow multiples and synchronicities of seventeen. You ask why this is so?

We ask for you to consider the patterns of creation and how patterns help to affect all potential outcomes and consequences. When a pattern is laid, for instance in a multiplicity of three, movement of energy then occurs in what we call a triangular basis. When energy is laid in multiplicities, shall we say, of one, energy moves in a circular shape. When we lay down creation, shall we say in multiplicities of four, we see movement in the shape of the square. There is a Divine Order that streams forth in all Divine Thought and patterns of humanity. So, study this of the seventeen, and you will then begin to understand how geo-energy relates to bio-energy and the human form.

HARMONIZATION OF EARTH

Now a continuation of this teaching: You know that the Heart Chakra of this planet, that center the Masters placed on the I AM America Map, extends straight through to the other side of the planet. Many of you have wondered and asked how this affects what is now occurring. To the northeastern side of this heart, all energetic adjustment shall occur to help influence a quantum change in spiritual consciousness.

Your own Pacific Northwest, as I have instructed, is the exact location of the forty-eighth parallel, affiliated with physical movement or an action body. This is a specific point, to bring an energetic adjustment to fields of consciousness on the present California coastlines. However, at this time, if you should organize a healing event to adjust all circumstances, travel to the more central parts of the northwest, what is known as the state of Oregon, into those areas covered with the basalt flows. To offer another finer adjustment, do this work very much as you would work acupressure and acupuncture points on the body. If there are those who wish to serve the Elohim, send your thought and your prayer to that location. Also send your thought and prayer continuously to other locations that have been harmonized.

Perhaps you are now all wondering when another working of the Divine Plan will be seen. In response, I tell you, tarry not in your internal self, for there is much challenge ahead. Tarry not in your work of consciousness here, Dear children and peace-makers of many planetary lifestreams. You are here to fulfill the destiny and evolution of consciousness. You are here, not only to realize and experience a Time of Change, but to utilize it to explore the consciousness within your own being. It is only through this example and demonstration that you can extend this, hopefully and willingly, to your Brother and Sister, with the purity of the greatest light.

Helios and Vesta call their children! This call reminds them that they are part of the whole and not exclusively limited from that whole. Helios and Vesta call each and every one of you, Dear ones, to the call of this ONE.

## INTERNALIZATION OF THE GREAT CHANGES

The prophecies of Earth Changes have been brought to each of you as a teaching of the ONE and for your own internal union. You are now called from the solar Logos to activate internally and externally your devotion to the Unfed Flame of Love, Wisdom, and Power. Each one of you is a Godship, prepared to travel through, shall we say, these times that require infinite mercy and infinite compassion. Do you hear the cries, the screams and the shudders of suffering? It is time for you now to walk through this and understand service to life that is ALL.

Perhaps you are now questioning what I have said. Does this energetic adjustment come through my personal joy and happiness? Joy and happiness are but another fraction, shall we say, of this experience of tempering the Eternal Self. All that is presented to you now, Dear Stewards of the Plan, is presented so that you grow from the seedling into that fine, strong grove of trees that can withstand the wind and rain of change. Change is ever-present around you. It is ever-present and Omnipotent. Change is the only way that we temper our internal divinity and keep, shall we call, a cosmic check and balance upon creation.

How long there has been the suffering of my shores and my waters. How long has been the suffering of my lungs and my breath. So now, I gently move to the side to breathe a little easier, to swallow instead of gulp. Do you understand the glorious gift that is now given? In awakening to the ONE, you know that life is eternal, infinite, and ceaseless. Yet all is changing, while you are changeless. This, again, is the teaching of the outer world. Change is necessary for you to understand the ceaseless and timeless Source. Again, a portal is now open and a Time of Change harkens. Your thoughts and feelings are restless. Do you have questions?

Question: "Would you give the optimum location for the energetic adjustment in the state of Oregon and the optimum ritual?".

The optimum location is in the central part of this state. The specific location you shall cross-reference in your written material.

*I am looking and I see, in the center of Oregon, a round circle coming up. It is northeast of Ashland, Oregon, and extends up and takes in a little bit of the circle of what we would call Eugene, Oregon, but it's, again, much more to the eastern side. It is almost as if this dot is in the center of the state of Oregon, that if you could get within the radius of the dot, it would be okay. Most important, what is being impressed in this teaching is to get to the central heart of Oregon.*

[Editor's Note: A group of eight joined in prayer and ceremony, as instructed by the Ascended Masters, in Bend, Oregon. The result was the shifting of energy to lessen the effects of volcanic activity in the Cascade Mountain range.]

ANCIENT, UNDERGROUND SEA OF OREGON

As you have studied and understand the geology of this state, you also know that resting underneath her lands is an ancient sea. These waters wash into what we know as the Pacific Ocean and in these waters, my whole electrical system can then be adjusted. Do you understand?

Question: "What ritual would you have us do?"

## THOUGHT AND PRAYER

As always, holding thought and prayer in a group has by far the strongest effect. Blending and merging your energies with the Mother in thought and prayer is always the best. Pour yourself into me at that location. Pour forth your heavenly energy and anchor the Father unto me. Look for other adjustments in your Earth field to occur. Questions?

Question: "How many in number shall we have for this healing event?"

Always two or more to hold the consciousness. Three or more to put it into activity. Six or more to form the Rays. Seven or more to bring completion.

Question: "As you wish, we shall do this. What thought, feeling, and action can be used as a focus and can be shared with the world?"

Thought brings balance.
All thought serves the next thought.
All is as ONE.
That is the thought, balance, harmony, and blending.

The feeling is purification.
Do not be afraid to allow your own change to erupt
or to move.
Perhaps that change is necessary.
It is the feeling.

Purify your being.
Place yourself in the heart of intent.
Action, let it come from the blend of these two.
Action in service, as has been stated, breathes the breath that
all may utilize.

These are the three premises now for this teaching and I shall close.

Response: "As you wish. Thank you and blessings."

# The Four Pillars

*"The internal self is transmigrating
through experience after experience
to gain quantum consciousness."*
– SAINT GERMAIN

*This chapter is a lesson received during class time at the School of the Four Pillars. After a breathtaking hike up the Barnhardt Trail, eleven students gathered for this teaching from Beloved Saint Germain. We began with the following invocation: Beloved Mighty I AM Presence, Great Host of Ascended Masters of the Spiritual Hierarchy of the Great White Brotherhood and Sisterhood of Light, Beloved Saint Germain, Beloved Kuan Yin, Beloved Mother Mary, Beloved Sananda, Beloved El Morya, Beloved Serapis Bey, Beloved Seven Mighty Elohims, and Archangels of Light and Sound come forth into my energy field, Dear ones.*

*The beloved Teachers of Light gently appear. Some are visibly outlined against the background of pine trees. Some can be felt through their magnetic vibration. A few stand behind the students that they sponsor, and others lovingly form a circle for the Master Teacher to come forward. A flash of ultraviolet light is seen by a few students and felt by all.*

Greetings, in that mighty Christ Light! I AM Saint Germain and I stream forth on that Violet Ray of Mercy and Forgiveness. As usual, Dear students and chelas of mine, I request permission to come forth.

Response: "Dear one, please come forth."

## THE SPIRITUAL PATH

You, Dear ones, students of the School of the Four Pillars, have, shall we say, climbed that highest mountain. You have climbed, shall we say, another step of adeptship. Did you note, Dear ones, each step along that path was another step forward in your Mastery in that mighty Law of Life? It is this Law of Life that each one of you is attempting, shall we say, to solve. Each one of you asking the question, "Is this the next road I shall take? Is this the next path I shall take?"

Let me assure you, Dear hearts, that a time will come when that Law of Life will be achieved throughout your being. The Law of Life is a law that is achieved through the breath, the light, and the sound. Each layer of your energy fields, each cell and subatomic particle expresses and achieves life. Each cell, expressing and achieving life, is also qualified, shall we say, by light and sound. Light and sound then blend into that mighty appearance. The Law of Life is the harmony of these aspects, shall we say, of light and sound, each light and sound Ray qualified with an aspect of divinity. When I mention the word Divinity, I talk about that flame anchored within your heart. And also, that Divine Essence, that Divine Being, which, shall we say, has chosen through a field of experience, a code, in an epochal manner, to express that Law of Life. All Divinity is an expression of this Law of Life.

Dear students of the School of the Four Pillars, it is important that you understand the heritage, or shall we say, the Divine-ship that you carry forth into the world. I pass this cup to you, each and every one of you. Now drink. As Dear Sananda has said, "Sup with me, Dear Brothers and Sisters of Light," for the time has come for us to share this energy with all who have eyes and ears open.

## THE FOUR PILLARS OF SOLOMON'S TEMPLE

The anchoring of the Four Pillars upon the Earth Plane and Planet began several epochs ago. In the Lemurian existence, the first pillar came through the development of the physical body. Then came the development of the emotional bodies through the Atlantean pillar. Now, you who are known as Aryan, apply through conscious choice and decision, the active intelligence which carries forth this work through the third sphere. The fourth pillar of vibrational energy awaits its completion in this new millennium. Through choice and intelligence these four mighty pillars are anchored to the planet and we have known them as "Solomon's Temple."

If your eyes and ears are open but your hand cannot intelli-gently do, what good is it, Dear ones? We ask each and every one of you to align, as El Morya has said, your will to that Divine Will and allow a breath of conscience to supersede your conscious-ness. The time of consciousness now comes to the planet. But, what good is consciousness without intelligence? Have you not known, Dear ones, the many who have developed awareness and consciousness, and yet, have not learned to guide that conscious awareness through the intellect.

Science and its application, as it has been given to humanity at this present time, is what we would call the disciplined approach to the development of the mind and an ordered rhythmic service to intelligence. As you have known, throughout this time on your Earth Plane and Planet and present history, many of those who are arriving at the transition of the Spiritual Awakening would blame the scientific community for the shutdown and breakdown that you are experiencing in society. However, we would like to remind you that science has rhythmically served the opening to Divine Conscious Awareness. Open up, Dear ones, to your Divine Inheritance and to your Divine Heritage. Consciousness has come to serve all and to serve all as one mighty breath in that Law of ONE.

## TEACHINGS ON THE FOUR-FOLD BREATH

I would like to teach you what we would call one of the first principals of breathing through the vertical power current, or what you would understand, as that mighty Golden Thread Axis. Let each breath represent what you have known as Mineral, Vegetable, Animal, and now your HU-man Kingdoms. We will start with a breath that will open up, shall we say, all Grounding Chakras to the planet.

Sit upright. Spine straight. First breath: Let us now anchor to the golden center, as we have called it, of the planet, your Beloved Sister and Sponsor, Babajeran. Breathing through the Golden Thread Axis, let us now recall the Lemurian vibration. Up from the pulsing core of the planet comes the energy. Feel this and direct your breath. In a series of breaths, move this energy first to the base of your spine. Upon achievement of this, you will first feel a burning and then a warmth will spread across your lower abdomen. Continue the draw of this pulsing energy as it develops from Lemurian to Atlantean.

From the base of the spine, again through a second series of breaths, direct the energy through your Golden Thread Axis to the Heart Center. Continue again, the breath, not as in one mighty draw, but directed in currents of threes and fours. Signal when your have achieved this through the Heart Center. Do you feel a broadness in the chest? Do you feel the opening, shall we say, of the Chakra Centers? Do you feel an adjustment of all Sub-Vortices (chakras)?

And now, the most important breath. The breath of active intelligence. First, let us direct the breath from the Heart Center to the center known as your Third Eye. This center of focus is the pineal gland. Now direct this in pulses of seven and eights. Do you understand? Once you have achieved this, please signal. Upon achievement of this movement of consciousness, you will notice a violet light streaming into your vision. Have you noticed this?

Dear chelas, stalwart students, practice this breath during this Time of Transition, for it opens your Third Eye, clarifies your fields, and allows for you to work fully in your capacity as a teacher and healer. There is one more breath. However, I would prefer to teach the fourth breath after you have achieved success with this lesson. After you have Mastered these, we will teach you the Breath of Cooperation to complete the Four-fold Breath. Instruction on this will be given too at a later date. This breath seals the masculine and feminine energy as one current running and pulsing in the fullness of electromagnetic energy. [Editor's Note: This is the *Twilight Breath*.]

Tarry not in your work upon the Earth Plane and Planet! There is a Time of Change that comes. Not only is there a change within the consciousness, there is a change that comes to the Earth Plane. As you have all experienced the recent rumblings and grumblings of our planet, we urge you, Dear students, to continue this breath work. In this breath a healing occurs, shall we say, an adjustment of your energy fields to the fields of Beloved Babajeran.

LESSEN THE PRESSURE

The prophecies that have been brought to you are prophecies of choice and change. Not only are we going to see further earthquake activity in the Los Angeles area, we will also see earthquake activity into northern California. There is also the potential and possibility for earthquake activities within the Vancouver, British Columbia and the Canadian border.

We ask all of you, Dear stalwart students of the Spiritual Hierarchy, to continue your healing work. For as each and every one of you adjusting your own magnetic fields, there is a lessening of the pressure in the tectonic plates of collective consciousness. As you have understood the Earth itself to be composed of fissures, fault lines, and moving plates, look again, for as above, so below; as below, so above. Collective consciousness moves much like a chakra works in the movement of energy in the human aura. Their compositions are much the same.

## "BIRTH" QUAKE

Have you not experienced those days when you are feeling a birthquake? When riots, violence, and wars break out among humanity is this not very similar to an earthquake? The planet's layers and fields are comprised of this collective consciousness, and we ask you to understand that this is also where all healing begins for the physical and tangible Earth. We have taught that the first layer of the auric field meshes and routes with the second, third, and onward up to thirty-three layers which manifest the appearance in the physical. Corresponding to each of these fields is also, what we would call, its collective energy. Let me explain.

Electromagnetic fields surround all of life, and how would we define electromagnetic energy? Electricity is the first layer of the field served by the Blue Ray. The second layer, magnetics, you have known as the bonding through the heart energy. This served in the Atlantean course of evolution developing the emotional energy. The third layer of the field is known as Divine Mind and this is where these two principles merge as ONE in electromagnetism. Sometimes, we refer to electromagnetism as Aryan.

Please understand, Dear ones, each layer of the field is accompanied by six others (seven total). In electromagnetism, each of these layers is subtly affected by different changes in fields. For instance, your thought can direct feeling; your feeling can direct action; and your action can move matter physically. When these three blend, shall we say, in that harmonic, then the fourth dimension is birthed. Access into that dimension is birthed of higher consciousness. We will further address higher consciousness in this discourse.

## YOU ARE MIDWIVES OF HIGHER CONSCIOUSNESS

All who are ready to serve the Earth Plane and Planet recognize you are all midwives of a higher consciousness. If there is, shall we say, movement and shaking of land, isn't this also an opportunity for consciousness to be birthed? Observe even fissures, shall we say, where the Earth has moved. Place your hand to feel the energy from these rocks and you will notice a consciousness that has pierced, or shook that spear of active intelligence. Now, perhaps, the first question that may come to your mind, "Is there active intelligence even in the smallest of rocks in the Mineral Kingdom?" There is an active intelligence carried in what we call Prana. Prana, as you know, is that movement or breath behind ALL. It is present within all things, much like the genetic blueprint. This genetic blueprint of the Divine Plan, as Divine Will or Force, known as breath, moves us forward into an activity.

Yes, even the smallest manifestation or expression of consciousness contains Prana, a consciousness comprised of ONE. When an Ascended Master has the ability, shall we say, to move a rock, to open up a wall, to hold back a river, or to walk upon water, he or she simply understands the consciousness of the ONE. He or she simply understands that all life takes command from life.

And now I shall open the floor, as I sense your questions.

Question: "What is the purpose of time and space?"

Time is given for experience. Space is given for the appearance, or the manifestation of the experience. Time and space, as you would understand them, are the key Creators of what is known as illusion. And yet, it is only through illusion, this mirror of consciousness, that we evolve and grow, shall we say, the internal reality.

Question: "How do the thirty-three layers that you mentioned relate to energy fields and our spiritual body?"

## LAYERS OF CONSCIOUS ENERGY

As you have evolved from mineral to animal and now to the HU-man, you have added layers or fields of consciousness. This results in an awareness through which you can extend your expression and qualification of light and sound. Currently you are all experiencing, what we shall call, the integration of the Eighth Ray. This is an initiation much of humanity is experiencing now. It is through this Eighth Ray that one then understands the work of the Violet Flame of Forgiveness, that brings the body, mind, and soul into transfiguration.

At the eleventh layer of the field one develops, what we call, the ability to transmigrate between dimensions. This has been confused with Ascension. The eleventh layer of the field allows the mind the choice to pick up the body at will or not. At the twenty-second layer of the field of expression, one becomes, what we know, as the world servant. Onward to the thirty-third layer of the field, one is ready for cosmic expression.

All appearance, of course, is guided through thought. All thought is guided through Divine Power, all Divine Power, through that known as the force of Will. Perhaps it is more important that we understand a quality, or what I would call, an awareness of consciousness aimed towards transfiguration. As I served that Ray of Transfiguration, that mighty Violet Ray of Mercy and Compassion, we experience, shall we say, at the inner level, our first Alchemy of soul. Look to that which you can change through this Violet Ray, as well as to the qualities it contains. This Ray extends itself in service, diplomacy, and Brotherhood.

It is our actions that determine the result, shall we say, of time and space. But a time now comes to the Earth Plane and Planet where the Vortices of the planet, which you understand to be the same as chakras in the human body, are activated. It is in this activation that an acceleration occurs at the cellular level. And it is in this acceleration that you will get the glimpses into what is known as a Fourth and a Fifth Dimensional reality. Do you understand?

Question: "What is soul transmigration?"

## THE ASCENSION BODY

The teaching of transmigration occurs simultaneously with the process of Ascension. Do you remember your Biblical teachings of forty days and forty nights? Dear Brother Jesus Sananda then experienced, what we shall call, transmigration. This was a cleansing of the physical, mental, and emotional body. Also this forty-day period is numerically significant. In the process of transmigration, an experience is achieved that is called dimensional shifting. The physical body is radically changed, burned sub-atomically through the Fire of Light. There is an explosive sound and the soul is released, shall we say, to travel dimensionally. In this particular case, a service was brought to humanity. Through this intentional purification through selfless service, a plane of dimensional consciousness now known as *The Christ* was anchored.

The internal self is transmigrating through, shall we say, experience after experience (lifetimes) as quickly as possible to gain "the quantum consciousness." Fourth Dimensional consciousness is soon to be anchored upon the Earth Plane and Planet. However, this time, it will not be achieved through the process as explained before as transmigration. It will be achieved through, what we call, a Cosmic Intervention, for the universe in which this Freedom Star is to exist is a universe that will be seen by many during the dimensional shifting.

Time, as you have asked, yes, is slowing down. Time, as you have asked, yes, is speeding up. Have you not noticed how many of the minutes seem to stop? Have you not noticed how many of the minutes seem to fly? When our planet and shared planes of consciousness enter into dimensional shifting, time as you know it, begins to implode.

Question: "Ethics and consciousness. How are these used? Where do they differ?"

EVOLUTION, CONSCIOUSNESS, AND CHOICE

Dear chelas, the course which you have completed is a course in achieving awareness. Awareness evolves into consciousness through choice. Are you now aware of the many paths you have traveled? Are you now aware when you reach that bend in the road and ask of yourself, "Do I travel to the left? Travel to the right?" that now in consciousness you make that decision. The evolution of consciousness is contingent upon the ethics of choice. The ethic of choice comes through the understanding of duality. And yet, it is duality that leads you back again to the expression of the Monad, the ONE. Left or right is really the same decision.

Evolution occurs through experience. Awareness begins through the Animal Kingdom and develops from instinct into intuition. Take this awareness and, like a general knowledge, develop it into a common sense. Common sense rules the pivotal point of choice. Through choice, consciousness is allowed to break through into the ONE. The consciousness of the ONE realizes that from that point of left or right, there are natural consequences. There are also, what we would call, a different karma or dharma involved in the direction of the point that you choose. However, as one evolves through the consciousness of choice, they begin to understand that either/or will suffice.

272

There is great joy in knowing that either/or is an ethic of consciousness. We have stated this in many prior teachings for a sense of non-judging, for a sense of union, for a sense of opening the heart for a love of all humanity and all circumstance. Understand the ONE, for only in the understanding of the ONE can consciousness then evolve. Choice is the taskmaster of the ONE, for only through the choice can you understand ALL.

Dear ones, I shall take my leave from your plane at this moment and will return for further discourse. Continue, at all times, with the Violet Flame. Call it forward, into, and around your body. Use it at all times to transmigrate and transfigure any circumstance. Almighty I AM!

# *Birthing Dimensionally*

"You have moved from a Third Dimensional expression
to a Fourth Dimensional aspiration."
- SAINT GERMAIN

*This is the continuation of the lesson for the students at the School
of the Four Pillars. The invocation begins: Oh Mighty Beloved I AM
Presence come forth. God I AM come forth. Great hosts of Ascended
Masters of the Spiritual Hierarchy of the Great White Lodge of the Great
Brotherhood and Sisterhood of service, come forward. Come forward in
this moment and bring your perfect service as I offer my service. Om
Manaya Patiya, Hitaka. Beloved El Morya, Beloved Kuthumi, Beloved
Sananda, Beloved Saint Germain, Beloved Mary, Beloved Portia, Beloved
Kuan Yin, Beloved Nada, come forward and bring your perfect service!
Beloved Michael, Jophiel, Chamuel, Raphael, Gabriel, Uriel, Zadkiel,
Crystiel, come forward and offer your perfect service. Oh Mighty I AM!
Oh Mighty I AM!*

*There is a great light as they come forward, approach, and stand among
us. They put a hand on our shoulders and ask us to offer our service
to this transition of humanity. The transition is geophysical, yes. The
transition is you and I; as the planet is in transition, as the chemicals
change, so too we are changing. The carbon-based consciousness that*

*we are is altering into the silicon. And, now I turn the floor over to Beloved Saint Germain. The beloved Master of the Violet Flame, Saint Germain, steps forward and speaks:*

Greetings Beloved chelas. I AM Saint Germain. I stream forth on that Violet Flame of Great Compassion. And it is the Laws of Compassion that bring you here today. As I return and bring forward this understanding, it is a consciousness shift of time and of space.

## THE INNER AND OUTER WORLD

You have asked for personal experience. This consciousness shift is your focus. Our beloved Brother El Morya will speak of focus, but it is the consciousness shift that each and every one of you experience at your personal level, in your day to day life, that is important. It is the shift of how you see yourself and others with whom you interact. In this transition, yes, the time does speed, the time does slow, the time does compact, and the time does expand. In doing all of these things, it is just as though you are stuck in a tunnel and you want to wriggle your way through. You might elongate a muscle, or stretch or compress it, pushing against the side as you wriggle your way through from one place to another. This time of transition feels like this.

This birth has been announced. This change, or birth, is a change of focus. No longer is the three dimensional world your focus. No longer is your everyday life your focus. You now have an inner and an outer world. As this inner world disciplines the outer, the experiences of the outer creates spaces for the inner to express. It is a paradox that flows from within and from without. You and I are going through this same transition. There is no difference. The transition of an expanded experience, in the Fifth or Sixth Dimension, is still affected by an experience from the Third or Fourth Dimension. Each and every one of you are birthing in this transition.

That which you have found to be stable in your life is no longer. You're asked many times to follow your bliss, to come to your heart. You're asked many times to look at this as your guiding light, to look at this as your inner guidance. You're asked many times to come to accept what is burning within your heart. This is your course, your path. You have heard technical explanations today, that as you expand from this inner desire, you create the outer expression.

You now understand that you have moved from a Third Dimensional expression to a Fourth Dimensional aspiration. It is in this expression that the aspiration becomes fulfilled to express in itself and of itself. It is the Source that expands from within and from without. This that you see as a paradox is how all creation flows. It flows in these understandings that the world is neither flat nor round, but it is round with flat spots! And the flat spots are not completely flat; some are sunken in, some are raised, some are not straight, and some are crooked! It is this understanding of the great diversity of creation that allows for an infinite amount of choice. This infinite amount of choice sustains the experience. We ask you to go within and choose within. And by doing this, it will temper the creation that is without.

As this creation that is without is continually tempered, it then disciplines the expansion that is continually sustained through the inner expression. It is a paradox, yes, but in the paradox, creation contains light and dark, below and above, front and back, and the understanding that voluntary and expressive manifestations flow and are sustained. It is how the cosmic identity stretches from personal experience to universal experience. This word that you call "personality" is the reality of all your personal experiences. It is that which has tempered your outer world and has created your Inner Self concept. We ask you to come to accept that the Inner Self concept is always of a Divine Source. You are not terrible people. You are not bad people. You have not lost your value because you are continually experiencing!

## POLARITY, CHOICE, AND THE ONE

There is a Master we know as the Herakhan Babaji who has said, "There is no saint without a past and that there is no sinner without a future." They are the same. How may one be a saint on this planet and plane without sin? How can one go forward without knowing what was behind? This is the experience of choice. In choice, you and I are the same. We all have levels of choice. We have levels of understanding. We have levels of discipline. We have levels of acceptance. This is the path of Mastery and the levels of acceptance are unlimited! All that is blocked will be freed! All that is dark will be made light! All that is dark somewhere contains the secret of light! It is through this understanding that creation comes forward and is sustained.

Have you ever considered that there is a dark side of the Moon? Have you ever considered that the Moon does not rotate on an axis as your planet does? Have you ever considered that your Sun, which is a physical manifestation of the Light of God which Never Fails, also has a rotation? By our perspective, from this planetary point, there is a dark side of the Sun and there is a dark side of the Moon. Have you ever considered there is the all-encompassing perspective of the ONE that transports one focus to an infinite focus? Consider that your life is all that you choose. You may choose to accept, you may choose to reject. It is part of your path and it is your Divine Right.

He that chooses to be a farmer may shun the lumber cutter. He that chooses a lumber cutter may shun the farmer. It is a choice. When you make a conscious choice, the outer experience disciplines your perspective of creation. It disciplines your viewpoint. It brings you to these points of understanding. Many of you who have grown gardens know nothing of lumbering. And many of you who have lumbered know nothing of gardening or farming. Choice is infinite experience.

We are all ONE in the sojourn of the experience of creation. We have all planted those seeds and reaped the bountiful harvest. We have all gone to war and conquered. We have all been conquered and have been the victims. This is the experience and there is not one that is more valuable than another! Understand that you are all of these! You are all unto your genetic coding. You and I are ONE. Our experiences are equal. Trials or tribulations, we are the same. It is the same path. It is the path of the Mastery of the self, to learn the discipline of infinite possibility and the expansion of choice.

If you choose to cook one type of food and that food only, that is your focus in that moment. If you neglect the completion of a focus and go to another focus, then that which you left will be spoiled. Finish what you start so your experience is not spoiled. Then, will your experience come to the full fruition, full breath, full life, and full understanding.

## MASTERING PATTERNS

Many times in your lives and embodiments you have the same thing occurring. Men have the same difficulties with women. Women will have the same difficulties with men. They move from one relationship to the next, move from one experience to another. And the same things are always occurring! Until one has Mastered and completed the experience, it will keep occurring again, again, and again. Step through the fire of your own fear, or of your own doubt, and meet your Divine Source. Consider that you are not only affecting yourself, you are also infinitely affecting others! Complete what you have started.

Fulfill the desires of your heart. Come forward! Wriggle through the tube to the other side! Ascension is the Mastery or completion of one energetic pattern after another. In this Mastery, we sustain and maintain our infinite focus. It may now seem challenging to move from one dimensional Ray System to another. Remember when you learned to ride a bicycle? Once you Mastered it, you now pick it up at any time! Once you have learned to play the piano and Mastered it, you pick it up at any time. It is no different with your emotions, with your actions, with your thoughts. They are the same and they are tools for your expression!

Do we have questions?

Question: "You mentioned in the earliest part of this discourse that when we went through a dimensional shift here, you were going through a dimensional shift as well. Does it occur in all of the dimensions simultaneously? Are you moving onward to another dimensional reality?"

## WE ALL GO TOGETHER

Dear one, you are the Master of the future, as are all these Dear ones with you. The future is already our present. We reach back through the experience to nurture, to guide, to protect, and assist the experience to its fulfillment, because it is, as we have said, the completion of the process. We started the water to boil, now you must place the vegetables in the pot! We serve the stew, but you must consume it! As you shift, so do we. And as we shift, so do you. These are the Laws of Balance and Harmony and Unity that govern all actions and activities infinitely sustained in this Divine Plan.[13]

The plan, yes, has variations. But the variations are only to accommodate individualized expression. When the individualized expression brings a unified service, known as Christ Consciousness, then this particular expression comes through a unified field. We have discussed this before. It is this unified field that creates a complete dimensional shift. As you said, many are awakening individually. When this awakening is affected by a certain percentage of your planetary inhabitants, a collective dimensional shift will occur. It is a momentum that is sustained. As this occurs, in what is like a twinkling of instantaneous light, those who are the last to understand are suddenly filled with light and understanding. We all go together.

It is the same here. There are those of us who are more active in service than others. Through service momentum is built. But there is no judgment and there is no keeping score, as you would say, as to who offers service and who does not, because, as you know, everything and everyone has its own time. In the time/space continuum, we are equally affected because there is only the reflection of the energetic patterns which are sustained. Our energetic patterns sustain and reach through into your dimensional collective and yours, as you come to your awakening, reach through into our dimensional collective. They go forth infinitely, for it is the continuum understanding that all life is for life.

Question: "Since we have been obtaining so much help from the other side, in this case, from you and from many others who have been of service to us, who's helping you? Do you have guides and teachers who help you through to the other side where you are going? And can you share what help is being given to you?"

THE UNIVERSAL FAMILY

The Masters, Lady Master Venus and Sanat Kumara, are our sponsors. It is their radiance, in individualized focus, that has brought them together in a unification. This uniting has brought them to a harmonic. This harmonic has created a pathway on which we, in this dimensional collective, may tread. It has created a path that we may follow. We, in turn, unite in the same manner of a focus and create a pathway to a space, opening in the inter-dimensional shifting, or as you have known it to be called in your text and in your sacred treaties, the veil. When this is opened, it becomes a pathway on which you will pass in our footsteps and on which we will pass in their footsteps. It is part of the homogenizing effect of the family. We are all ONE family. We are of any race, creed, or color. We are assigned to this experience of creation in this universal structure that is, in and of itself, a family.

It is the Central Sun System that you remember from other teachings. This system is expanded and expounded upon and the consciousness continues. Many times, from one family system to another, aid is given because there is a larger system to which all the families, or you may call them tribes in your world, come together. But still, there is a basis upon which the creation is founded. As you come into our world, your carbon-based molecular structures will then become reflections of carbon and come into what you have known and experienced as silicon-based. Look at your computers systems. Look into those basic silicon structures and observe the ease with which information is processed and assimilated. It is far faster than your memory system or your own brain function.

However, if you carefully analyze your own brain function, there are many silicon-based cell structures already in existence, which have come through many evolutions during eons of creation. You have expanded from one Ray System to another. In our world, we have expanded and expressed into the Twelfth Ray System, and the Thirteenth is coming into radiance. In your world, the Eighth Ray is now coming into radiance to sustain your creation. These world radiance harmonics come forward, based only on the collective acceptance and movement of consciousness uniting in a harmony. Yes, we have our Masters and our teachers, and this will continue until we have completed into the Thirty-third Ray System. Once that has been completed, there is an additional Ray pattern sequence set into motion and we will complete these together. As this is fulfilled, at some point, we all return to that which you call the ONE.

Question: "On each of the Rays, when we speak of either the Eighth Ray or the Fourteenth Ray, are these Ray harmonics or are they specific Rays with their own tonal quality and attributes?"

HARMONIZING SELF

Each Ray has its own tonal quality and attribute. This is the nature of the expression of consciousness. As far as harmonics, those which you call odd and even numbers are harmonics for your Third Dimensional world. The odd and even numbers together are harmonics in our dimensional world. It is the harmonizing of energetic patterns that we ask you to sustain.

As Brother Sananda has asked you to love one another, that is a focus, a focus to learn, a focus to Master, to sustain, and to express the fullness of your creation. We know it is a great challenge for you. We know this has created great trial and tribulation on your planet. Even for those most dear to you, this is difficult to sustain. It is this sustainment with which we now charge you, with which you are now empowered. Only in accepting that this is the only law, will you be allowed to wriggle through from one dimension to another. We ask you to continue on in your search. Continue in your joy! Continue on and understand that, yes, what you call suffering is based on harmonics of energetic patterns in your emotional and intellectual fields! What you would call joy is based on the same harmonic systems! It is the acceptance that these can be redirected and focused as you choose that creates the pattern that you will call the Self Master. We are here only to Master the self, then to bring that Self-Mastery to the whole. Question?

Question: "Does an imbalance in the positive and negative charges of magnetics cause disease? Are we in control of the molecular balance that we have?"

FREEING SELF FROM BELIEF SYSTEMS

Dear one, consider this. There are times when you may push on a point and your headache will leave. This is the result of expanded consciousness, that the headache no longer need trouble you. Consider too that those diseases in your planetary system which are a lack of ease indicate imbalance. That which may be highly positively charged can be as much dis-ease as that which is negatively charged. It is the balancing of each of these charging systems that brings you to the point that we have called a non-judgment, a Mastery, an understanding. There is no disease in any human physical body that cannot be transmuted and brought to balance. This is a Law of Creation, because the physical world must be obedient to the focus.

When first diagnosed with a dreaded disease that is termed in your world as "fatal," the emotional charge creates adrenaline that feeds the growth of this disease at a very rapid rate. This great fear then sustains and maintains the charging of the electromagnetic field and the particles that compose the physical body are then responsive and must be obedient to the focus of this charge. When one steps and looks through a different focus and chooses a different path, then the charge is brought to a neutral point and re-directed to the place of choice

.

Yes, to answer this unequivocally, all disease can be re-directed, can be un-made, can be transmuted, can be undone, can be left forever. It is a choice. It is the doubt you all have in your plane and planet that creates a collective acceptance which allows individuals, as you have thought yourself to be, to bend as a tree in a great wind and your leaves blow in a whirlwind. The great storm that pushes you about is about acceptance. The storm provides the opportunity to accept that the leaf and the tree come from a much stronger source. The tree grows, freeing itself from belief systems through acceptance. Soon, it can withstand the harshest wind, the most violent storm. Then the tree evolves to a different consciousness. The tree is self-determining, a sovereign Master. It will then become apparent that your choices expand possibilities. You are in command. Do you have questions?

Question: "With this major earthquake in Japan, do we do a disservice by focusing our energy upon it, or how do we deal with being magnetized into this awareness of change?"

## CHANGE ASSISTS GROWTH

Change is an inevitable part of existence in this universal structure. Without the change, there is no path for anyone to travel. There are no lessons for our teachers to share, and then, in turn, none to be shared with you. Change is the only thing that you may be guaranteed will continue. Yes, there was great destruction, loss, and sadness, but it is through this, that people pull together in harmony. No longer will they sit in a freeway traffic jam and look at each other with disdain. No longer will they have the luxury of hating one another. To transform this cataclysm that they have experienced, they must come together in a harmony. What you see as a great tragedy is a great blessing for humanity's spirit to experience true, sincere love.

Through cataclysm, the human spirit will become creative and tap into the infinite choices that exist. That which you see as destruction is truly a blessing, for it brings about change. There could have been great destruction and all could have perished without the lessons of growing together, of becoming Brother and Sister, of working together, of uniting in a focus to improve all the life systems. But there is great compassion. There is great mercy and understanding. There is a great willingness in the human spirit to find the best, to live life for life.

Question: "Choice and a change in consciousness seem to be interwoven. How does this relate to the sound waves that are extending from Sedona to Taos and Santa Fe? Is this a geophysical event, a consciousness event, or is this related to a secret government activity?"

THE EARTH SINGS

There are those in your planet who would undermine your transition. There are those who would choose to slow your process. This is a Law of Balance. This is a law that brings the universal structure to take a momentary breath on the path to self-analysis. The configurations of the movement of land masses will create pitches. It is the creation of these harmonics that can be taken advantage of by those who wish to slow the process, or by those who wish to speed the process. It is a state of which both groups are aware and in which both are active.

The planet sings with great joy many times. It is at this moment, when the collective has such an intense doubt, that she groans in her song. She moves to become more at ease with herself in the creation. There are new pitches and new songs being brought forth into this sphere. Just as a mother rocks a child to sleep, so too the Mother Planet rocks herself to bring forth the same calm and peace. You may see these as earthquakes. You may see these as a tidal wave or storm. However, they are songs that bring her ease. Your focus can also bring forth an easing for Mother Earth. She is your Sister and she is your Mother. She has sponsored you in this great journey in the densities of Ray

Systems. She has sponsored you so you may understand creation and your creations.

## DISSIPATE CONFLICT

Now, there are choices for you to make. All peace and harmony on your planet exist in one set of choices, all conflict and destruction in another set of choices. Your worldwide, collective choice system lies somewhere in the middle. There are places of great peace and joy and other places of great conflict. One of these places, New Mexico, carries choice systems that have been greatly challenged for some fifty years in your Earth time, and these choice systems have been taken advantage of. It is wise to find no conflict in the choices that others make. It is wise to come to a level of acceptance and to direct your focus to your own choices.

You may bring peace and harmony with six to ten people, or eleven to fifteen people, or twenty-one to thirty-three people, holding a sustained focus for any area of your planet. Conflicts slowly dissipate because there is no longer a charge that will magnetically hold together that great feeling of mistrust, control, or suppression, for that too is a magnetic attraction. We will discourse on ritual, creating the perfect harmony in any area of your planet, if you so choose.

Question: "Thank you, Saint Germain. I want to refer back to the discourse that you gave us today about our changing from carbon-base to silicon-base. Does glass have anything to do with dimensional shifting, the actual composition of glass?"

## CARBON-BASED TO SILICON-BASED CONSCIOUSNESS

Glass, as you know, is a silica-base liquid. It is formulated by the regulation of temperature to bring this alchemical process into a solid. It is in this state that this solid allows the refraction of many types of Ray lights. Glass, which is the silica-base, as you have succinctly discovered, is the veil through which all is passed. You have seen in pictures, as you have seen in glass, the electric light refraction and the existence of my own personage. Was it not also through many other refractive silica-based solids (mirrors, crystals, camera lenses) that there is the appearance of those you call Master, those you call angel, or those you call saint or teacher?

[Editor's Note: Saint Germain's face has unexpectedly appeared several times in photographs taken by the authors.]

It is a veil and an access point, symbolizing that patterns within the human auric system are ready for dimensional change and Ascension. It is the symbology that what is held in the glass can no longer be held by the glass alone. It is the symbology that the inner is not separated from the outer. Glass is a type of magnetic attraction. It also creates separation of water to air, or air to air, or dimension to dimension. Have you not looked into a mirror, one that faces another, and seen yourself through many, many refractive points? Have you not seen yourself forward? Have you not seen yourself behind? These refractive points are part of the silica transition. The light is captured and then refracted and enhanced in the membrane system.

I ask you to consider that the human auric structure has a silica-base. It is the loosely structured silica-based atomic pulsations that make it difficult for it to be seen without the dimensional interfacing of the pineal gland. It is this gland that adjusts the lens of the eyes, cones and rods. This allows one to see through the veils of the dimensions. There you will find that we never leave you. We have always been with you from the beginning of your sojourn here. We have always sponsored you and we too have always been sponsored. You, in turn, do the same for those who come to you. Sponsor them to find the peace in their heart. The joy that will bring them to that birth change! If there are no further questions, I will take my leave.

Response: "Thank you Saint Germain."

# The Key

*"You as limited body are mortal.
The consciousness that beats your heart is immortal.."*
- SAINT GERMAIN

The work upon the Earth Plane and Planet at times may seem to you to be so tedious and you ask, "Can I take any more of this?" But Dear hearts, be gladdened, for a time now comes where we ease through this transition. As you have observed, it is much like squeezing through a key hole or the eye of a needle, and you are nearing now the end of this tunnel.

## AWAKENING TO THE EVOLUTION OF CONSCIOUSNESS

Dear hearts, I would like to remind you, that you, at this time, have been chosen to bring forth a great body of work that will help those who are easing through, shall we say, that keyhole of life. The time has come upon the Earth Plane and Planet that eyes and ears are open, ready, and receptive. Eyes are seeing so much more clearly than they did five years ago, and now the ears are open and ready to hear the message through the voice. As

I stated before, this is known as an evolution of consciousness, and I would like to explain this idea further.

Consciousness has always existed and it is infinite. Each and every one of you are given the consciousness of this Infinite ONE. When we say consciousness, we refer to Universal Mind or Source, which all of you, at all times, can contact. Mineral, Vegetable, Animal, Human Kingdoms, and onward to Cosmic Man, each and every one of you has the ability to reach into what is known as Universal Mind. Through the evolution of consciousness, you awaken to the great potential that lies in front of you.

When we refer to the feast, we are referring to the great table of consciousness that lies in front of you, each and every one of you choosing from its tasty morsels. The time has come upon the Earth Plane and Planet that we awaken consciousness to what it truly is, to what it truly holds, and the potential and possibilities that it can produce in your world of thought and feeling.
Dear ones, many of you think that you must perfect the consciousness, but understand that consciousness is already perfected. Many of you think you must discipline yourselves to find consciousness, but let me assure you that it requires not discipline, but simply surrender.

Each and every one of you think of yourself as holding a space in your already permeated consciousness, that you are mortal and therefore must sustain and rise to another place in order to access the stream of Universal Consciousness. But let me explain Dear ones, that each and every one of you are filled with consciousness through the atomic levels. You are functioning with a conscious intent. Dear hearts, consciousness is in, through, and around you. There is nothing that is changeable about consciousness. However, it is through your willingness to use consciousness that you realize and understand your creations.

I hope I make myself clear regarding the topic of consciousness. When I refer to the evolution of consciousness, I am not stating that you are imperfect and must rise to another condition. I am stating that you have the ability to use Universal Consciousness for creation. The path of Mastery requires the use of Universal Consciousness, for it frees up the creative consciousness to be used for further, shall we say, consequences. In your world of thought and feeling, through the Law of Attraction and the Law of Repulsion, you are filled with an electromagnetic vibration. This electromagnetic vibration attracts and fulfills the call of consciousness, or what I would like to refer to as the Law of Creative Consciousness. It repels and attracts according to the desire of consciousness. When we speak about the concept of desire, it is a teaching that leads the soul to freedom, for eventually consciousness will no longer desire. This is the unfoldment and transformation of consciousness. Do you understand?

Response: "Yes, so far I do."

Let me state that at this time upon the Earth Plane and Planet, many who are following the path of Adeptship see themselves, in the moment, imperfect. But let me assure you Dear hearts, that each and everyone of you is Divine and carries a perfection, as Kuan Yin has stated, which "Fills the heart with joy." Consciousness upon the Earth Plane and Planet is as it always has been. However, it is life, through its appearance and qualification, or sensing ability, that prepares and examines consciousness in a fuller scope. Consciousness is the key to all of creation. It is the key to transfiguration. It is the key to Ascension.

When I speak of consciousness, I refer to Divine Mind, that which is the first manifestation upon the Earth Plane and Planet. When I say manifestation, I refer to the Omnipotent Presence of the Mighty I AM. In appearance, it is known and directed, shall we say, through thought, for thought finds its vehicle through the mind of man. There are thoughts that exist throughout the Mineral, the Vegetable, the Animal, and the Human Kingdoms. Even the smallest part contains the great consciousness of the Mighty I AM. So understand Dear ones, that all contains a portion of Divine Mind.

OPEN TO DIVINE MIND

When you approach the idea of Alchemy, turning lead into gold, understand that it is only through Divine Mind or the Universal Mind, or Universal Consciousness, as we have referred to it, that you are allowed to access and transmit thought to bring forth transformative and transmutative qualities. If, in your world of thought and feeling, you are experiencing a time where you doubt yourself or no longer chose to walk the same path, the first place to enact change is within your consciousness. Simply hold the thought. When we say, "hold the thought," we are talking about training yourself to open to Divine Mind, for potential lies within this mighty law. This Law of Consciousness is a Law of Life that you are filled with and will respond to instantly.

## OUTPICTURING

In our dispensation of work which came in to the Earth Plane in the early 1930's, and even the dispensation of work that came in the 1860's to the 1920's, was a teaching of a discipline of consciousness through the spoken word. Now we ask you to raise this energy from the throat chakra into that of the third eye. Hold the out-picturing of consciousness. See, as we would call it, in your mind's eye, yourself performing those tasks in front of you.

Let me give you an example. Many of you in that outer world tire so of the jobs you hold. At times, it is not only a matter of having enough money, but it is a matter of having enough time. You wish to have leisure time to develop yourself, to spend the time with your spiritual work, to spend the time in spiritual camaraderie with friends and relatives. You wish to have the time to develop into that family of ONE, the Family of Light. However, you see yourself as also needing, shall we say, the amount of money so that you can continue in the world that you have created. And yet, are not these two desires in conflict within your world?

Desire is not the achievement. Desire shall set you free. Hold in your mind's eye perfect out-picturing. See yourself utilizing consciousness and the process of visualization to achieve your goal. See yourself in the camaraderie of your friends. See yourself in the camaraderie of the desires of your heart. In this perfect out-picturing, project the energies from the Throat Chakra into the pineal area and let the energy of this visualization pour through the Third Eye, much as a projector would project a motion picture. Out-picturing is one of the first ways that you will learn the openings to the potential of consciousness. Through the pineal gland, we have full contact with Universal Consciousness.

Have you not experienced, through the dream state, a time when you have contacted others known to you in this embodiment, as well as others who have now passed-over through dropping the body? This is achieved through out-picturing and the pineal gland. It is your divinity to realize the gifts of the human body and their respective potentials and possibilities. But one must understand the disciplines that develop such an opening.

## YOU ARE TIMELESS, IMMORTAL, AND DIVINE

I have instructed you in what we call the Aryan Breath, given to you to open, through consciousness and visualization, manifestation in your world of thought and feeling. Now, I would like to discuss with you, Dear ones, a further evolution regarding transfiguration and Ascension. Perhaps we could address this topic as immortality. I would like each and everyone to consider that you are already immortal. Has not your soul migrated from density to density, from the Mineral through to the Human Kingdom, throughout different solar systems of light and sound to find itself planted firmly on Mother Terra? And you are now concerned about your immortality? You are timeless, immortal, and divine. From the perspective of eons, see yourself as a light being traveling from the great out-picturing of the Mighty I AM.

Many chelas and initiates upon the path feel they must discipline the body in order to raise it into a transfiguration. This methodology does indeed work; however, we would ask you to consider that there are other ways that this can be achieved. You can discipline the body to follow, shall we say, the soul, for the soul directs the body. Either way, the achievement is the same. However, understand what is the Source and what is only a qualification of the Source. Since you know the body to be the end result of your soul, receiving and transmitting a matrix of Rays of light and sound, common sense urges you to consider that your body is only an out-picturing of consciousness.

There have been those who have simply stated, "Now, I shall drop this body to take on a new sheath," and this has been achieved. This is transfiguration and Ascension through the soul. There are those who have raised the body by accelerating it at the atomic level, dissipating it at will into other dimensions and raising it into another field of unified conscious reality. Either way, we are looking for a vehicle to raise the soul into a fuller extension and expansion of Universal Consciousness. In past discourses, we have given you instructions regarding both of these techniques. Those who choose to discipline the body, find the practice to be a little more tedious, slower in its performance. Those who choose to awaken the consciousness, will find that the body transfigures effortlessly.

These are two ways of looking or perceiving. Use this transformational work for the burning away of grosser images in order to refine your creation. Allow a New Day and a fuller creation. Do you have questions?

Question: "At this moment, you are asking us to consider that there are two paths for a dimensional change or a dimensional shift. The physical body can be disciplined to follow the soul, or there is another method that can be employed that does not require the movement of the physical body in a disciplined state. Is this correct?"

This is correct, for the Light of God Never Fails and it is the Light that we must concern ourselves with regarding the teaching of Divine Consciousness.

Question: "Many people have the great desire of Ascension and have been exposed to Ascended Master teachings and the existence of the I AM Presence, yet in reaching their latter years, still come to a place of despair, loneliness, and feeling as though they have failed in their great mission of desire. Would you please give us a simple technique they may use so that their hearts will not be in such despair?"

The teachings of immortality are primarily intended to open the mind, which is cloaked in the embodiment. I have explained that consciousness is and always will be. The consciousness chooses its circumstances, embodiment after embodiment. For those who have not yet raised this body are those whom we put our focus upon to discipline the soul. In that discipline of the soul, immortality is perceived as continuous, infinite. Let me explain. Have you had ever the sensation known as déjà vu?

Response: "Most certainly, yes."

## CONSCIOUSNESS OF SOUL

This experience is offered as an opportunity to understand the fullness of consciousness, its immortal destiny. It is in that one fleeting moment that all men and women upon the Earth Plane and Planet shake their heads with wonder and question their lives. Déjà vu is a slippage, shall we say, of time and space fields. In that moment of slippage, the soul speaks deeply to the consciousness and says "I AM."

In reference to those for whom you request a technique, it is always important to keep the physical body balanced while occupying it. It is difficult for those who have become ravaged by old age and disease, for once the body is uncomfortable and unbalanced, it is hard to keep the attention upon the consciousness of soul. Soul directs the consciousness and, through out-picturing, we ask you to find contact with the soul.

I have described another path to achieve this union and, of course, we always impart complementary techniques that may raise the body through vibrational circumstance. Perhaps the soul has developed to a point where it requires a new body in order to continue its conscious awakening. Then the body is simply laid aside. Oftentimes you have heard of the different yogis who have so disciplined the soul, they know the minute they must step out of the body to transmigrate (much like the sensation of déjà vu) to that new sheath. You have heard of the instances where they left in a matter of an hour, sometimes two hours, and sometimes, for those who are listening to the urgings of the soul, within ten seconds. Dropping of the body is another technique. It is not the technique many have understood as physical death, for physical death is a technique of taking a great rest.

Many of those who have fallen asleep and have not yet awakened the consciousness to hear the urgings of soul, live their lives as if this embodiment is all that has been granted to them. Upon completion of the time period in which the body houses their soul energy, they simply close their eyes and rest within the shell of death. Those who accept the concept of physical death shall have this experience; for again, it is a conscious out-picturing. Many will go through this process of death and believe, shall we say, that death is their path. They have allotted a time period for death.

Let me explain further. Those who have accepted death into their consciousness, once entering the death process they have out-pictured, some hover near the body after death and some enter into the great rest for up to two hundred years. [Editor's Note: This is an Earthly, physical plane timing.] Some have gathered energy developed through religious teachings and go onward into the creation of that teaching. Some see their paradise as achieving all those things they were never allowed to achieve while in the body. Some see their paradise as simply living out the requirement of that religious teaching. This is known as a *devachan*. The devachan is the creation that remains. The mental activity then closes the creation of the out-picturing from that embodiment.

Those who have disciplined and listened to the wantings of the soul and project through the consciousness, may achieve the dropping of the body and the ability to take on a new Body of Light without entering into what is known as devachan. Each of these stages of evolution is the unfoldment of consciousness. Each of these are necessary and essential for the chela, the initiate, the adept, to understand the road of Mastery that is traveled.

For those who have noticed a weakening of the body, of course it is always best to use the out-picturing through thought, to bring forth a healing result. If you are filled with the illusions of the world, it is most important for you to gain full contact with your Source for your own perfect out-picturing. The use of the Violet Flame was brought to the Earth Plane and Planet so that we could address the out-picturings of the past and those mental thoughts that are no longer wanted, so they could be consumed, transmuted, and recirculated into Universal Mind. I hope I have given you a clear understanding as to what is known as the dropping of the body. Do you see Dear ones, the difference between death and the dropping of the body?

Question: "It would seem that death is a choice of rest and the dropping of the body is a choice to go on when the body no longer serves the purpose of creation, correct?"

DESIRE FOR FREEDOM

This is correct, Dear one. And there are those who wish to take the body with them and discipline the body, so that atomically, through the alchemical process, much like changing lead into gold, the body is then transformed from one dimension to the next. In either case, this transfiguration is through the opening of consciousness, the wanting of soul, and this comes through a natural course. So the path of desire is still important Dear one, for ultimately it is the path of desire that will lead you all to freedom. It is the path of the Spiritual Hierarchy, the Great White Brotherhood and Sisterhood of Light, to teach and to hold freedom as one of the first principles and concepts for chelas, initiates, and adepts. It is only in our desire for freedom that we become purified, transformed, and ONE with Universal Mind. Questions?

Question: "Referring back to the explanation of déjà vu, it would seem that it is an experience that is acknowledged in this outer world, but since the soul is the interface of the creation of what we call the outer world, the experience already is in existence. Is this accurate?"

DISSOLVING THE PAST THROUGH THE FLAME

This is completely accurate. For each out-picturing of consciousness very much impresses that picture. When we say out-picturing, it is pictured, it is photographed, it is, shall we say, burned in a sense upon that plane of consciousness. When there is use of the Violet Flame, what you are out-picturing is the dissolving of those past out-picturings. For instance, have you noted that when you use the Violet Flame, you lose your past life recall? What is gained is the teaching brought into unity, ONE with soul.

Response: "Yes, I have noted this. It is something I have not understood."

This is because with each use of the Violet Flame you are dissolving, through your conscious out-picturing, all of those activities that existed as old tapes, old movies, and old recordings which no longer serve you.

Question: "Can you literally, through this Violet Flame procedure, alter that which is the past and the future?"

If you have out-pictured to the future, of course this would work.

Question: "I understand. So things that you think are inevitable, you can change with Violet Flame decrees?"

Have you not met those who feel that death is inevitable? Have you not met those who feel that an end is inevitable? Yes, this is a use for the Violet Flame, for it dissolves those records, those imprints upon the unified field of consciousness, so that a perfection of consciousness can exist and the soul is then freed. Desire, in its wantings and trappings, is a servant to freedom, and yet, it leaves its imprint. Have you not noticed that those who desire something, upon achievement, desire something else? It is very important, if you are following the path of desire, to use the Violet Flame to blaze and transmute the past desires. It is as if, each time that you step forward on the path, you must forget the path that was behind you. You also ignore the path that is in front of you. Your focus and attention is given to where you stand today.

Question: "In your Self-Mastery, has your path come from the same desire as the other Brothers and Sisters of the Great White Lodge?"

Of course it has been desire, for desire bridges the Animal Kingdom to the Human.

Question: "Then the question I have is, why are there many teachings upon the planet and religious structures that ask for the dismissal of desire or ask for, shall we say, turning away from desire?"

## EVOLUTION THROUGH DESIRE

There is no way to turn away from desire. Desire is a natural course and we encourage each and every one of you to understand its completeness. Desire raises the Mineral to the Vegetable Kingdom. Through desire, Mineral and Vegetable Kingdoms are contained within your atomic cells. Desire understands the human condition, the unfoldment of soul. One day, you will desire nothing but contact with soul and Source. It will be the one desire that you hold and no other.

Question: "So, you are saying that the little desires that we have in the human condition are important for the experience. When we fulfill them, then we may move on?"

There are those who think that out-picturing can replace experience and we have proven that this can be so. However, there are those who understand that experience trains the body; therefore, it is simply a matter of choice. Those who wish to raise the body, generally follow the path of experience. Those who are looking to drop the body, look for the path of out-picturing. Both of these work; however, there is a time in evolution, through an awakening of consciousness, that both are required. This is known as bi-location and achieved by those who wish to take their body to other dimensions.

This was one of the teachings taught in the mystery schools of Egypt and at the end times of Atlantis. At that time, there was an understanding that the world was in great change, alongside a great shifting of dimensional consciousness. Many wished to keep the body types, for those body types had served them well. Again, it is a matter of choice. The body types then allowed for further evolution of consciousness. Some of those who even raised that body type, shall we say, to the other dimensional out-picturing, also ended up dropping that body and taking on yet another new sheath. When we refer to a sheath or a body, we are referring to the spacial confinement of consciousness, traveling from dimension to dimension, with each dimension having its different qualifications. Do you understand?

Response: "Yes, I understand. If I were to model the experience, or the path as you have just outlined, it would seem you have done both the out-picturing and the discipline, each one serving a purpose for your service."

DOWN WITH DEATH!

This is so, Dear one. This is so. That is why I teach both, for both contain the elements of Mastery that will set you free. Keep the quality of freedom in your hearts at all times. This is the quality that I represent and the teaching and service that I bring.

Question: "This is understood. So for those who have reached this great age and have found themselves in a position where they feel they can go no further, then the suggestion is to meditate and use this out-picturing that you have just described?"

Remember Dear ones, that you as limited body are mortal. The consciousness that beats your heart is immortal.

Down with death!
Down with the slumber!
Awaken to the life that fills all with the MIGHTY I AM!

Response: "Thank you Dear one."

# *Earth Changes*

> *"An exchange of life comes forward; that which controls and holds now exchanges for freedom. The freedom that each of us in the heart of this realm know, we now refer to as Unana."*
> - EL MORYA

*Beloved Mighty God Presence I AM, come forward and bring your perfect service, that the information is pure and clear. Beloved Archangels, come forward and bring your perfect service. El Morya, Sananda, Kuthumi, Nada, Portia, Kuan Yin, and Mary, please bring forth your perfect service, so that this information provides transitions for humankind. OM MANAYA PATIYA, HITAKA.*

*Once again, it is as though I am floating above the planet, traveling over the Atlantic Ocean, headed eastward towards Europe and Africa. I will describe what I am seeing.*

## NUCLEAR INTERVENTION

I've come to a place over the water that is very blue and all of the land masses look very white. It is as though they are painted onto this blue seascape, but they are three-dimensional with their mountains and valleys still showing. I've come to where the Azores have been and they are now six to seven hundred feet below the ocean. As I travel, in what was the northern direction but is now the southern direction, I can see that Ireland is several hundred feet below the water also.

Looking into the Mediterranean Sea, land mass is still clearly visible below the surface of the rising water. There have been discussions from the Masters as to how this cataclysm and the sinking of the Sahara Desert occurred. They have explained, in no uncertain terms, that it was something that mankind did. It was a collective decision made by the German, Italian, and French governments to use a nuclear detonation in the sea bottom of the Mediterranean to widen a fissure, to allow the water from the melting ice caps to recede. Also, the technology of the time revealed that beneath the Sahara Desert there was a fresh water inland sea still contained within the continent. With the aid of their satellite microwave transmissions, oceans and other mineral deposits on the plane were easily detected.

This detonation caused further sinking of Europe at a much more rapid rate because it upset the natural flow of Earth coming to a place of balance as the poles were shifting. It was after this second pole shift detonation occurred, creating this great cataclysm, that there was an acceleration which submerged most of France, the coastlines of all of the European continent, and the north African continent. The center of the detonation was located near the Middle East.

I have seen great tidal waves and continental plates which dropped and no longer interlocked with one another. They fell because of the disruption of the hard lava and granite flows that were literally holding these continental sections in place in northern Africa. This explosion sent out a rippling effect, like a rock thrown into a pond. Then the water below, on the bottom, rushed into areas where it had not been before and undermined the continental structures. This man-made detonation is certainly more traumatic and tragic than all of the other naturally occurring Earth Changes on the planet.

I am now going to turn the floor over to El Morya, since he is the bridge for this African and European information.

*El Morya steps forward. Lady Nada is to one side of him and Kuthumi is to the other. Sananda, Portia, Mary, Saint Germain, and Kuan Yin are surrounding them. El Morya, his aura a piercing electric blue color, speaks:*

Greetings Dear students of the Divine Light of the ONE. I AM the focus of El Morya and I ask for permission to come to you and bring the discourse about these lands. It is this time that you know as Transition, that all Earth, as you have called it, comes into a focus with the breath of Prana and this changes the frequency of all cell structures in the human consciousness and physical body. As this planet is changing so too is your physical body going through its change. As you see yourselves become more lighted in manner, you will see that the planet too is coming to this great, great Divine Light.

## CESSATION OF STRUGGLE AND VIOLENCE

The eastern European countries that have had great conflict and continue to, even at the moment of this transmission, will experience the cessation of violence. It is our purpose and focus to bring to you now (and we will continue to bring this service), an understanding that the emotional body of the human and the emotional body of the planet are the places where the transition is most clearly expressed. It is important to remember that phrase "Changing the heart, the world will change."

As you have most succinctly pointed out in understanding the concept of Divine Mind, we too ask that the world become more clearly focused on the Divine Mind. Our world, which is the same as this Divine Mind, is a realm not unlike yours. It is the harmony of Divine Mind that brings about the complete clarity of focus. Life in this realm that we inhabit is without conflict and has only the activity of focus. In lands of great conflict, concerned with who is right and who is wrong, the world can see examples that where there is no concern for the truth, there is only the struggle for control. The lands of this greatest struggle, especially in Europe, are the lands that will be brought to rest and released from control.

The western coasts of Bulgaria, Czechoslovakia, Greece through Turkey, and into that which you know as Austria and Hungary, up into Poland and Estonia have had great struggle for control and these lands are greatly altered. This struggle continues on through your Scandinavian countries and Germany, the Netherlands and Belgium, France and Italy. It is in the areas of this great, intense struggle which are brought to rest. It is so on this map. The lands of the Arabic Nations that struggle with the Israel Nation are also brought to rest. It is not as though we are sending a punishment forth but only a rest. They will emerge as the planet transitions again. They will emerge in the most pristine perfection that could ever be achieved.

ONE GOD, ONE HEART

It is the purpose of this great exchange that once again, an exchange of life comes forward; that which controls and holds now exchanges for freedom. The freedom that each of us in the heart of this realm know, we now refer to as Unana. In this realm, all will come to know the ONE. It is this understanding that your kingdom of your human creation is of All That Is, ONE. It is the acceptance that your separation is no more. You are set upon the path to return to your Home, to your heart, the Source of the ONE God.

You who come to exchange your bondage for freedom . . . you who exchange your hatred . . . you who exchange your greed . . . you who exchange your dominance and suppression for your freedom will find a heart that has truly changed and is guided by Divine Mind. The focus becomes clear and no longer does the emotional body dominate on your planet. It is the acceptance that each of you have, this clear focus as part of your Divine Purpose, that brings forth this change in the world. Prana is brought back to glory and furthers Earth onto the path of Freedom Star.

Each of you who hold tight to your money, hold tight to your rules, hold tight to your sovereignship over others; each of you who have sampled this through many, many centuries of conflict, this is your day to know that it is over. No longer will there be governments that control individual freedoms of the ONE. No longer will there be economic systems that control and suppress individual freedom of the ONE. Unana comes forward from this moment. It is the day that the heart of humanity changes to ONE heart. It is through this ONE that freedom is infinite and sustains the Kingdom of God.

You and I in this kingdom are ONE. It is in the separation of the human that we lack understanding and harmony. However, this is very temporary in your world, for the plan calls forward that you experience this separation; but then, in the understanding of the ONE, you will return full circle. As this is prophesied for each of these countries, transitions occur in their economies, their governments, and their lands; these institutions are only reflective to how steadfastly you hold on to them, how resistant you are to the flow of new energy. We ask you to allow your heart to flow, to give freely, to come to this Divine understanding that there is Oneness in creation and that one has no power over another, or a group of others. May peace come forward to each of your hearts.

*The Master El Morya points to the Earth Changes Map of the World and continues to teach:*

As we travel further into the northern lands of Africa, these lands have shifted their poles (rotation reversal). The north is no longer north and the south is no longer south. The poles will return in this transition, at the third and final resting, where the north will again be north and the south will again be the south. I now turn the floor over to our beloved Kuthumi, who will address the great movement of water through each of these new coastlines.

*The Master Kuthumi of the Elemental Forces and the Sixth Ray of Ruby and Gold steps forward to give his teaching. He is clothed simply in a brown robe and speaks with deep humility:*

Greetings Dear Children in the ONE Unana. I AM Kuthumi. I ask in service that you understand your true nature, for as it has been said, the human contains both the Mineral and the Animal Kingdoms. I ask that you find this understanding with nature, for as animals are of nature, so too are minerals.

## THE SAHARA DESERT

I ask you to see in these lands that you refer to as Africa, that each of these changes that occur comes in a sequence. They come in a sequence that brings about the cosmic understanding that the change that you experience is quite beautiful. It is not totally of sadness or grief. Those who will stand on the edge of a coastline as it alters will find themselves untouched in the alteration. Indeed, they may find themselves witnesses to the great miracle of creation. We come to the most eastern part of the African continent. This area south of the Nile goes through much transition. This area, once known as the Sahara Desert, becomes a great seed for all of creation in your world. A large forest once again grows and covers this area in great abundance at the time when this transition is complete.

As we travel further into the areas that you know as the Rift Valley, there is this great opening of the Earth, for she now opens her heart and allows this flowing of water, so that all of the interior land is now accessible in the simplest of means by water travel. The mountains heave and move further towards the sky and the lakes pour into the valley. It is during the settling of Africa that this perfect, pristine waterway is formed. This waterway is formed in such a manner that all vegetation that has been lost in the northern lands will be again be abundant.

## NEW AFRICAN LANDS

In traveling further to the south, Earth movements cause tidal wave activity and volcanoes erupt. Fissures within the ocean move as well. This will break up the land in this southern area of the continent. It will break into many islands. These islands will serve many purposes when this transition is complete. Agriculture will be very abundant and then there will be occasional flooding of the sea on a cyclical basis, which will bring silt and sand to these islands. This will be done in a fifty-year cycle. As we move further south to the tip of this great continent Africa, there is a description of rising lands. Lands rise through volcanic activity and the sea bed is a buildup of a continent which exists now. Fifteen hundred years into the future these lands raise into great plains that are very abundant in the growing of certain grains.

## CONGO RIVER

After the completion of the final pole shift, we again turn our attention north. That area, which you know as the Congo River, will open up and flow to the interior of this large continent. This continent, which has for many, many millennia been cut off from the rest of the world, now will have complete access in the completion of this cycle. There will be a complete understanding and fulfillment of the Oneness throughout the continent. Brothers and Sisters of this land now focus on the Divine Mind and will have within their ability, the simplest methods by which to travel, to communicate, and to continue to grow crops to sustain their cultures.

It is through this flow of harmonic Oneness, this great balance and perfect understanding, that conflict and control no longer seize the world. Your world of conflict is only the agitation of your emotional body and the emotional body in this global transition will, as you have suspected, be brought to rest and peace.

We move forward to the western coast and see the lands continue to rise up and move. Small islands, formed from erosion, continue to surface throughout the peripheral part of this continent. The Sahara Desert is now a great sea, and this land will be extremely abundant for those who wish to fish and trade in this area.

The world, as we have known it coming to a technological pinnacle, will look upon technology in the future in a simpler manner. As consciousness moves into the realm of Unana, technology will not be used in a self-serving manner, but will be used in joint efforts for the community, the ONE.

Question: "Thank you, Brother Kuthumi. In the prophecy, the Niger River seems to erode the lands away on the western side of Africa and opens further to the east, to the Bay of Protection, which opens the country of Chad. This enables it to have seaport cities. Would you elaborate on this change?"

The continent that once was closed becomes open. These seaport cities will serve to transport crops, such as papaya and coconut, and there will be large growing areas for many types of fruit in these regions. The world's dietary charge will no longer be based on proteins. It will come to a time when the Animal Kingdom will no longer be put into submission and the Mineral Kingdom will become of greater service. Questions?

THE NIGER RIVER

Question: "Regarding the Niger River, specifically where the first African seaport will come into existence in the New Age, there are those who would like to know if the Niger River floods? Is this part of the great global warming, or is this due to earthquakes or tectonic plate movements?"

The opening of this river is due to a combination of tsunamis and tectonic movement. Yes, there will be some volcanic activity, but it will always be in the sea bed of this area. It is the tectonic movement that causes this erosion and the opening of this waterway.

## AFRICAN WEST COAST

Question: "The next area that I have questions about would be on the west coast of Africa. There is a small area that forms a sort of peninsula and, comparing the current map with the Map of Exchanges, it looks like we loose bits and pieces of Morocco and areas nearby. Can you elaborate on that change? It looks like part of the Atlantic tectonic movement or possibly part of the raising of the lands of Portugal."

The movement of this western coast that you refer to, along the borders of Morocco and continuing into Tunisia to the east and further into the southern areas, is tectonic movement. It is part of the activities that occur in Portugal, Ireland, and Iceland. However, this tectonic movement is due mostly to the global warming of the ice caps, which have now raised the water level, resulting in a recession of these particular coastline areas. Small earthquake activity breaks up the rockiness of the existing shores, but it is mostly the rising waters and the continuation of the man-made cataclysm that occurs in the Mediterranean, that will most affect this western coast. It is these in combination that form this new coast line. The formation of this new coastline also brings about a change in the long-term weather pattern. Since it is now a smaller land mass, rain waters come for a fifteen hundred-year period that will bring agriculture and usefulness again of this land. The people in this area will be self-sufficient.

Question: "Will the Canary Islands, which are of course off the west coast of Africa, be under water?"

It is the island chains that follow the long Atlantic ridge between the two continents, these island chains on this pathway will be submerged as the waters rise on a global scale.

## A NEW LAND

Question: "My next question will take us to the south of Africa. Somewhere along the Tropic of Capricorn there seems to be a rising of lands off the coast of Madagascar. Could you tell us more about this incredible Earth Change?"

It is the experience of the planet, having volcanic activity in the ocean waters, which causes the rising of these eastern and northern sections of Madagascar. These activities bring forth a new land that will serve humankind and animal-kind equally, but each will have a separate purpose on the planet. In the times when the transition is complete, there will be large farms setup for the re-population of certain animals on this island. These farms will be done in a manner so that your ecosystem will be brought back to a place of harmony, instead of conflict.

It is truly not the intent of humankind to be self seeking and self serving, as it has become in this evolution, but rather to be of service to the creation. That is the intention of dominion. It is to be of service in the domain. To serve the Animal Kingdom, to serve the Mineral Kingdom, to serve the Plant Kingdom, to serve all of these brings you to the next step of being able to serve the Divine Kingdom. These great farms which develop in this area will help to repopulate those depleted species on this planet which have been, up to this moment, treated dishonorably.

GONDWANALAND

Question: "The next question that I have Dear Brother, is about the Rift Valley, which I have read is one of the major geophysical wonders of the world, taking up one sixteenth of the entire Earths' circumference. The theory behind the Rift Valley is that it was formed when a subcontinent in the Indian Ocean sank, causing a great tear in the continents. Can you share some of the ancient wisdom about the sinking of what is known as Gondwanaland?

Gondwanaland, which you know as the great Arabian continent, was once a continuous continent, spreading as far as Madagascar, and south to points as far as Australia. This great continent, which did break up and change, was home to a great race of people. This race of people reached certain technological advancement in which they exploited the planet. When great achievements are built upon the sweat of other species and other members of humanity, the universal structure can no longer support this.

The lands which rise in Madagascar and the lands which run through this Rift Valley are part of this same mass (Gondwanaland), a plate that runs under the seabed to what you know as your South Pole. This plate is not visible with our present technology because it sank below certain underwater volcanic activities which now exist. Only the individual areas broke up and holes within the plate allowed such areas to come forward and up through the volcanic activity. This situation existed throughout all of these areas and as far east as the Philippines. To illustrate this Earth movement and separation of these plates, visualize a large parchment torn at one corner and slowly ripped upward toward the African continent, through the Mediterranean, and further to the North Pole.

We have seen changes happen millennium after millennium through many cycles. It is the working of these cycles that allows for worn-out perspectives of creation to be released and no longer held in collective consciousness. Understand the purpose of each of these changes on the planet is not to destroy that which is already built, but rather to further the growth of Divine Mind and the understanding of the Divine ONE.

EARTH'S ROTATION AND POLE SHIFT

Question: "H. P. Blavatsky spoke in her work in the *Secret Doctrine* about sidereal years, containing within them 25,000 of our Earthly years. Each sidereal year represented a great breath and each breath, a portion of a teaching from the Hierarchy. Is it possible that you could share your knowledge on this?"

Please consider that which you refer to as a "sidereal" is that which is on one side that will then reel to the other. The Polar Shift Prophecy, as you understand it, is the movement of the poles from one point on the planetary sphere to another. This happens when the planet rotation ceases and then reverses its rotational spin around its gyroscopic axis. When the rotation ceases, the planetary gyro loses stability and the poles shift. In the last "side reel" year, the poles were aligned to what is now your equator. So, as you see, the poles are now one quarter the distance around the planetary sphere, or ninety degrees from their last position with the gyroscopic rotation reversed.

It is the reversal of rotation that has caused the complete cessation of life, as you know it, on this planet. The polar shifts which occur now are not as drastic. These shifts are not the cessation of an epoch, but rather, they are the adjustment of the Ray patterns within the epoch. This is not to be confused with a complete cessation. It is this adjustment, from one pattern to another, that allows the consciousness to come to a complete understanding of self. The great conflict that occurs at all levels in your world comes from the search of who you are, what you are, and from where you have come.

The Lemurian epoch ceased when Gondwanaland no longer served the purpose or the sustainment of life. And in this cessation all was changed from one epoch to another. Still, we are coming to the completion of the Atlantean epoch. It is still not complete and will not be for several thousand years, but we are indeed moving forward to the Ray System in this epoch. You and I, being of this same epoch, share this understanding. The Master system, which is understood here, is all of the same growth, the same great development.

The time that you refer to as 25,000 years, the "side reel" year, is much different than the time system you perceive. If you will consider the old Biblical text, from the perspective of God, a thousand years was one day. And if you were to take 365,000 of those days and calculate those by 25,000 years, you will have the approximate length of an epoch. It will not be exact, but it is an approximation. Consider that in this world, the time you have in the life cycle of a human body is very, very minute. Even the time cycles in the realms of Mastery are merely minutes compared to the great Source. We are all passing through this epoch together, one stage at a time. The completion is drawing near in the Mind of the Great Source. We are now coming to the cessation of the exhale, so to speak, and we are about to begin the inhale, the return to the ONE. However, in the human experience of time, this is several million years into what you would refer to as "in your future." Do you have any question?

THE CYCLES OF HUMAN EVOLUTION

Question: "You stated that we were at the end of the affect of the Atlantean epoch. Now as I have understood it, the Lemurian emerged into the Atlantean, the Atlantean moved into the Aryan. Are we not the Atlantean merging into the Aryan?"

It is the Divine Plan that is programmed into the plan of all creation. In the next 25,000 years, the transition should come to its complete cycle into the Aryan. It will be the understanding that the Divine Mind will live in the simplest form, will have the least technology, will have the greatest unity in the Mineral, Vegetable, Animal, and Human Kingdoms, which will bring back the spiritual mind. [Editor's Note: After the Aryan Cycle, we will experience the "HU-man" Cycle.]

If you look at the examples of the Masters' lives, they have modeled for all of us the concept of the Divine Spiritual Mind. They have lived their lives with simplicity. They have had no need for that which you refer to as technology, water, or food. They came to Divine Understanding and that is their complete interaction in creation.

Question: "Would you clarify the prophecies of Mozambique and Somalia?"

Mozambique breaks into a series of islands called the Isles of Africa and portions of South Africa. A large island is formed also to the east.

# *Infinite Garden*

*"The Plant Kingdom will abound with new species and will replace the animal protein-based consciousness. Grains, fruits, and vegetables nurture the simplistic attitude of the ONE Unana Mind. "*
- KUTHUMI

*After a short break, we return to the Map Room. It feels as if this room is suspended in the air, surrounded by clouds. The Master Teachers, El Morya and Kuthumi, are studying the map that will contain the next teaching. Beloved El Morya steps forward and addresses me telepathically through his piercing blue eyes.*

Greetings Beloved chelas and students. I AM El Morya. I come forward as a bridge to this transition. Do we have permission once again to continue and to enter your energy?

Response: "Proceed Dear one. You always have permission."

Let the mighty Christ Light come forward and bring perfection! In this Time of Transition the consciousness awakens! Understand that each detail symbolizes Earth movement, movement in your own physiology, and a continuation of movement in your energy. I now turn the floor over to our Beloved Kuthumi for continuation of this discourse.

*Master Kuthumi steps away from the Map Table and addresses us with his gentle brown eyes.*

Greetings Dear students of the mighty ONE. I AM Kuthumi and ask for permission to come forward.

Response: "Come forward Dear one."

## MOZAMBIQUE AND SOMALIA

The land of Mozambique is pivotal and contains a rich history. These lands were part of Lemuria prior to the continental shift. In the changes, these lands are changed and then stabilized into the new epoch. The lands of Somalia erode because of crushing tsunamis and changes in continental plates. Each plate has a unique consciousness that attracts or repels, maintaining infinite balance in your geophysical ecosystem. This principal charts the course of all the changes that come to the face of your planet. Infinite balance opens the consciousness of freedom to continue on its path of Divine Mind.

As the waters change their currents and tides, not only is the African continent affected, but the Earth's rotation on its axis points continuously fluctuates, affecting the Mineral Kingdom. This fluctuation of the Mineral Kingdom then affects the human physical species and evolves the consciousness across the African continent. This brings the planet further into its own alignment and plan. There will be the abolishment of all types of servitude. Only the free thought that is the ONE will exist as the dominating energetic pattern. The world will be realigned.

This is accomplished by the alignment of all of the Golden Cities through the expanded consciousness of the Mineral, Plant, Animal kingdoms, and culminating in the Human Kingdom.

As we travel further down the map's coastline, you see disintegrating lands and alterations that create balance in your great sphere of consciousness. Each disintegration, when numerically counted in kilometers, measures the transformation of the Earth.

## ISLANDS OF SOUTH AFRICA

Further down this map, changes in South Africa rise and break the lands into large and small islands. When an island is formed, the continent floats on a cushion of water above and below it (again, an example of the balancing of the energies). Just as leaves on a tree distribute energy to the trunk and the roots, laws of physics distribute new energies to the planet.

## LAW OF BALANCE

Currently, wealth and political power are centered in certain areas of your world. As the Earth Changes occur, these energies will become evenly distributed and no longer centered in one place. The current consolidation of political and economic power is the consciousness that throws the planet's rotation off. Through the consciousness of ONE, there will be an even distribution throughout the world. Understand that even the most extremely conflicting political scene is a servant to the Law of Balance. Each conflict will inevitably be brought to ONE harmony. This great activity of change and the Law of Balance assures this.

## UNIVERSAL SOVEREIGNTY

Through these mighty laws, you will see that a small group will no longer rule a large group. As the world evolves to self-understanding, self-rule evolves the consciousness to universal sovereignty. This altering of consciousness will literally alter genetic codes. Consciousness rearranges the grand design! The world and its social structures, religions, and economies are designed for transition. The things that were important to you as a child cease to interest you as you matured into an adult. This same transition happened again when you entered into old age; you became wiser. You become wiser through experience and understand that experience serves the true purpose of who you are. This is much like the planet's cycle of consciousness. The planetary changes remain the destiny of this planet as long as the consciousness maintains its current focus and perception.

The breaking up of these lands of southeastern Africa create a larger island that will serve a great purpose. It will happen after the tidal waves have receded. The purpose is that all is ONE in understanding. The Island of ONE and the Unity Islands will demonstrate peoples interacting with a sense of Oneship, a sense of family. Individual racial discontentment will cease. We will find ourselves blending into an understanding of the unity of creation. From this perception, all will grow—Mineral, Vegetable, Animal, and Human Kingdoms—to experience the harmony as described in the very first Jurisdiction. As each kingdom is harmonized on this planet, attention is given to the ONE Source. This creates honor, blessings, and joy to the ONE Source. This expands and abounds in fruitfulness!

A great fissure opens along the Saudi Arabian coast, as well as in the Somalian lands. This forms a peninsula. Movements in the Rift Valley raise the peninsula in elevation. This area will shake and the land will rise immensely. During another two thousand-year cycle, this land will again rise. However, this is for another changing cycle that is yet to be explained. The opening of this land to the water brings a healing effect. For as you know, salt water, of which your bodies are made, brings balance to the world. As more lands are exposed to salt water, all is made pure; all is made pristine; all is made in the understanding that the ONE Source has created all. Questions?

Question: "My question is in regard to the Arabian peninsula, which is one of the largest peninsulas in the world. The prophecies state that the Bay of Holy Prayer widens through the shifting of tectonic plates. Does this correlate with the great conflicts in this area?"

TECTONIC MOVEMENT IN THE MIDDLE EAST

The small republics on this Arabic peninsula of Oman and Yemen, the Arab lands of Emeritus, Iran, and Iraq that all border their neighbor Saudi Arabia, these Brothers and Sisters of the great tradition of Islam see themselves in a light that is now to be transformed. It is prophesied by their prophet, and our Brother, that these changes occur by the movement of the tectonic plates.

This is a symbol that they have widened their perception of themselves and the Oneness. These changes are a cleansing, to eliminate conflict that has come about in this geographic area. There will be more than sufficient time during these sequential changes for those who wish to move from the coast to do so. This change will be gradual, in part, with the rising of the water and also through several earthquakes. This change is much like labor pains, coming closer and closer together, bringing about the birth of a new understanding.

In this world birth change, you will have some activity and then a duration of time before more activity and again, a duration of time. Then again, there will be some activity and a shorter duration of time, activity and a shorter duration, and continually shorter durations until there is activity after activity, one after another, much like labor. The birth of the new consciousness makes its appearance into the material world, into emotion and feeling, into thought, and Divine Wisdom.

## LOVE ONE ANOTHER

Brothers and Sisters of these lands, hear these words: LOVE ONE ANOTHER, beyond the boundaries of your nation. Love each other beyond the perspective of your religions. Love each other as you are of the same Light Source. Spread this love to all who come to you. Spread this to those who are Christian. Spread this to those who are Jewish. Spread this to your Hindu Brother and to your Buddhist Brother. See no nation as separate from you. See no one as impure. Only see the ONE that you are. There is only ONE Source of creation. There is only ONE God of understanding. You and all of creation are ONE. Through this understanding, the world may move beyond squabbling, beyond who is right, beyond who is impure, beyond who is just and who is unjust, and on to the ONE love that is the purpose of creation. It is only love that will sustain you. Love one another.

In moving north toward Jordan, Lebanon, and Israel, the activities of science may self-destruct, as was described earlier in this prophetic material (in the detonation of the nuclear devices in the fissures of the Mediterranean Sea). Dear Children of the ONE God, of the ONE Creation, Mother/Father God loves you equally and will not abandon you, will not think of one of you over the other. These prophecies are given to assist your understanding that there is no preference of one religion; there is no preference of one economic system. All are equally affected. No one is chosen. No one is spared. All are equally loved. Questions?

Question: "Dear Brother, could you give us information about the devastating disease of Aids, which is affecting so many in North and South America and Africa? How could this suffering be lessened?"

Truly, it is the design of men to control others that has caused this plague to once again come to your planet. It is believed in many world circles that govern economies, food, and the military, that there are certain members of the world community who are less desirable than others because of their perceived lack of contribution. It is therefore accepted and understood in these world community organizations that there are those who are quite expendable to the survival of the planet. However, there is a Divine Plan that loosens the grip of those who have such great fear and base their decisions on this controlling fear.

This planet's destiny is to understand the ONE. It is therefore understood, there will be those activities to thwart this destiny. These are choices based on fear. But do not worry, those who breathe and dance fear will be brought to an understanding above the struggle of fear. They will breathe and dance ONE service. This land of Africa is blessed. As the navel of creation, it is the beginning of the Aryan Race. From the stress and upheaval from these birth pangs will come forward the Divine Mind of ONE consciousness.

The greatest conflict creates the greatest harmony! This is the paradox. The world will no longer suffer from the denial of true Spirit and knowing Spirit as the ONE. There is always one last dance before the final movement. We are in attendance to receive those who choose this in this transition.

NEW SEEDS OF CREATION

Question: "Would you tell us more about the story behind the purpose of Africa, known in the prophecies as the Infinite Garden?"

The Infinite Garden will contain, as we have spoken earlier, all of the new seeds of the creation. The Plant Kingdom will abound with new species and will replace the animal protein-based consciousness. Grains, fruits, and vegetables nurture the simplistic attitude of the ONE Unana Mind. This Infinite Garden also springs forth a new understanding of the Aryan. It is the nursery, so to speak, of the beginning of the new epoch. It is where these seeds will completely abound. Technology will develop from complete harmony with the Natural Law and the spiritual principals of the Twelve Jurisdictions. It is here, in this Infinite Garden, peace and harmony will prevail. This land is transiting out of its conflict and into a land of great freedom. The Infinite Garden is a gem of consciousness. In this garden, all forms of life spring forth renewed! The Infinite Garden is the new land of Africa!

Response: "Thank you, Dear one. I have no more questions on Africa."

# *Europe*

*"There is an exchange of fear for love, and there is the great exchange that brings us from the separation to the ONE."*
- LADY NADA

*Again, after a brief break, we resume our studies with the Master Teachers, Kuthumi and El Morya. Master Kuthumi places his hands into his brown robe and steps back from the marble table, covered with the maps of Africa and Europe. Lady Nada has joined the group to transmit a teaching about Europe. She is tall and graceful, dressed in an aquamarine gown. Kuthumi speaks first:*

I must turn this floor over to our Beloved El Morya.

*Master El Morya of the Blue Ray walks forward, along with the stunning Lady Master Nada. The energy of their two auras intermingle, creating shooting stars in hues of green, turquoise, and royal blue. He places his hand softly on her shoulder and his eyes again address us:*

Greetings Dear ones. I AM El Morya and ask you to come and stroll through this Garden, into these lands that have been known as Europe. I will now turn the teaching of these maps over to our Beloved Nada. She will bring forth the necessary discourse and you may ask questions.

*El Morya steps back and Lady Nada assumes the position of teacher in front of the map of Europe.*

Greetings Dear students of the ONE in the mighty Christ. I AM Nada. I ask for your permission to come forward and bring discourse.

Response: "Come forward Dear Sister. You have permission."

GREAT BRITAIN

We turn to the great lands that you know as Great Britain. Ireland has continued its conflict and will be brought to purity in the changes, for the fight of Brother against Brother will be brought to rest. Small earthquakes will affect the English channel. The tunnel that is built from continental Europe to the English channel will sink during this change. The cities that are along the southeastern coasts, including the lands in Wales, will also be enveloped by the rising waters and the earthquake activity that shakes the coastline into rubble. It is this shaking that will affect the seat of power in the British Empire and bring all to a place of service again. The time of rulership is over. The time of service is now. The western and eastern coasts of Scotland are eroded; yet still, the core of the Scottish land will be held in a continuum as the new Golden City arises and over this land a perfection is sustained.

## SPAIN AND FRANCE

Spanish lands remain relatively intact, although there is some erosion in some coastal areas. There is also some loss of cities along these coastlines. Spanish lands rise to a greater height, or a plateau, shall we say.

French lands are devastated and broken into islands. Those lands, up into the Alps, will be broken and very little will remain of the French territory. In this land that was once an ancient sea bed, where the water of the Mediterranean flowed from the present North Sea, only the highest areas will have dry land. These remaining lands of France will still be populated with those who have moved from cities and lower lands. These islands will learn the great Laws of Harmony. They will learn the great understanding of the ONE.

## GERMANY, POLAND, SWITZERLAND

We come to the breakup of Germany and Poland, this land devastated by the changing of the water levels. These water levels are brought forth by the melting of the caps and a small geothermal activity that will occur in the northern areas of the tundra of Russia. Springs will begin to thaw and warm this tundra, which will continue to bring about the rising of the waters.

Switzerland remains unchanged, except that small movements in the plates will cause the Alps to rise gently, and the mountain lakes, including Geneva, will empty out over the mountains. The lakes will break up into smaller lakes and much of the ice that is formed in the Alps will start to melt during the global warming.

## ITALY

Many of the Italian islands will be several hundred feet below the new sea. Parts of the area of the Italian coasts, such as Rome, Milan, and parts of Venice will have rising waters which will cover them completely. These rising waters will force the population from the coastal areas into the interior of the peninsula and further towards the mountainous areas of the Alps.

## ICE SHEETS IN EUROPE

In Hungary, Austria, and Bulgaria, sheets of ice will come from the sky and crash upon the European continent. These ice sheets will also affect Germany and Poland, and will continue into the areas currently on the southern border of Russia. Russia, with the rising of the waters, will lose many of its northern areas and break into islands. These islands, that are the remains of the Ural Mountains, become a long peninsula. It is also in this prophecy that the great sheets of ice continue to fall from the sky and cover much of this area. The ice melts and adds to the water level of these areas.

The geothermal activity that occurs in the northern tundra area allows the growth of large, pampas types of grasses. Continuous condensation, freezing and thawing activity in the middle and upper atmosphere, creates further sheeting of ice throughout northern and eastern Europe.

Through change, freedom comes. The planet will come to infinite harmony. In this moment, we will stop for questions.

## THE SHINY PEARL

Question: "One question that I do have is about the Ural mountains, which appears as a large peninsula of land known in the prophecy as a large island called the "Shiny Pearl." The prophecy states that this island becomes a large trade center for the Ocean of Balance, with seaport cities covering her coastline. Could you tell us more about the Shiny Pearl?"

The Shiny Pearl is the Ural Mountains, connected by a large vein of white marble. As the mountains rise in height for the greatest distance of approximately one thousand kilometers, they are seen as a peninsula. There will be the ability to see this great ridge of land far off, as it will stand as a beaming glow for all seafaring activity, so much so, that due to the angle of the axis that has adjusted the north and south poles, the sky will stay bright as much as eighteen hours per day. This makes navigation extremely easy and it will make the movement of large amounts of crops from one place to another by barge extremely simple. Again, we will see the use of wind power for sailing and the shipping of crops, and great storehouses of grains to feed the world.

World economics will be balanced in such a manner that it will come to a ONE World understanding. There will be no dominion of one economy over another; only a great sharing will take place. In this area, the Ural mountains provide a beacon, much like a natural lighthouse, for a long period of time. The glowing pearl of this shiny landmass gives to humankind the sense of true harmony and balance and all will share in abundance. The days of the "haves and have nots" has come to an end. The time is now for lands in northern Russia that were once barren places of great suffering, to serve all of humankind through agriculture and economic strength, shared by all.

## ICELAND: THE BRIDGE

Question: "One Earth Change Prophecy that we found quite fascinating addresses the metaphor of the Map of Exchanges. Saint Germain has often spoken of the Map of Exchanges as the masculine and feminine energies uniting for the creation of the child, or the birth of the Christ Consciousness. Iceland is very unique in the Earth Changes. Would you elaborate on Iceland's role in this?"

Iceland, which long has had green pastures and many geysers in its northern latitude in order to keep warm, has suffered great abuse over the centuries. It now comes to a place of world trade and commerce and is a stopping place in the main route from areas such as the Ural Mountains through to the United States and Canada. The day is coming when this particular land mass rises from the Atlantic Ridge and will support many types of shipping and will be warm enough to support many types of retreats.

It will be great when your world understands that the technology at your fingertips is, shall we say, for the inspiration and achievement of Divine Mind, for the growth of wisdom and a step towards Mastery. Iceland will serve as a bridge from one continent to another. It will be one of the main shipping ports.

The activity that raises this island will occur sometime during the beginning of the Earth Changes in your current United States. There will be small, underground, or underwater movement of volcanic origin. This will be measured very easily toward the end of the transition of your Americas. So too, as these exchanges start, the Iceland area will be one of the great focusing points and exhibit phenomenon that many will marvel to watch as these lands start to gently rise out of warm, bubbling waters in the North Atlantic. It will be a signaling point that the next step is soon to occur upon your plane and planet. Iceland serves as a great marker upon your history.

Question: "The second series of events that occur in the Map of Exchanges is the prophesied uniting of the Ural and Caspian Seas into one large sea known as the Sea of Grace. Could you elaborate on this, Lady Nada?"

There is a great movement in this continent near a fissure. This will open and the lands will succumb to the rising waters and the times of conflict and distress will come to an end.

Question: "Does this correlate with the rising of the Himalayan Mountains?"

The movement in the Himalayan Mountains will cause a small reaction, which creates activity into the area of Australia and the Arabian coast.

Question: "So, in essence, the rising of those mountains will activate the joining of these seas into a larger body of water?"

## A CRESCENDO OF CREATION

It will signal the same coincidental time, for as the birth pangs become closer and closer, there will be more simultaneous activity on the planet. It will bring a crescendo of creation, as though you are listening to a symphony that comes to a great and final, abrupt end. Upon the last chord and from that point, is only the sense of peace and completion.

## LETTING GO

Question: "Lady Nada, the prophecies, particularly for Eastern Europe are quite severe. Gone are the cities of Leningrad and Moscow. The Volga River is nonexistent, covered by the Ocean of Balance. The Ukraine, USSR, and White Russia are all gone. Do you have any suggestions, kind words, or prophecies of hope that we can share in relating this message to the peoples in these lands, so that this cataclysm can be averted?"

LET YOUR PEOPLE GO! Hold no longer the iron fist. If there was one thing that I would ask of the world governments, it is LET YOUR PEOPLE GO! Find no reason to hem them. Find no reason to chain walls for them. LET THE PEOPLE GO! Find no reason for them to create war. LET THEM GO!

It is in the letting go, as Beloved El Morya has stated, that freedom will come. The cities of Moscow and St. Petersburg need not suffer the rising waters and the destruction of all history and culture. But neither is it necessary for any great city on this planet, such as Paris, or London, or Rome, to lose its heritage. Any city may honor its heritage and move into the next epoch.

## EXCHANGE FEAR FOR LOVE

When you come to a personal change in your life, do you not honor the path that has brought you to this place? Do you not see the role your path has played? But, you may chose to dishonor that. And, it is this dishonoring that creates this great conflict of the worlds. Have you not seen that all these people, regardless of any structure, were all born free? No matter what race, religion, belief, or geographical location, all are born free. It is only in the acceptance of freedom and the lessening of any ties that hamper or enslave, that create these changes.

Every change on this planet can be stopped in the ONE breath by letting people go, by allowing freedom, by business and government no longer holding ties over individuals or groups. We request only that you see and acknowledge this, so you are no longer governed by fear. Be governed by the Divine and True

Mind. Understand that your world is subject to change. There are times when "subject to change" means without notification. It is in these world prophesies that "subject to change" is notification that your elements of choice may be expounded upon.

It is just as easy to let go ... to allow the free movement of the Divine Plan ... to let the joy of your existence and your Divine Natures be the great guidance ... and allow this to be the focus of the ONE Mind of this creation. It is just as easy to inspire as to enslave, economically or politically. Again, as an exchange of energy through the Map of Exchanges, not only does the masculine tyranny cease, but the feminine creation comes into balance. There is an exchange of fear for love, and there is the great exchange that brings us from the separation to the ONE. It is at this pivotal point of balance through these exchanges that you no longer work as a child of God, throwing temper tantrums across the political boundaries. These boundaries are ceasing because that which creates them is ceasing.

## THE PATH OF SERVICE

Come to the ONE understanding and work in harmony as a mature society. Evolve your childlike nature to the maturity of your Divinity. Exchange your childish shoes and walk the path of service. No longer will you pray, whine, and scream to be taken care of by angels and benevolent gods. You may offer, "How may I be of service to you and to my Brothers and Sisters?" No longer will you have the concept of "me, my, mine." It is the I AM to be filled. You will say, "I exchange this to be of service. I give this up to share my life, my love, my Oneness, for I AM as you are."

Dear ones, consider this: We are exchanging many things. We are exchanging all that hampers and holds us back. We are exchanging one path for another to create the Freedom Star and our greater service in this universe. Do you have further questions?

Question: "Not at this moment, Dear Nada. Would you return tomorrow to discuss the lands of New Lemuria and the Golden Cities?"

## LET CREATION STREAM FORTH

It will be a great joy to return. At the first hour after the midday, we shall gather, and the discussion of all these new lands throughout your plane and planet will bring the awakening of who you are and why you have come here.

Let the creation stream forth!
Let the feminine balance bring to this world the
understanding that all is ONE.
Hitaka!

# New Lemuria

*"As we move in these exchanges, so too these new lands arise through continental plate movement in the expansion of the planet through the growth of consciousness."*
- EL MORYA

*In the name of I AM that I AM, Beloved Mighty I AM Presence, God I AM, come forward and bring perfect service to this channeling. Let Beloved El Morya, Kuthumi, Sananda, and Saint Germain come forward and bring their perfect service. Let Beloved Nada, Portia, Kuan Yin, and Mary come forward and bring their perfect service. Let this be sustained and maintained infinitely, in perfect alignment to the Divine Plan. Almighty I AM THAT I AM.*

*I am looking to an area known as Antarctica. I will describe what I see.*

NEW LOCATION OF THE POLES

The Golden City of Cresta shines as a beautiful golden star! Looking at the Antarctic Continent, it is no longer covered by ice and snow. This is also the case in the North Pole area, where the Arctic Continent is most visible. Much of the ice and snow has moved. Glaciers that have receded from each of these north and south continents reveal usable tundra land. Looking above the planet, there are distinctive mountains, valleys, and some inland waters. The poles have moved to different locations, one in the vicinity of Baffin Island and the other closer toward the New Lemurian lands and the lands of Australia. The continental lands that were once completely covered, still have many remnants of glaciers following the melting of the poles.

The sphere of the Earth has adjusted its configuration to a more symmetrical shape. Previously, scientific explanations theorized that the spherical shape was more elongated in one area than another, forming a shape like a pear. Now, the Earth seems to have a more expanded shape, a rounded, complete sphere.

*Several Masters are now present and Beloved El Morya steps forward for the teaching. The Earth Changes Maps of new lands that were once ancient lands of Lemuria are rolled out on the Map Table.*

Greetings Beloved students of the ONE Golden Light. I AM El Morya and I ask for permission to come into your energy field, into your plane of consciousness, and to bring you discourse.

Response: "Welcome Mahatma El Morya. You have permission."

THE NEW LANDS

In this time that you have referred to as Transition, awareness and focus become distinctively understood, but it is a process. Awareness, many times, acts as a pebble in the shoe. One may be very aware, and yet the clear picture of what purpose the pebble serves may be elusive. It is the complete understanding of this awareness that offers the mind an understanding of the outer world's activities as well. The inner world's activity attracts to itself those paths, those teachings, those formats of experience which bring balance and harmony. This is exchange, for what is within will direct the focus of what is without.

As we move in these exchanges, so too these new lands arise through continental plate movement in the expansion of the planet through the growth of consciousness. As this expansion continues, the planet, once again, comes into this new era. The new lands in the north and south, and the lands of New Lemuria, inspire the acceptance that change is a constant activity in this plane. In this plane, it is readjustment that allows for the understanding of the infinite possibility of your focus coming to the ONE.

When the lands of New Zealand rise as a new continent, there is much discussion about how these lands will serve to move the consciousness of the planet forward. The Sea of Infinite Wisdom will bring about the separation of current Australia and New Lemuria. These continental lands will serve humanity in the capacity of integrating science and the mind. They will serve the science of creation. Science in your world has many times served the ego of the individual scientist, or it has served the greed of a great corporate entity. Now the focus will no longer be of a self-serving nature. Freedom and understanding exist only in the Divine Mind's experience of creation, integrated completely through the entire plane of consciousness.

## INTELLIGENCE OF DIVINE MIND

In considering the world's changing elements, separation now comes to unity. There were times when information was kept cloistered and most others kept in ignorance. In the focus of the Divine Mind, there is no ignorance; there is no cloistering of information. Each Golden City on the planet brings about the quality of a Ray and a quality of consciousness working together in harmony. Harmony forms a union of the Divine understanding and world consciousness. This union brought forward is the state of Unana. Through understanding the service each land brings and the quality of consciousness each land holds, each work, as a piece of the puzzle, is now set into place, by which all other pieces may fulfill their purpose.

As one Golden City activates, so too others activate in succession, and the picture comes into clear focus. The understanding and purpose of this creation is now integrated in all levels of Divine Mind, consciousness, and into the cellular structure of all being. This is also reflected in the activity of the Oneness that is in the Human, the Plant, the Animal, and the Mineral Kingdoms. Here in these new lands, which you will refer to as New Lemuria, each continent that arises within this continental chain has a purpose of focus in this creation, has a purpose in the creation of the development of the Divine Wisdom.

## "BE" THE ONE IN SERVICE

Here in this new land that is forming near New Zealand, as stated in previous prophetic teachings, science and technology will serve humanity, unlike our present state of affairs wherein humanity must serve science and technology. This role for science is known strictly in our world as Divine Service and Purpose of All Being. All serve the ONE.

Moving northward on the map to these new areas where this fiery eye is growing, is the understanding that this illumination comes to activity and complete integration. The existing coding system of the human species, as explained by your current sciences, is an incomplete explanation of the existence of creation. Preexisting creative forces and patterns also must be understood. In the world that you refer to as the Realm of Mastery, these preexisting forces of creation work in a harmonic. In your world, defined forces of creation have been used for self-service and enslavement. These days are over. The time, as you know, is now. Freedom is to be of service, not servitude. Here in this world, all is changing. The Divine Focus is redirecting each individual flame that has joyfully accepted purposeful understanding.

After the changes, these new lands that have lain fallow under the sea will be pure and pristine. Other lands will come under the gentle healing waters of great salt oceans of purity. The changes bring about new opportunities for service, as each of these lands contains new minerals. Each of these lands contains new seeds of plants. Each of these lands will contain animals and humans in a new directive of service to the ONE. This directive has always been the purpose of the creation of this great planet of Prana. It is the level of the freedom of choice that exists here which creates divergent or conflicting realities. These realities of your daily lives, through eons and eons of evolution, have now come to a level of acceptance and non-judgment towards the ONE. Now, be the ONE service!

If we, in our service to each and every one of you, can in the simplest way, activate an acceptance and response to this ONE service, then the success of this great transition will come to a wonderful fruition. All will move once again as the great hands of a clock, moving in the perfect and complete timing of the universe to the next hour. In your daily life, you keep track and meter your life experience by the hour, the minute, the second, and it is in each of these that you make new choices in creation. It is in each of these that you step and move to the next place. Likewise, in this hour new Earth Change activity occurs. We are at this verge of the next step. It is a step that is quite wondrous . . . one that is quite fruitful . . . one that is quite loving.

NEW PLANTS, NEW FISHES

Vegetation in these areas will have different forms. Those plants lost in the transition will be replaced by new plants, as well as new minerals, substances that will restructure consciousness and evolve species genetically. This will happen first in the new lands and then will continue during the transition to proliferate throughout the remaining lands. It is the hope that as each of these layers of awareness are altered and redirected to the ONE service, little by little the existing genetic coding that creates conflict will be replaced. This transition will be done in a most gentle manner. Worlds will come to the understanding of a ONE world and eliminate separation. Here in this realm, all will come to the fruition, integration, and completion of that which you refer to as Mastery. This will become a global activity. Through this change, service to all of creation will spring forward. Seeds of this consciousness will proliferate throughout the entire universal structure.

In these lands north and south, tundra and lakes will be prevalent. As the years go by, fish will populate them. As the years move on, agriculture will also be possible in these areas. The New Lemurian lands will take approximately 2,000 years to reach their service. However, their very presence and existence, forming through volcanic activity and out of former continents, will make available minerals that have been resting, so to speak, in the planet's core. There will be a great expansion in your scientific understanding of what elements exist. These minerals are usable by all who work within the sciences and the services to humanity. The Mineral Kingdom that has been at rest in this area will bring forth no less than twenty-two additional elements. These elements will completely alter consciousness and the current sciences.

A NEW SCIENCE

You have, at this point, dabbled very slowly in your creation science. When these new elements are discovered, all will change. The exact definition of these elements can be given at a later time. The dispensation of this material will be taught by Beloved Saint Germain, for Alchemy and its application is his area of expertise. Those who choose to inhabit these lands and embrace the ONE understanding will have joy and great longevity. Life will be untiring and completely fulfilling.

Note also, the relationship between your Sun and your planet will alter. Daylight will be longer than a twelve-hour segment. Night will be shorter. The planetary experience of half light and half dark will cease as time moves on. In this secession, the light that is the Source of this creation in this plane of understanding and conscious awareness will come to a place that is perfect service. Here, the Infinite is always that which is within.

Come to this place of great joy! Sharpen your focus, choices, and understanding to create balance. This is the fulfillment of Divine Service. Do you have questions?

HEAVEN ON EARTH

Question: "Yes, Dear El Morya. I have a few questions. But first, I would like to start with the metaphor of the Map of Exchanges. In previous prophecies, the Spiritual Hierarchy has spoken of the metaphor for exchange in the phrase: "as above, so below." I have interpreted this to mean the anchoring of heaven on Earth in these lands. Would you explain?"

As the planet exchanges a self-serving focus for a service to the ONE, all who do not serve the ONE will be relinquished, as you say, freed and let go. The focus will come to the service to this ONE. Humanity will see itself as ONE. The planet will be part of this ONE. The Plant, Animal, and Mineral Kingdoms will be understood as ONE. The lands which inflicted the greatest enslavement and servitude will bring forth the greatest service. Those lands which have held and cracked the whip, will release it in perfect service.

Anchoring the service of the ONE is heaven on Earth. It is from this Heaven that I AM of service. It is from this understanding that I AM in activity. It is from this great desire and focus that I AM the vision of the ONE creation. As you have asked, rest assured, Heaven and Earth will be completely anchored as ONE realm.

MASS ASCENSION

Question: "Will there be a mass Ascension?"

The universal structure of a system with twelve planets contains the experience of Ascension, or the movement in dimensional awareness. It is practiced on a planetary scale, one which has previously occurred on Venus and on Mars. It is in this transition that the entire focus brings about infinite acceptance into the ONE. It is as though you move from one grade to another. Once you had the eyes of a child; you had the thoughts of a child; you made the sounds of a child; you spoke the words of a child; and you had the actions of a child. But, it is in the movement, as you become a woman, that you have the eyes of a woman; you speak the words of a woman; you live the life of a woman. It is so for all the inhabitants of the planet that we dearly love as Prana. She and her inhabitants move forward into the next step of the path.

Mass Ascension has been achieved by those who have the eyes of the servant, the ears of the servant, the words and the activities of the servant, and have truly sustained, understood, and moved forward into that realm. It is the same for the entire planet. All will move forward. This is the plan. It is not one which I have designed, but it is one which I have embraced.

## UNITY OF ALL KINGDOMS

Question: "Freedom begins from unity within. The harmony and bliss of heaven radiates from this center. Is this an appropriate interpretation of the Map of Exchanges?"

Dear one, you are prepared for all that you have brought forth. Your interpretation is the result of your preparedness and the result of your Master Guide. It is this guidance which works through you and with you. There is nothing imperfect in your presentation. It speaks of the acceptance of unity and through unification we step forward on the path.

It is time that humanity comes to the unification of Self. Accept the unity of the Mineral, Plant, and Animal Kingdoms. Accept the Divine Spark and breath that forms the human. And so, in this understanding, you ask, "Who am I? Where am I? How did I get here? What is my purpose? Why do I have this life?" Through experience, the understanding of freedom is released. Through freedom, there is understanding of unity, the Divine Spark and the service of the ONE. And so, it is the ONE that makes all kingdoms. It is the ONE that breathes out the spark. It is the ONE that creates individual petals of flowers, leaves of trees, minerals, stars, the skies, birds, animals, and waters. Freedom ends the search for the self-identity.

Response: "Thank you, El Morya. I have no more questions."

Then it is with great, glad tidings that we bring to a close this Map of Exchanges. It is with the dearest love and attention to the ONE that we bring to a close this time of discourse.

Let this go forward,
So that the eyes and ears may be opened.
May feet step forward in action
And let it be done with a glad heart.
Hitaka!

# *Heaven on Earth*

*"We will shatter the belief systems that are outdated and worn,
and birth the potential of consciousness."*
- SAINT GERMAIN

Greetings in that mighty Christ. I AM Saint Germain and I stream forth on that mighty Violet Ray of Mercy and Forgiveness. As usual Dear hearts, students, and chelas of mine, I request permission to come forth.

Response: "Dear Beloved Saint Germain, please come forward. It is with great, glad tidings that we greet you."

It is with joy that I greet all of you, stalwart students of the heart of this Dispensation of the Fifth Ray during the Time of Transition. And it is with great joy that I greet all of you Dear ones, for the completion of this material. This material marks the end of an epoch, shall we say, an end of the influence of Atlantis. And it now opens the gates to those who embrace Divine Mind, that Oneship of the Aryan.

## ONESHIP AND ASCENSION

Dear ones, the times upon the Earth Plane and Planet that are to come, are times where one must truly open the ears in order to hear the full content of what has been received. This information has been brought forth to serve those of the Spiritual Awakening and to awaken mankind to that mighty Unfed Flame of Love, Wisdom, and Power within the heart, the divinity, the Oneship that we all share in.

This Time of Awakening is now transiting across the planet, much as the Moon spreads a shadow across the planet at night. And in this shadow, shall we say, there is a physical representation of this awakening. Dear ones, rejoice and be gladdened in your hearts, for a time comes where, yes, this planet shall change, and it shall be accompanied by the music of a change in consciousness. This change in consciousness will open each and every one of you to that new Kingdom of God. All of you who have longed for your Ascension in light and sound, now open to the potential that awaits you. Dear one, the time comes too for you to understand the kingdom that exists in that Fifth Dimension. We are approaching a time when the Human Kingdom will embrace, not only other elementary kingdoms which are a part of this Divine Plan, but also expand the vision, consciousness, and perception into the aggregate Body of Understanding.

The Earth will be surrounded by the choirs of angels from the Kingdom of God, for you are Divine, Dear Beings, blessed in this Oneship! Find your position as a Cosmic Being, Ascended Master, Beloved Elohim, or Archangel. Each and every one of these positions in the Kingdom of God is of equal importance, one not less than another. Each holds a piece of the puzzle of which you spoke. Each and every one of them plays, shall we say, a harmony that is soothing to your ears and rests your weary hands and feet.


## THE TRANSMISSION CLOSES

The Time of Change is a blessing now for those who walk on the planet in this epoch. The transmission of this material began in the early 1980's and today, I close the book on the transmission of this particular Dispensation. Let me explain. This material was brought forth to bring a synergistic and synchronistic plan among humanity, one which would involve the synergy of the sciences, psychologies, religions, and the fine arts. All of these have been brought forth in a teaching known as the Four Pillars. The spiritual message opens not only eyes, ears, and hands, but hearts. The vibration of this Earth Changes material will first touch the heart. This is first felt in that intuitive manner. Intuition raises the instinctual bodies into intelligence. Intelligence paves the way for wisdom.

The Aryan will bring forth the full expression of the combination of the Ray Forces, culminating in Divine Wisdom. Long has humanity sought the application of wisdom and now a time comes where the Ray combinations will allow this to be so. It is only through Divine Wisdom that one understands a responsible choice. Each choice anchors Heaven upon Earth; As above, so below. The Kingdom of God deals daily with the implementation of the plan working through the hands of humanity. Dear ones, we rely upon the instinctual forces of your intelligence to make those choices each and every day which allows the Divine Plan to work to its fullest perfection.

## THE POTENTIAL OF CONSCIOUSNESS

The time which comes to the Earth Plane and Planet is a time, yes, of catastrophe and a time of cataclysm; yet, it is also a time where we will shatter the belief systems that are outdated and worn, and birth the potential of consciousness. This potential of consciousness is based upon the truth expressed by Dear Sananda, Lord of the Transition, Teacher in the Kingdom of God of humanity and angels alike. It is simple: "Love one another." Love one another, Brothers and Sisters of the Planet. Let love be the end result of all activities. Love is the binding force of that aggregate Body of Light of which you and the planet are comprised.

Tracing previous Earth Changes upon the Earth Plane and Planet, it is time for you to understand, Dear students and chelas of mine, that change is inevitable and always will be. This is a course which not only prepares your consciousness for the idea of change, but also promotes an elasticity or flexibility within the being and expands your consciousness into what Beloved Kuan Yin has called a Oneship.

## EXPANSION REQUIRES FLEXIBILITY

Study the three series of maps that have been dispensed in this Spiritual Teaching and you will begin to see a beautiful interplay, the arcing of each of the Rays, and a fresh perspective which allows a flexibility of your consciousness. Expansion requires flexibility. Humanity is now asked to develop flexibility; for this is needed in order to assure humanity's complete survival.

It is important that you listen to all of these prophecies as they have been given. It is important to listen to the heart of the message contained within each and every one of them. This is a Time of Prophecy. Many prophets will appear after the presentation of this material. Many prophets have existed before the presentation of this material. Mark these words of mine: That shining Star of Freedom will see a time of seven moons within the skies.

Ceres and Portia, Lady Master Venus shall all appear.
And who of humanity now will hear?
But listen Dear students, the heart of the rose,
This is the time that now I prose.
Fourteen kings and eighteen queens,
Is this a time for angels seen?
Listen to these prophecies.
Mark each word.
They are yours to see,
Yours to hear.
Open your soul and open your mind.
Deep within is the find,
Not of gold and yet of value.
Open your hearts! Open your hearts!

## CHANGE IS INEVITIABLE

Is there much more that I can say to accompany this time? Do we choose the violence of wars and hatred? Or, will we break down our individual intolerances of one another and simply love. This plan I now place into your hands. Work this among you. The leaders will rise and the leaders will fall. As I have said, there is one thing of which you can be assured, change is inevitable. This is also the inevitable path, the lighted path that you, Dear ones, have traveled. I reach my hand across this veil and offer it in service, for I too know how this path can be.

I encourage you, Dear ones, to study this prophecy. Understand each detail contained within it, for not only is it a prophecy that will flex your consciousness, it is a prophecy filled with the light of a New Day and hope for a future for all of us. The Kingdom of Light and Sound is continuously expanding upon the Earth Plane and Planet. It is now a time of major expansion, Dear ones. It is time where consciousness is now, shall we say, at that pivotal point of departure.

You may say, "How close I now come to the Light of the Source, and it is as if my waxen wings are melting, tinged with fire." You, who now cross this Dark River, know what lies on the other side. It is a valley of rest and peace. This knowledge too is contained within this material.

## THE GOLDEN CITIES ARE ANCHORED

Each of the Golden Cities, all fifty-one of them, are now anchored into their geophysical locations. This ends over fifteen thousand years of planning on the part of the Spiritual Hierarchy. I celebrate this day, for the anchoring in of the consciousness of Unana. For each and every one of you, Brothers and Sisters of the Golden Flame, the light of this path now shines! Dear hearts, I raise my cup, filled with the memories of my journey, and the hope and faith of the journeys to come! I raise my cup and drink of this effervescent life! We take our rest from this material and we close the golden-leafed books.

## RETURN OF THE GOLDEN-LEAFED BOOKS

*Saint Germain stands at the lectern. His aura radiates an immense light, flooding the area with infinite wisdom, love, and a feeling of complete peace. In front of him is the book from which he has read the poem. He quietly closes the large cover of the book, the pages of which are edged in pure gold. On either side are two angelic assistants, and they too are surrounded by an immense gold and white light. Saint Germain lifts the book into the glow of luminous light and an even brighter beam of light appears.*

Lords of Venus, of the Flame, I now return your wisdom long ago imparted. For now, we serve that plan that was held in the conception of your mind's eye. May it stream forth into the hearts of men, those who now awaken to serve the Divine Plan I AM.

*The book begins to disappear and becomes one with the light. Soon the beam of light dissipates.*

Dear students and chelas, I AM your Brother Saint Germain. I thank you and acknowledge your assistance. I shall return, shall I say, and bid Adieu to you. Do not tarry with your work. The work is priceless. I bid you all peace.

Response: "Peace to you, Elder Brother."

# Global Warming Update: North America

*"All elements will be involved in the great purification of the Earth, not only earth, but water, fire, and wind will all come together to give their service to lift the human into a greater state of knowledge and to a greater consciousness."*

\- SAINT GERMAIN

Greetings Beloved chelas in that mighty Violet Flame and the Flame of Unana. I AM Saint Germain and I request permission to come forward.

Response: "Please Saint Germain, come forward. You are most welcome."

And present today with me are also Lord Sananda, Beloved Mother Mary, Beloved El Morya, and Beloved Brother Kuthumi. We will, upon occasion, be presenting information through the presence of Unana, through the Unity Consciousness of ONE. And through this, we ask permission to come forward.

Response: "Please, come forward. You are all most welcome."

*Saint Germain is stepping back and Lord Sananda is now coming forward.*

Greetings, my Beloved Brothers and Sisters of the Golden Flame. I AM Sananda and I request permission to come forward into your energy fields.

Response: "Please Lord Sananda come forward. You are most welcome."

As you have known, Dear ones and Dear hearts, there is much peril upon the Earth Plane and Planet at this time. We are now coming forward in order to give a group effort of energy to the Earth Plane and Planet, to give our guidance, and to give our insight upon the times to come.

## THE I AM AMERICA MAP

When the first I AM America Map was presented and unrolled for humanity, it was brought forward to show the probabilities of human consciousness at that time and what is the possibility of its creation. This was presented based upon the collective consciousness reading of the time. It was also presented as a point of gathering, to bring people of like mind together, so possible solutions could be contemplated and then acted upon.

At this time, we are willing to give more possibilities, not as predictions, but as possibilities of events that may happen upon the Earth Plane and Planet. Again, this information is based upon the collective consciousness as it is being read at this time. It is important Dear ones, Dear hearts, to apply, at all times, the laws of Co-creation as they have been given to you. It is most important to always apply, in that Law of the Best and Highest Good, the teachings of the Twelve Jurisdictions. For you see Beloved Dear ones, Dear hearts, Brothers and Sisters, students and chelas on the path, these are teachings that have been brought forward to raise consciousness into a new understanding. This is the Age of Cooperation that we speak of. This is the time that we are now all moving into.

## TIME OF TESTING

When I first spoke at this lectern, giving the information that was to become the basis of the I AM America Map and spiritual information, we came during a time that is known now as the Time of Transition. During that time, a group Spiritual Awakening occurred among many souls, awakening to their Divine Destiny and inherent divinity. At this time, humanity is experiencing what we have termed the Time of Testing. The Time of Testing is not unlike a Time of Transition; however, it is a time where we will see the compacting of time itself, a period where humanity will begin to understand the choices that are presented in front of them and at what direction the Earth will then continue in its own evolution and sojourn.

Today, we will talk about the United States, some of the changes that will happen in Canada, and some of the changes that will happen in Central and South America. Altogether these are known as the Americas. Beloved El Morya and Beloved Kuthumi have come forward to also offer information about Europe and Africa. Beloved Mother Mary has come forward to offer information about the incoming pouring of the new vibration, the new souls that are known as the Seventh Manu, often called in the Earth Plane and Planet, the Indigo Children or the New Children.

## HIGHER VIBRATION OF LIGHT

All of these factors are playing a very critical and important role in moving the Earth into a higher vibration and frequency of light. The Golden City material will also be shared by Beloved Saint Germain, as he has always held this in his intention, that humanity would have a choice during the Time of great Change, that there would be an opportunity to use this as a platform for spiritual evolution and growth.

We will first start with prophecies for the United States. Beloved Saint Germain will take the podium.

## A REVIEW WITH SAINT GERMAIN

Greetings Beloved chelas in that mighty Violet Ray and Fire. I AM Saint Germain. I've spoken so many times about the Prophecies of Change for the United States. It is first important to understand that why I speak of these prophecies, I will not assign a timeline to them. See them only as events that may or may not occur. They are given primarily as guidelines for you, so adjustments and changes in consciousness can be your choice and call for action.

## WASHINGTON STATE

*I'm now observing a finger that is going down the coastline of Washington State.*

The prophecies for these areas stay somewhat intact and the same. You will see that there will be volcanic explosions in this area, starting first with Mount Baker and then proceeding onward to the Grand Chain. When I refer to this Grand Chain, I am speaking of Mount Rainier onward to Mount Hood. These form within themselves a triangular event, which possibly proceeds into other mountain volcanoes. However, it is important in terms of looking at the eruption of this chain, to keep your eye upon Mount Baker, for it serves as a guardian post to alert one first as to what could occur within the future.

*He is now moving on down.*

A series of islands were the result of the global warming. This is what remains now of the Puget Sound area.

*He is showing a series of islands where Seattle once was. He is showing a large island that is the Olympic Peninsula.*

As you will see, a small bay forms on the Washington Central Coast. This forms a smaller peninsula of land which will later erode away.

*He is now showing a fault line that moves from Vancouver Island near Victoria underneath, drawing a line directly to Vancouver near Portland, Oregon.*

This is an important fault to know and to understand, for within the Times of Changes, especially during and after the global warming, we will see an activation of this fault line. This will bring a further activation of fault lines that exist within the triangle area, as I have earlier identified, in the area of Ellensburg, Washington. Refer to the past prophecies if you wish to obtain further insight into this information.

## THE UNDERGROUND SEA

*He's showing another bay that occurs through the triangular area.*

This is the bay of underground water of Oregon. As I've explained before, there is a complete underground sea that exists underneath Oregon and parts of Washington State. As we enter into the Times of Changes, we will see a constant eroding and shake up of these lands which eventually will sink the areas of Washington and Oregon altogether.

A pyramid of land, you see, remains. When I speak of the sacred pyramid, I'm speaking of the mountain that is known as Mount Shasta. This, you see Dear ones, Dear hearts, was in another time the location of a very sacred city, which existed and held consciousness very much in the same way that Shamballa once held this consciousness for Beloved Babajeran, Mother Earth. This comes from another time period, but because of this great and mighty service that was brought forward from that time period, this mountain now stays intact and it will throughout all global changes.

## ON FACING FEARS AND THE FUTURE

I must remind you Dear ones, Dear hearts, to use the Violet Flame if you feel fear of any of these events. You must understand that these events are being brought forward and shown to you so that a conscious awareness of them would allow you to make empowering choices now. It is a Time of Choice, Dear ones, Dear hearts, a time where, within your own heart, as it has been stated so many times before, you can redirect the course of such events. However, it is important to not keep our heads in the sand, is it not Dear ones, Dear hearts? We must face what is in front of us and make the appropriate choices.

Before I proceed into the state of California, do you have questions?

Response: "No, I do not. Please proceed."

As you see Dear ones, the coastline as it now appears moves into the state of Idaho and into some sections of Utah. However, as you well know, some of this is also prophesied to disappear as we enter into the Times of Changes. As you know, the Times of Changes can last anywhere between fifty years to 250 years and we may even see them continually for 2,000 years.

## THE PLUMED SERPENT

As you well understand, the Cooperation Mountains are destined to make their appearance within the 200th year of the Times of Changes. This performs a great advantage for the people of the United States, for it produces a new energy which erupts, you see, throughout all of North America. It creates a new form of telepathy that will exist between the people of the United States and South America. It creates an anchoring, if you will, of a greater energy, to bring about a unity of consciousness between the people of both of these continents. They will unite again, as they were in another time as the I AM Race, Ameru, as you may remember it.

This is a symbol of the plumed serpent, as she arose at one time in greater glory, and it is the destiny of these people that they will rise again into a new understanding and bring about a celebration of this higher consciousness. It exists, not only of Unana, but exists of the mighty Golden Flame and as a tribute to the Golden Age of Kali Yuga.

These mountains will extend on down into parts of Mexico, but they will primarily be felt within Central America, within the Islands of Cuba, forming, as I have stated before, a great freshwater lake. And the mountains will be felt all into South America to the final tip. This will bring about a new type of energy which will usher in the New Times and a new consciousness.

## CHANGES IN CALIFORNIA

As I continue into the state of California, it is true that a series of quakes will be involved in the overall disappearance of these lands, but it is also important to understand that global warming will play one of the greater roles in the flooding of the inland land of California. It is true that your government has information regarding this series of events and this is not to be taken lightly. It is to be taken with great sincerity and also to be considered as your movement into prayer and intention, which, as I have always stated, is the highest form of ceremony.

As we have shown in the Six-Map Scenario, many of these lands will continue into their erosion into the Grand Canyon, and you will see a new coastline that will evolve into the state of Arizona and into some areas of even Texas. It is important to understand the erosion of the Baja Peninsula and the effect that this will have on the migrations of people, the migrations moving first through Arizona and New Mexico. Into New Mexico, we'll see the underground caverns and their susceptibility to explosion. But it is also important to understand that during the global warming that we will see many forest fires that will erupt throughout all of the Southwest and much of Southern California. This too will cause a great migration, many people leaving these lands into Arizona, Utah, and Colorado.

It is important always to keep your consciousness fixed upon the Law of the Greatest and the Highest Good, if you wish to perform any type of adjustment to the prophecies that you hear. This is the ideal purpose for the Golden Cities, as they have been brought forward to bring that perfect inter-action between Earth and spiritual law. That is why we have identified the Stars as the best location for prayer, medita-tion, and ceremonies. This is a place where Mother Earth's ears are open and can hear the request of those who are spon-sored during this Time of Testing. There is a great response, as I have identified so many times before, of the unique reciprocity that exists between each Star of every Golden City upon the planet. And I assure you Dear ones, Dear hearts, as the Ascended Master energy is focused into each of these Stars, that all are activated in their glory and intent. It is true that each comes into a physical activation in a two-year incre-ment, but it is important to understand that all are activated in terms of their ability to receive, know, and understand the important spiritual essence.

Before I proceed, are there questions?

## YELLOWSTONE CALDERA

Question: "Yes, I have a question about the Cooperation Mountains. In the area of Yellowstone, evidently the lake has a volcano forming in it. Could you give some explanation of that?"

Indeed, it has a link to the first three volcanoes, as I have mentioned before. If one is to keep their eye upon Mount Baker, they will notice a difference on a daily basis in its re-lationship to Yellowstone. In terms of probability, it is a high chance that this will enter into eruption, for this serves as one of the central causes for the beginning of the development of the Cooperation Mountains. See this change as a birth change into the Age of Cooperation. Know and trust that the Golden Age is well within its birthing order. To hold back a change is to hold back the birth of a wondrous new soul who can give much to the Earth Plane and Planet.

Dear ones, proceed without fear and know that the New Times await.

## COOPERATION AND COMPASSION

Question: "You have brought up an interesting point. To hold back an Earth Change is to stop the birth of a new soul. Could you explain that?"

The changes will also coincidentally birth a new Time of Cooperation. For you see Dear ones, Dear hearts, as recent events have been illustrated upon the Earth Plane and Planet, until the United States can understand the grief of other nations, compassion will not be built among the hearts of humanity.

Question: "I see. So it is the soul of compassion you're referring to?"

This is the Heart of the Dove. The Heart of the Dove is born of compassion, of love for one another as Brothers and Sisters and the human condition itself. As I've stated, the Heart of the

Dove is one of the finest spiritual areas that one may travel to, to open the heart of compassion within at an individual level, and great leaps of spiritual growth can occur there. But this is also one of the greatest locations to affect world peace and to bring about a soothing and calming effect to enflamed world conditions.

The Heart of the Dove has been given as a great gift to humanity by Avatar Master Babaji. This was his request and his input for this Time of Change.

Response: "I understand. I have no questions at this point. Please proceed."

## MISSISSIPPI AND MISSOURI RIVERS

The Mississippi and the Missouri Rivers and their tributaries, as you all know within the time of global warming, will also nearly split the nation in two. This has been carefully illustrated within the Six-Map Scenario. This is a prophecy that illustrates the weeping of Mother Earth and the opening of compassion. For again, is it not the open heart that cries the open tears and bleeds upon the seed, that knows then the price of compassion? As it has always been stated in these spiritual teachings, that until the eyes can see and the ears can hear, compassion is only a belief. When one truly understands the glory and the beauty of the human condition, then one is ready to take up the cross of compassion. This was clearly illustrated in the life of Brother Jesus, as we know him as Sananda. It is through compassion that we open to a new vibration and a new understanding.


## GLOBAL WARMING AND CLIMATE CHANGE

This global warming, you see, will change forever the face of the state of Texas, opening up cities such as Houston and San Antonio to the waters of the ocean. Also, alongside the coastline will be the beautiful bay of the Golden Sun, as brought through Mother Mary. We will see the coastline now changing and expanding, going in at inland levels up to 120 miles in places.

The East Coast Dear ones, Dear hearts, as it has already been stated by your government, will see a change in climate. This will bring about great changes in cities such as Washington, D.C., New York City, also Philadelphia, and other cities that are located in New Jersey, Delaware, Rhode Island, and Massachusetts.

The seesawing of seasons, as it was spoken of in the Six-Map Scenario, will be illustrated quite clearly and this will bring about a difference within the oceanic currents. This is also well known and documented by your scientific community. This will bring about a series of migrations of many people, fleeing these lands and moving to the inland lands of Ohio, alongside some areas of Indiana and Illinois. This will bring about the great awakening of Malton, for indeed this was always her purpose.

And now, unless there are further questions, I would like to turn the discussion over to Brother Kuthumi.

Response: "There are no further questions."

## THE SONG OF MALTON

Greetings stewards of the plan. I AM Kuthumi of the Golden and Ruby Ray. I request permission to come forward.

Response: "Please, Kuthumi, you are most welcome. Come forward."

There is a song that is sung in Malton. It is the sweet song of nature. It is the song of leaves. It is the song of the grass. It is the song of flowers and birds and trees. It is the balance of nature, the balance of all things as they exist on this Earth. Malton exists for this great love and aligns itself to the Golden City of Denasha. This, long in its planning, is of no mistake for humanity. Malton, you see, will have some of the brightest communities of the Earth and the balance of the Earth. You will see communities that will erupt within this Golden City that will be more modeled after the times of the Celtic tradition.

There will also be religious communities, almost mirroring those of monasteries. But there will also be many new gardens and croplands that will be used to feed many people during the Times of great Changes. It is true, that it may be difficult at times to bring the proper transportation forward because of the shutdown of so many of the systems. But new ideas in agriculture will be developed in this Golden City, as the co-operation of all the kingdoms will ensue. We will see here the cooperation of all Elemental Life Forces, the cooperation of gnomes and kingdoms of fairies, the cooperation of the Mineral Kingdom, the Plant Kingdom, and the Animal Kingdom.

This is a Golden City of great fruition. It is true that many of the people of Washington, D.C. and New York will flee to these lands and these communities will set forward a new consciousness. Malton will always be known as a city of balance, for indeed this is the destiny of this land. There will be some flooding that will come from the draining of Lake Michigan into the lands to the northwest. Many of these communities will establish themselves on the southern and eastern sides of the Malton Golden City. This Dear ones, Brothers and Sisters of mine, will have a great influence over the Earth. Questions?

Question: "Yes. My only question is will you be returning more frequently?"

My work has been one of preparing balance for the Earth. I have been working diligently within the Ring of Fire. I will return at your request.

Question: "I will need to have you return at the appropriate time when we are planning the communities for Malton. Will you be available for this?"

It would be my honor to serve.

Response: "It would be a great blessing to see you again."

*He is now backing away. Saint Germain is coming forward.*

## THE EAST COAST MIGRATIONS

As Beloved Brother Kuthumi has explained Dear ones, Dear hearts, this will be a location of many migrations of the East Coast. There will be a cooling that will extend first from Canada down into Maine and into Massachusetts, New Hampshire, and Vermont. You will see a chilling effect that will happen within the waters. This of course starts as the seesawing of the seasons. We will see snow that will fall in July and warm and hot muggy days in December. We will see an extension of seasons. An even greater balance can come forward for the Earth through your prayers in the Star of Malton. For those who wish to serve the Earth in this matter, this is the greatest location to state your prayer and intent.

Great winds are scheduled to hit the East Coast. These winds are the winds of change, essential winds to bring about the change in consciousness. This change, you see Dear ones, is nothing to be feared at all, as it brings an alchemizing effect. It settles across the lands of all of America. It is true, there can be death and destruction through such terrible global super storms, but it is also important to understand, that as many souls leave and move into the higher dimensions, they will know and understand the New Times. They will later partake of this in future embodiments upon these beloved lands of I AM America. Many of them know and understand at this level of consciousness, the greater purification and how it works together as ONE consciousness, in the same way as we all stand today here on this podium.

*He's now lighting a candle.*

I light this candle as a symbol of the Light of God that Never, Never Faileth. Dear ones, Dear hearts, as we talk of such changes, it is important to keep your focus upon the mighty Light of God that dwells within you and is expressed everyday through your thought, your feeling, and your action. All life, as you know upon the Earth Plane and Planet, is purposeful. Keep your focus always upon the Violet Flame and know within the mighty sound of HU, a one vibration comes forward for all of mankind. It is no mistake that the human is one of the highest forms of life that has yet to walk upon the Earth, raising from a consciousness of the animal now into the Divine God Being. Questions?

Question: "The human, are you referring to a more developed sense of who we are?"

A SHIFT OF LIGHT

Not only a more developed sense, but a longer lifespan to match the longer periods of light. This was one of the prophecies of Canada, on the plateau of the Rising Sun. This will be one of the first locations where the Earth will experience the continuous light. It will be a flooding of light which will come to the planet to lift it from the changes, to know, see, and understand the great shift in consciousness that has occurred through such purification. As I have stated so many times before, all elements will be involved in the great purification of the Earth, not only earth, but water, fire, and wind will all come together to give their service to lift the human into a greater state of knowledge and to a greater consciousness.

Question: "I understand. So we are yet to evolve to the human state?"

You are within the human state, the Unfed Flame of Love, Wisdom, and Power is planted within the heart, the sacred chamber. But know this Dear one, the human has yet to be fully actualized, to be fully expressed in its higher form. There were times, yes of course upon the Earth, where the soul of the human reached to great heights in understanding, but the evolution of the human body was yet to be understood in its fullness. The Golden Age of Kali Yuga will bring this forward into a greater understanding. And beyond the Age of Cooperation, we will enter into the Time of Transportation, an age where one will begin to understand time travel and moving between the dimensions.

Now, unless if there are further questions, I will proceed with information for Canada.

Response: "Please proceed."

## CHANGES IN CANADA

The lands of Canada are lands of Co-creation. These are lands that within their Alchemy hold the destiny for the human. For you see Dear ones, it is true that the human is indeed a Creator, a Co-creator, or as you laughingly call it, a Creator in training. Each of the Golden Cities of Canada will express this creativity in some form or another and many souls that reincarnate upon the Earth in the Golden Age will come to these Golden Cities, where they will openly practice their more astute abilities of Co-creation.

Canada, during the changes, will see many of the lands melting within the Northern Slope. We will see many lands of the west coast go under water during massive earthquakes, flooding, and volcanic eruptions. But it is also important to know and understand the great destiny of this land, for it holds the flame of true Creatorship.

You see, it is the land that is closest to the North Pole and so it holds within it a more masculine energy and the great draw of the breath [Editor's Note: Entering the North Pole and exiting the South Pole]. This great creativity is destined then to be taught all over the world for the unfoldment of the true HU-man . . . the HU-man with the God spark . . . the HU-man who creates as God creates . . . the HU-man who is self-actualized. Each of these Golden Cities will serve in one aspect or another for the Co-creation process.

Pashacino will serve through the scientific development of Co-creatorship and it is there that many new classes will be taught upon levels of Co-creation and the unfoldment of the human spirit. There will be great studies and research that will come from this particular Golden City Vortex because of this greater influence.

There may be, during the Times of Changes, fires that will erupt in some of the forests of British Columbia; but know this, that in this purification process, a greater energy is also expressing itself and allowing for the new souls to come forward which will grace these lands. Questions?

Response: "I have no questions at this time."

## AFTER THE CHANGES

Eabra, extending somewhat into the lands of Alaska, so it is treated as a mutual Golden City between Canada and the United States, is brought forward for the creative aspect of uniting the feminine and masculine energies within a person. This, at a spiritual level, allows for a greater expression of the unity of consciousness and the understanding that the human form is not as limited as one may think it to be. There I serve with my Beloved Portia, who stands for equality, balance, and justice. This is an important principle as we move into the Age of Cooperation.

There will come a time period after the changes where the Earth will move back into balance again. It is important to know this and trust in this mighty Law of Balance. Eabra will hold this energy, for this prophecy to be seen with great and depth of clarity.

As we move into the lands of Canada, the energies from Malton will emit a finer energy, which will have a great effect upon the interior land of Canada and we will see the planting of many new types of crops, where hybrid seeds will be developed to bring greater food stuffs for the people of the planet during the New Times. A new type of crop will be developed there which will be very, very high in vibration. The eating of this type of grain will assist the opening of the pituitary and pineal glands and bring about a greater opening of the Third Eye and knowledge of the true Divine Inheritor. It functions much as the white gold functions. In the beginning it will be known as a Food of the Gods but it is a grain that has been able to properly process the monatomic elements within the plant substance itself. This will come after the full development of Malton and will express itself in the Song of God of Uverno. Questions?

Response: "I would prefer that we continued on and I'll hold my questions until the end."

*He is now stepping back and Mother Mary is coming forward.*

Greetings children, stewards of the Violet Flame and the Golden Flame, of which I cradle and hold. I AM Mary. I ask permission to enter.

Response: "Please come forward. You are most welcome."

## LANDS OF THE GOLDEN SUN

Within the lands of the Golden Sun I come. As I have spoken before in the prophecies of the water, the salinity of the seas will change near Texas and onward into South America. It is to this change that many weather patterns then change within Central and South America. As it has always been stated so many times, much of these lands will remain protected. There will be changes naturally of course within the Amazon region but this is also an evolutionary process. Many of the trees of the Amazon forest are moving above in their collective consciousness and some will take embodiment as nature spirits, which will be seen clearly and freely in the Golden Age in the New Times to come.

There will be a great interaction in South America between the Deva and the Nature Kingdoms and the human. It will be seen as a natural course of life and those who wish to understand this communion with the Earth through the nature spirits may do so through their travels to the Three Sisters. I refer to them as the three beautiful Golden City Vortices of South America. Of course, there will be some flooding that will occur to many of the sea coastlines of South America. There will also be changes to the western coastline, this brought about through the tectonic shifts that are linked to California, Washington, and Oregon States, and onward to Vancouver and British Columbia.

## MARY AND THE NEW CHILDREN

But know, as Beloved Brother Saint Germain has stated, these changes bring about a New Time. I rock this cradle of humanity. I hold it close to my heart, for I know that while this New Time comes and that there is fear within of losing your life, know that life is lost only at a physical level and it moves on into its immortal life.

Many new souls will come within the Swaddling Cloth. These are children of my heart. Many of them have never incarnated before upon the Earth Plane and Planet and they will have this closer connection to Mother Earth and the nature and the deva spirits. A few are also scattering in incarnations across the United States and to the lands of Canada, but the largest focus and group of them will be born into the Swaddling Cloth. This will allow for a new vibration to enter the Earth, where a sensitivity to the Earth will be developed and a balance then can be achieved for the Golden Age of Kali Yuga.

It is important for those who wish to sponsor the children of the new Manu (we call them children of the Seventh Ray, the Indigo Children, the New Children), to enter into meditation everyday at 6 AM from their time zone. Focus only upon this one mantra.

Beloved beings of the Seventh Manu,
Come forth and bring your enlightenment and your
upliftment for humanity.
So Be It.

Response: "So Be It."

It is a simple prayer. It is a rosary that can be repeated, if you wish. It is a mantra that can be stated, if you wish. It is a prayer that can be given, if you wish. It is an intent that can be held within your heart, if you wish.

These new children who come forward have an increased telepathic ability. They come from galaxies far away, some as far as the Dahl Universe. At one time, a few of them incarnated upon the Earth Plane and Planet and they are recorded in your Greek mythology. So, if one would like to study about these new children who are coming to bring such upliftment to the Earth, that gives some historical reference. A few came before for Atlantis and a few before for Lemuria, but by and large, most of these children are of a pure and more pristine higher vibration. Their sole purpose is to uplift the planet at this time, to bring about a new culture and a new energy which will lift the Earth into the shining Star of Freedom.

The consciousness of Unana is implanted within them. Within their heart is an additional flame. It is the White Flame, which represents purity and freedom of expression. The incarnation of these great souls will secure peace for many, many, many generations upon the Earth Plane and Planet. Questions?

Response: "Thank you very much for coming. We would like to enjoy your presence more frequently. You have been a great mother."

I shall withdraw.

*Saint Germain is coming forward.*

Dear chelas, I shall end this discourse for the channel tires. I realize I have additional information from Beloved El Morya and Kuthumi for Europe and Africa but if you so choose that may be given later today or at the appointed time

Response: "As you wish. I hope that you all return soon. Thank you."

Om Manaya Pitaya, Hitaka.

May the Light of God Never Fail.
May the Light of Unana now be lit among
the hearts of humanity.
So Be It.

Response: "So Be It."

# Global Warming Update: Europe and Africa

*"There are seventeen Golden City Vortices per map,
each of them carrying through their sacred geometry
and numerology, an intention of golden light to flood the Earth."*
- THE PROPHETS FOR THE MAP OF EXCHANGES

Greetings Beloved chelas. I AM Saint Germain and I stream forth on that mighty Violet Ray of Mercy, Compassion, and Forgiveness. As usual Dear hearts, I ask permission to come forward.

Response: "Please Saint Germain, come forward. You are most welcome."

Before I proceed, let me perform another energetic adjustment of the room.

*There are many Masters entering now with Saint Germain; Lord Sananda, Mother Mary, Beloved El Morya, Kuthumi, and another Master is coming in who will be introduced. Sananda is coming forward to the lectern.*

Greetings Dear Brothers and Sisters of the Golden Flame. I AM Sananda. Do I have permission to enter your energy fields?

Response: "You most certainly do. Come forward. You are welcome."

Let us now continue with our work for the world. When I call this world work, I say this with all compassion and all love for all of humanity. This message and this work is being given with great love. You are indeed moving in a Time of Transition, a Time of Testing; yet also, it is a Time of Cooperation. The great changes that are about to come to the Earth Plane and Planet will birth this period of cooperation for humanity. It will bring forward a Golden Age, a New Time, for humanity will grow upon the Earth Plane and Planet, not only at a level of soul growth, but will also grow in their understanding of the Earth environment itself.

SOULS OF THE NEW EARTH

Many new souls will be coming to the Earth Plane and Planet in this 7,000 to 8,000 year period. Many will come to join the round of birth and learning and many will come to experience, for the first time, the Earth Plane and Planet, to assist Beloved Babajeran, the Earth Mother herself in her own evolution and growth experience.

Alongside this is a great opportunity for many souls to balance lifetimes after lifetimes of karmic imbalances. It will also provide the necessary growth for good karma and dharma, or purpose of the soul. It is a blessed time indeed. As you see Dear ones, Dear hearts, there are many other Master Teachers and spiritual advisors who are present for this lesson today. Of particular importance is Beloved El Morya and Brother Kuthumi. They are coming forth to hold a focus for Europe and the lands of Africa. I will now turn over to Beloved El Morya.

*El Morya is stepping forward. He's wearing a long blue robe.*

Greetings stalwart chelas of the Blue Flame. I AM El Morya. I request permission to come forward.

Response: "Please El Morya, come forward. You are most welcome. "

I would also like to add that Lady Nada had intended to come forward this day but Brother Kuthumi is carrying the mantle of her consciousness for this lesson today. And at this moment Brother Kuthumi will join me and we shall merge our consciousness as ONE, also with the mantle of consciousness of Lady Nada, to give this information for the Map of Exchanges. Do we all have permission?

Response: "You all have permission and Lady Nada can come at anytime she so chooses. You are all welcome."

*They are all now merging their energy as one golden light. This force begins to speak.*

Greetings in the Flame of Unana. It is the consciousness of Unana that we speak today. Unana comes forward as one of the mighty eight principles that will serve the Age of Cooperation. Present alongside us, as our merged consciousness and united as one energy system, is Lord Macaw. As you know and understand, Lord Macaw was the Lord of the last World, that is, the world as you knew it prior to your incarnations into this world, the world of the Sixth Manu. He served that world of the Fifth Manu.

## THE ACCELERATION OF LIGHT

Many of you carried out your soul's sojourn during that time as well, learning and growing through the schoolroom we know as Earth. As we have taught before, Earth is not the highest of the dimensions or lokas of experience, but it is not the lowest as well. In the times that are coming, the Time of great Change, a Time of Cooperation, there will be an acceleration of the energies of the Earth. Much of this acceleration is occurring through the Golden City Vortices. And it is of no mistake that there are seventeen Golden City Vortices per map, each of them carrying out, through their sacred geometry and numerology, an intention of golden light to flood the Earth. This will bring about a higher vibration. This vibration, in its timing and intention, will lead each and every individual soul into a higher understanding of choice and how choice creates experiences. Experiences, raising in vibration, lead the soul, then ready, to enjoy a heightened state of consciousness.

## THE SECOND SUN

The Earth in its overall journey then will increase in energy and vibration. A second Sun will reveal itself and the dualistic Sun system will then allow a new dimension to erupt in full force. This is a new dimension, brought about in harmony to the Divine Plan and all other lokas and dimensions of experience. This will cause a type of overlapping between Third, Fourth, and Fifth Dimensional states of consciousness. All of these dimensions simultaneously will be discernable and easy to know and understand. There will be many souls who will be incarnating during this Age of Cooperation who will embody Third, Fourth, and Fifth Dimensional experiences simultaneously. Some of these souls will take on an appearance of a parallel life. However, they will be linked in this holy trinity as such, carrying forward their Divine Plan and their understanding of the Christhood and its ability to bring a greater unity to the self.

Of course there will be, as I have mentioned, the souls that will be incoming during this Time of great Change upon the Earth Plane and Planet, to experience the changes themselves. This will allow a transmutation effect for them of many, many lifetimes. Some will come in for a short amount of time and then leave the planet and go off to other planetary systems which will serve their evolutionary process better. But this opportunity allows them to bring forward a balance of their lifestreams and their choices. There are many changes that will occur geophysically to the planet in the Times of Changes. Of course I have focused and outlined for you the changes that will be happening to humanity, but there are also changes that will simultaneously happen to mirror such an effect on the Earth itself.

## MELTING ICE

Humanity will see, know, and experience an overall global warming. This has been suggested and prophesied before. There will also be, through this overall global melting of ice caps, a flooding that will occur throughout Europe. This of course will change the face of Europe forever. For this reason Lord Macaw has come forward. I will allow him now to speak.

*The force is stepping back.*

## LORD MACAW AND THE ANCIENT EARTH

Greetings chelas and students. I AM Lord Macaw. I serve upon the Sixth and Golden Ray. I come forward now in service of the Golden Ray. Do I have permission to speak?

Response: "You do have permission to speak and to come forward."

You have known me before, Dear students, as a Keeper of the Map of the Ancients. It is important to understand the Map of the Ancients when you're examining the Map of Exchanges, for some will not understand why so much of this land is being brought for a rest. Do you remember Dear ones, how I showed and drew for you the bridge that is now a part of the lands agreement? [Editor's Note: "The Map of the Ancients" and its provenance is featured in "Divine Destiny."]

Response: "Yes, I do remember that."

This land bridge, you see, at one time existed even prior before the days of Atlantis. This land bridge was once a beautiful tropical forest and within it, many souls incarnated and enjoyed the peace and pleasure of worldly life upon the Earth. This was in a time of greater light upon the Earth and in some instances, the souls encased themselves in globes of light, much as the unity consciousness of El Morya, Kuthumi, and Lady Nada now present to you. From time to time, they would take on the various forms of the animals that were in this beautiful land, the form of a tiger, the form of a bird, even the form of fishes, as it was necessary to experience the Earth Plane and Planet in vibration and energy. This legacy was brought through many of the myths onto the people of Europe. With the sinking of the continent of Atlantis, a darkness fell upon the planet and a great tsunami erupted.

Before this, there had been other sinkings of land and eventually the land bridge, which held the tropical paradise, eroded away and iced over as oceanic currents changed and shifted to accommodate the shifting change and loss of light into the Time of Kali. Yet the teachings were kept in a purity and clarity within the heart of the tribal lords and these teachings were carried throughout the lands of Europe, kept, as what would appear to historians today, in a more pagan or prehistoric understanding. Yet these teachings have kept their depths and have kept their clarity.

KALI YUGA AND THE FORGETTING

This brought about a linkage through bloodlines, understanding the close relationship of the globe of light onward
into the genetic seed. These various tribes began to place an
emphasis upon the relationship of one another through blood
and thus became each tribe established unto each land. And
yet the ones who carried the knowledge within knew that all
were connected as ONE to the holy Light of Unana. But as the
light receded and receded from the Suns, this too brought
about a dark forgetting.

Prior to this, there raised great Golden Cities that served the
Earth well. Many of the myths, as you have heard of Camelot
and Avalon, are not myths at all, but yet contain and know
of the great cities of light that once existed in these areas of
Europe. There were also cities which existed in areas that are
now known as Hungary, in areas that are now known as Germany, in areas that are now known as Austria, and areas that
are now known as Slavic Nations. All of these held cities that
not only contained these original teachings from the tropical
land bridge, but also brought forth spiritual growth and development for those who chose to retain the knowledge.

However, as time continued, as it does in all things, and with
the sinking of Atlantis, the doors of knowledge were shut and
the energies from the land retreated back into their primal
state of elemental and devic qualities. I shall now step back.

*The globe of light comprised of El Morya, Kuthumi, and Lady Nada is
coming forward.*

FEMININE ENERGY AND AWAKENING TO THE ONE

As it has been stated Dear ones, these lands then will be given a rest. That is not to say that the energies of the seventeen Golden City Vortices will not be built upon the Map of Exchanges, for indeed it shall be so. It is a Time of Awakening of the feminine energies within the Map of Exchanges and in such a way, South America has retained more land mass and Africa shall retain more land mass, which will allow for an opening of feminine energy current to circulate within this Map of Exchanges in the Earth Changes and times to come.

We will see many of the European cities underwater, such as Rome, such as London, such as Paris. We will also see a shaking of the land which will extend from the Scandinavian nations, a fault line that extends on into areas of Germany and south on into Spain. New lands will appear off of Spain, as this has always been prophesied, and this will represent a new energy that will birth forth Europe and a Map of Exchanges.

The new souls, which will be born into the Golden City Vortices of these areas, will be reincarnated souls from the tropical land bridge. As it has always been stated to you by Master Saint Germain, there is no mistake ever, ever. There is a group right now upon the Earth Plane and Planet within Europe that is working diligently towards a united coalition of Europe. These too are the reincarnated souls who once enjoyed the tropical bliss and are coming forward to address the state of the human condition and the time of lesser light and will raise the energy of Europe into a finer glory and understanding.

Europe has long been divided, nation by nation, and yet they do express, know, and understand the unity of which they are all born. This is one of the purposes of the changes which will unite Europe as ONE. It too then shall represent the Age of Cooperation. The changes as they happen will accelerate this political, social, and cultural current as it moves along the nations of Europe. Questions?

Question: "Is this change basically one of compassion, unification, and acknowledgment of the planet and all the peoples?"

Indeed, it will also allow for a higher and finer vibration and the returning of the Fifth Manu to these lands where they once lived. For some time, the lands will be given a rest, some of the lands under ice, some of the lands under water. But in the middle of the Golden Age of Kali Yuga, after the climate has adjusted itself, these lands will thaw and return again to the tropical glory where once they were in another time. This overall heightening of vibration of the Earth will serve all. [Editor's Note: To learn more about Kali Yuga and the Golden Age see, "The Ever Present Now."]

Response: "I see."

The days of the monarchy were meant for the time where it was experienced. Now the leadership of these lands will come under a greater understanding of the needs of the HU-man, the God-man, who receives sustenance from the source of his God-being, the monarch and king of all, the Mighty I AM.

## CONTINUED TURMOIL IN THE MIDDLE EAST

Within the area of the Middle East, there is much turmoil and at this time, we will not release information, for it is yet still to be determined by the outcome within the next ten years. However, the choices that humanity is now making are perilous and deadly indeed. Everyday, call upon harmony, peace, and hope for these lands. Everyday, call upon a Divine Intervention of each spiritual and Master Teacher to come forward with the focus of their energy of light and sound to bring forth harmonious solutions.

## INCOMING SOULS

It is important to understand within the overall global warming that many of the coastlines will be reduced for up to 100 to 120 miles inland. This is of no mistake. This will promote a greater unity among the cause for humanity and Africa itself; as you've seen, it holds an energy like the Motherland of South America. Many of the incoming souls who will later incarnate in the tropical lands of Europe will begin their incarnation process there. Many of the new plants and animals of the Earth, who are destined to come forward at this time to raise the vibrational frequency, will come forward in the Infinite Garden of Gandawan. It is indeed a paradise. One who does incarnate in this area will again feel a connection to the Earth in beauty and in glory. Questions?

Response: "I have no questions at this time."

## GOLDEN CITIES: CALIBRATION OF NEW ENERGY

The energies upon the Earth, which are shifting and changing through each of the Golden City Vortices, can be utilized today for those who wish to understand them. Though subtle in their overtone, they create a solid foundation within the core, being a connection to the sacred chamber of the heart and a connection within the Star of one's own being and focus of purpose. We shall withdraw our energies.

*They are now separating their energies from one another. Sananda is coming forward.*

As usual Dear chelas, students, stewards of mine, send this message to the Earth with love, as I have always stated; for love is truly the one energy that can change any and all circumstance and situation. Dear Sisters and Brothers, heal your hearts as ONE within the energy of Unana. Heal your minds as ONE within the energy of love for one another. Come together as ONE into the Time of Cooperation, beyond the Time of Testing, beyond the Time of tumultuous Change.

I offer you all the Cup, this Holy Grail, as a field of neutrality, which comes forward to offer you a new vibration, a new energy, and a New Time. Hitaka.

Response: "Hitaka."

*He's stepping back. Saint Germain is coming forward.*

Dear students, chelas of mine, I AM Saint Germain. And now if there are questions, I will answer. Proceed.

A DECREE FOR THE "ONE"

Question: "Thank you. Regarding Europe and Africa, is there a decree that can be said that will help to efficiently move that energy into cooperation and harmony, into the ONE?"

I AM the light of cooperation.
Blaze forth the Golden Ray from the Heart of Unana
And light within the heart of humanity,
a golden time to come.
So Be It.

Response: "So Be It. This decree seems as though it would work for all parts of the world."

All work that I give Dear ones, Dear hearts, the decrees that are mantras that I give, are designed to help all as Brothers and Sisters of mine. My work comes forward for all of humanity. It comes forward to raise all into the birth and glory of the New Times. But most importantly, my work comes forward to free you . . . to free you from the bonds of limited thoughts . . . to free you from avarice . . . to free you from lack . . . to free you from disharmony.

As I've always stated Dear ones Dear hearts, it is not my intention to improve the food and water within the prison that is self created. As Dear Sananda has often said, "I offer you that most refreshing drink. Come and sup with me Brother, Sister. Come and sit. The table is ready. The fires are lit. Let us celebrate. We are as ONE."

Response: "And I will be there every day to sup with you all and I ask for that freedom."

It is yours but only for the asking, as now you know the law.

Response: "Then I ask to be free and to free all of humanity, all peoples of the world."

With effort and energy, it is achieved. With love indeed it is sealed.

Response: "So Be It."

Hitaka.

Response: "Hitaka."

I shall now take my leave from your frequency and will return upon your request.

Response: "Thank you."

# Epilogue

In 1992 we published the first version of *New World Atlas, Volume One*, that would later become Book One of the *New World Wisdom Series*. Since that time, we have seen many Earth Changes, and gratefully, nothing like what we originally thought could be possible. It is important, however, to remember that while the most extreme changes have yet to occur, that some of the events prophesied and explained by the Spiritual Teachers have transpired and many are occurring now, such as global warming, climate change, and extreme weather. Climate scientists point the finger at trapped heat radiating from our Earth en route to space, held by the long-lived gases of water vapor (clouds and precipitation), carbon dioxide (mostly caused by the burning of fossil fuels), nitrous oxide (caused by certain agricultural practices), and chlorofluorocarbons (gases from refrigerants and aerosols). Some politicians argue that the Earth is experiencing a natural warming trend that may be explained by our Sun's irradiance—the energy emitted by the Sun. The holistic perspective of the Spiritual Teachers of the *I AM America* material does not point fingers of blame, but understands the esoteric law of how human consciousness plays a pivotal role in creation, both individually and globally. A distillation of this philosophy affirms that, "Group consciousness creates climate." From this notion, we can understand that our individual consciousness is not a cause, but rather results in stagnation and destruction of the whole when we choose to do nothing to change our individual movements to affect the dance of group consciousness.

This Co-creative viewpoint, while seemingly simplistic, is not. There are some lightworkers that believe that the Earth Changes probabilities have been entirely transmuted through positive thinking and consciousness shift, and that the prophecies are no longer valid. I wholeheartedly agree that both of these qualities are tremendously helpful, both personally and collectively, however I find this viewpoint naive. First, the length of this period of tremendous change is not carved in stone. According to the Spiritual Teachers, it could be as short as seven years or as long as seven hundred. At times it may seem that this cycle is passive and other times strong and forceful. The mature understanding is that prophecy is likened to a constant, perpetual warning, and that we hone our spiritual development and insight so we are continuously open, awake, astute, and aware during this important *Time of Change*. In straightforward terms, Earth's cautionary yellow light is continuously blinking.

The reality is that change is upon us, and no amount of fairy dust will alter this fact. Since the late '80s we have witnessed tremendous changes in our global social structures and economies. Socially we enjoy technological connection, but we often feel even more separate and alone. During the Great Recession, as worldwide currencies lost value, the cost of housing swelled, spiked, and then collapsed, and this has become an insidious pattern. The volatility of this market further bred economic inequality, with eight percent of the world's population holding 82 percent of our global wealth. Today our culture is undoubtedly more polarized and complex than ever, with record numbers of whole populations displaced through conflict or violence. We have experienced the 9-11 terrorist attack, Hurricane Katrina, the continued flooding of the Mississippi and Missouri Rivers with extreme weather events, and the melting of Earth's ice caps and glaciers alongside the rise of the Internet and use of wireless technology, continuous consumerism, even the mapping of the human genome. And what used to be considered fringe, conspiracy-based theories, now appear to contain wide-eyed truths: Monsanto and GMOs, Chemtrails, Black Budgets, the Corporatocracy. Today the idea of UFOs almost seems conservative.

Through this complex, convoluted time of tipping past almost every point of no return, where are we heading—individually and globally? Can we make a difference, or for that matter, in this world of continuous fragmentation and ecological imbalance, should we even try? The Spiritual Teachers of these three books who prophesied these difficult times know differently. Through their ancient accounts of humanity's history on Earth, a provenance that seems to date back not thousands but *hundreds* of thousands of years, we've been here before. Our elder brothers and sisters, who obviously know every twist and turn of the human condition, offer their best advice: it is time for *our* spiritual growth and evolution.

The Time of Change is Now!

*Lori Toye*

# Afterword

I know this series quite well. In fact, this is its fourth published version of *Book One* and the third edition of *Books Two* and
*Three*. I first began the production of *Book One* of this series in
1990. I carefully chose selections and passages of Earth Changes
information in the transcripts from my archive of channeled
works—the treasured "Blue Book" that I have written about
in the *I AM America Trilogy*. Fortunately a group of volunteers
appeared at critical junctures to help craft the book through its
seminal stages. My friend Sherry Takala proofread the manuscript several times; however it was apparent that the book
needed an editor. After a trip to Edinburgh, Texas, for an Earth
Changes workshop, Dorothy Maville, a retired Latin teacher,
volunteered for the job. When the first book rolled off the press
in the spring of 1991, it included an eight-page signature of colored pages in the center, featuring a small version of the *I AM
America Map*, and full-color oil paintings by Sherry Takala de-
picting the Earth Changes Maps for Mexico, Central, and South
America. We also included full color images of Sananda and
Saint Germain painted by San Francisco artist Avedis Dermaka-
lian, and we featured the *Awakening Prayer* on the final page,
framed by the Eight-sided cell of Perfection.

After the publication of the *I AM America Freedom Star World
Map* in 1994, we included black and white scans of this map to

match the prophetic information for Japan, Australia, China, and India in *New World Atlas, Volume Two*. At that time digital scanning technology was entirely new, so I engaged a cartography company to produce these files for inclusion. Staff members from our office once again volunteered to proofread the manuscript, but I was unable to hire a suitable editor. And this book was small compared to the first volume of prophecies; it was just under 140 pages.

The following year, I explored a new channeling technique, via a remote generator, to produce seven spiritual lessons on the Rays by the Master K. H. You might remember how I've described this technique in *Sisters of the Flame*, whereby an individual *sits* for channeled sessions and feeds vital energy to a medium for the channel's greater energy and health during and after the sessions. Developed *sitters* can also influence the quality of the information, since their abundant, vital energy helps to sustain the length and clarity of a session. *I AM America* volunteer Jan was certain she could do this, but the only drawback was that she lived over a hundred miles from Payson, in Flagstaff, Arizona. Since I already knew that I would receive the information clairaudiently, and would type the information as it was dictated telepathically, she asked, "How about if I meditate while you type? I just *know* I can do this." Jan was an avid early morning meditator, and I was eager to try the new technique. Plus I was intrigued regarding receiving the new information since Saint Germain had asked me personally if I would help. So we agreed that we would begin each morning at 4:30 a.m. Jan would meditate and send me energy, and I would use this spiritual energy to support each telepathic session. Undoubtedly Jan and I were connected as one flowing energy, similar to the *Oneship*, which Kuan Yin has taught and described. We easily had completed about one-half of the lessons when one morning I overslept. By 6 a.m. the phone rang with Jan asking, "Where were you?"

When a donation appeared in 1996 from a European donor to help with the publication of the European and African prophecies to be featured in *New World Atlas, Volume Three*, I immediately organized its nineteen chapters. Financially assisted by a small family inheritance, I was able to hire the editing team of Barbara and Clark Hockabout, personal friends and mutual students of Ascended Master Teaching. They worked at our home for over a week to help polish the manuscript that would open with the Seven Lessons on the Rays by Master K. H. The third volume was published in September 1996.

By Y2K, we had published two more maps: the *I AM America 6-Map Scenario* and the *I AM America United States Golden Cities Map*, and we had a total of four books in publication. We decided to invest in our own print-on-demand system, which would allow us to print the *New World Atlas Series* ourselves, and save important funds that had been used to floor book inventory. In order to meet the specifications of this system, all of the books in the *Atlas Series* would need to be reformatted and would be printed larger—larger than the conventionally printed versions—so we decided to add black and white scans of all of the Earth Changes Maps to this series. By this time, technology had evolved significantly, so I scanned the maps myself.

This new system presented a different set of challenges for our business. While this was economically better for us, it was labor intensive. Len and I were often on the job by 5 o'clock in the morning, printing books and newsletters, plus packing and mailing orders. We trained our volunteer staff how to properly print and collate books and prepare individual copies for bindery. Fortunately, by 2005 print-on-demand technology had improved significantly and lowered costs per book. We decided once again to outsource our printing needs.

Yet again, we needed updated versions of the *New World Atlas Series*, especially Volume One. Through the process of working with a trio of professional editors throughout the first three books of the *Golden City Series*, new editorial formats and styles were established. Glossary terms for the *I AM America Teachings* were identified, written, and honed; appendices and indices added additional educational support to the material.

In 2010 I received a phone call from an I AM America student who had recently started an Ascended Master study group in the Golden City of Malton. Elaine Cardall and I immediately clicked. We both shared a deep love of the Ascended Masters and their teachings, the sacred energies of a Golden City, the solitude and beauty of nature, and the same birthday—although we were born a decade apart. Our monthly calls continued and I revealed study tips and offered casual mentoring. In one of these calls in late 2011, I mentioned that I had at my fingertips a complete archive of information where I could research some of her questions. Elaine was intrigued, "You know . . ." her voice broke and I detected a hint of emotion, even shyness, "I can help you with this material, that is, if you need me." And she immediately added, "I would like to be of service."

I excitedly shared with her my vision for the material, that included an introductory series of books based on never before published transcripts that dated back to my beginning days and dozens of transcribed lessons that could be organized into four more books for the *Golden City Series*, plus a final book describing a form of *Kriya Yoga*—breathwork—that prepares the human energy system for Ascension. "Can you send all of it to me?"

Elaine politely asked after my lengthy explanation. "Of course," I responded and in the next hour I drove to our local Wal-Mart, purchased a thumb drive, copied all the files, and mailed it to her the next day.

I patiently waited for her call that came about a week later. "It's absolutely amazing," she exclaimed as we spoke. She confirmed what I had known for years: "This is a complete body of information from the Ascended Masters . . . but I'm a bit uncertain just *where* to start." Undoubtedly these were teachings for a disciplined student—a true *chela*. And the Earth Changes Prophecies that originally played a central role with the Earth Changes Maps, in reality, only comprised a small amount of the teaching that contained detailed information on Ascension, the role of the Golden Cities, the Seven Rays of Light and Sound, energy fields and the human aura, health and healing, personal growth and transformation, decree and meditation, and literally hundreds of spiritual techniques. The I AM America Archive contained the complete teachings of a mystery school. Now, unquestionably, the task before us was how to properly organize and present this unique information.

I suggested that we first arrange the material by date, a method that in the past had worked well for me. We agreed to begin our work on the first book of the introductory teachings, "A Teacher Appears."

Several days later I received an email from Elaine titled "First Impressions." Here are some excerpts:

> "I was very excited to see that there were 51 transmissions. I am so thoroughly embedded now with the 51 Vortices that, though late at night, I had to read through the first seventeen.

I love numbers and geometric shapes and the
magic of underlying structures . . . I am already
feeling an emerging rhythm."

Regarding the channelings, she wrote:

"I will underline the first wave (for me) of
magical information (as if I were teaching a
class) and write down my questions about
what I cannot decipher in the presentation and
things which I cannot grasp. I will try to work
with those concepts at a few different levels
before forming questions for you."

Certainly some of the information was challenging and presented many new ideas and scientific concepts neither of us
had ever been exposed to in our spiritual journeys. Between the
two of us, we had over sixty years of intense spiritual experience. Like me, Elaine had started early with the inner journey,
retreating to live alone in a mountain cabin in her twenties,
after the untimely death of her mother. Her father had been
tragically killed when she was a young girl, but her work ethic
and sharp intellect led her to an Ivy League education at Brown
University, where she obtained an undergraduate degree in
psychology. "I've done a little bit of everything," Elaine hum-
bly chuckled. "I've been a secretary; I've waitressed . . . right
now I'm a caregiver, and have done this for several years." This
practical and thorough side of her nature securely anchored
her consciousness as she would spend several hours each day
conversing with Master Teachers and traveling in her light
bodies to various Golden Cities. In fact, her ability to contact

these sublime teachers and levels of consciousness would prove invaluable to our work together, especially as we began the painstaking structural edit of the transcripts.

We organized and arranged the transcripts into eleven titles. This would include the three new introductory books of the *I AM America Trilogy*, four new books that would complete the seven books of the *Golden Cities Series*. This left one important, remaining question: what should we do with the *New World Atlas Series*?

First, I wanted to remove the black and white maps. Since print-on-demand now offered color printing at reasonable rates, the idea was to print a separate atlas of all of the *I AM America Maps*. This would allow the addition of the individual maps from the *6-Map Scenario* and the *Golden City Map*. Also, after examining the material, we discovered that only about one-half of the pages were dedicated to Earth Changes information. The other half comprised New World Teachings such as the *Twelve Jurisdictions*, the *New Endeavor*, the *Christ Body*, *Shamballa*, *Anugram*, *Courage to Heal*, and Master K. H.'s teachings on the Seven Rays. Elaine wrote:

> "I find the need for the Prophecy Teachings
> to be together with the New World Teachings
> to reiterate the importance of global conscious-
> ness and choice. Each part of the world has a
> message that impacts our own inner changes.
> As I see the sequence of the three maps, this is
> the essential trinity for the planetary Ascension
> and should not be overlooked."

I wholeheartedly agreed. Originally we thought about publishing the former series in two large volumes, but this would require a large format that was a bit cumbersome. We would add the transcripts for the *6-Map Scenario* and a never published two-part session that focused on Earth Changes updates with a focus on global warming and climate change. Plus, I had recently discovered about a dozen cassette tapes of recorded sessions that had never been transcribed, and if pertinent, we would add this information, too.

So I spent time perusing bookstores getting ideas and designed a cover idea and sent it to Elaine for her input. She called within minutes after receiving the graphic. "I love the new title for the series," she exclaimed. I responded, "Yes, it seems to fit the material best, since this is spiritual wisdom for the New Times." And we agreed there would be three books total for the *New World Wisdom Series*, and another separate title, the *I AM America Atlas*, for the full-color map collection.

It took about a full year in our schedule to revisit this series, and each teaching, each phrase, and sometimes each word became filled with vibrant new meaning and nuance. It appeared as if the revised manuscript was alive and it would subtly recalibrate our consciousness to inspire the next level of spiritual growth. I mentioned this to Elaine, and she commented that she considered the book a sacred text. We also noted that the *Wisdom Series* was filled with the energy of every Ascended Master and reading its teachings instantly evoked their guiding presence or crucial overshadowing. Elaine described this process in an email:

> "Upon returning to the material and pressing
> onward, I began receiving it from a different

point of view. There was a swift upturning of
energies and a sensing that our beloved Saint
Germain, in a fatherly fashion, had actually
taken my hand and pulled me through a mis-
alignment."

And in several days, she added this:

"I am lit up. I am blessed and I am feeling
his (Sananda's) love more and more. He comes
through when I am doing this work. And Saint
Germain has been there for me often as well."

As Elaine completed her finishing touches on the manu-
scripts, I explored the design of the books. I wanted the typography simple, and purposely set the text with a large amount
of space that would immediately rest and relax the reader to
provoke a state of reception and contemplation. I wrote new
subtitles for the text so that crucial topics would be immediately identified and not missed.

When the first book was complete, I pressed three copies. One
for me, one for Len, and I mailed Elaine the third copy.

About four weeks later, I received her comments:

"This book is a rhapsody, a dazzling emanation for all of time, and so are you! Its scope is
truly incredible, a veritable roadmap for entering into the Golden Age."

Then I read her criticism voicing concerns about the preface.
This was totally unlike Elaine, so I gave her a quick call. "I don't

want you to make any apologies to the reader," she stated, "I want you to move enthusiastically into the book."

For a brief moment, I could not respond. For several years now, the two of us had been joined together on a remarkable spiritual voyage through the crafting of these transcripts into books. And for the most part, the waters had been calm and the wind blew at a comfortable pace. Unlike Elaine, I had endured many years of working with the public and understood the skeptics and those who might be uncertain regarding this type information, even a few lightworkers that believed the prophecies had been transmuted! I purposely wanted the piece to address doubts. And I also knew something else was bothering her, so I asked. She immediately responded, "How about if I write a small, two page introduction? I agreed, and without asking any further questions, got to work adjusting the pagination of the front matter to accommodate her opening words.

At the time I thought she had an emotional need to say something about her participation in the publication of this series. For some writers, publishing a book is like giving birth to a child, and from this viewpoint we were finally sending our triplets off to college; however now I know that is likely not the entire reason. What Elaine did not tell me, or for that matter, could not tell me was that she would soon transition from this physical plane. Elaine's health had been challenged for several years and she had successfully balanced her spirit, mind, and body with a deep, holistic healing based on her intimate relationship with spiritual principles. Her Higher Self likely understood what we could not in that moment. This important introduction to the *New World Wisdom Series* would be her last written contribution to the *I AM America Teachings* that had filled both of our lives with wonder, excitement, curiosity, and above all, love and enduring friendship.

I now treasure this introduction as one of my last memories of our work together, at least in this plane. During this time, which was almost six years, we processed eleven books of *I AM America Teachings*. Six of these books have been released in the last three years, including the *I AM America Trilogy* and the *New World Wisdom Series*. The remaining five will be published soon.

A close friend who had known Elaine for over twenty years called and was not surprised to learn how much work we had accomplished in such a short time. She told me that she had never known anyone who worked harder than Elaine, and then paraphrased a saying most of us have read before: "In the end, it's not the years in your life, it's the life in your years."

In our short time together, Elaine and I filled our days with the joy of our work and service, and a profound comradery and unity that comes through sharing a commitment to a higher purpose. I know with certainty that Elaine Cardall's loving contribution to this work will be appreciated and cherished for many, many years to come.

*Lori Toye*

# Spiritual Lineage of the Violet Flame

The teachings of the Violet Flame, as taught in the work of I AM America, come through the Goddess of Compassion and Mercy Kuan Yin. She holds the feminine aspects of the flame, which are Compassion, Mercy, Forgiveness, and Peace. Her work with the Violet Flame is well documented in the history of Ascended Master teachings, and it is said that the altar of the etheric Temple of Mercy holds the flame in a Lotus Cup. She became Saint Germain's teacher of the Sacred Fire in the inner realms, and he carried the masculine aspect of the flame into human activity through Purification, Alchemy, and Transmutation. One of the best means to attract the beneficent activities of the Violet Flame is through the use of decrees and invocation. However, you can meditate on the flame, visualize the flame, and receive its transmuting energies like "the light of a thousand suns," radiant and vibrant as the first day that the Elohim Arcturus and Diana drew it forth from our solar Sun at the creation of the earth. Whatever form, each time you use the Violet Flame these two Master Teachers hold you in the loving arms of its action and power.

The following is an invocation for the Violet Flame to be used at sunrise or sunset. It is utilized while experiencing the visible change of night to day, and day to night. In fact, if you observe the horizon at these times, you will witness light transitioning from pinks to blues, and then a subtle violet strip adorning the sky. We have used this invocation for years in varying scenes and circumstances, overlooking lakes, rivers, mountaintops, deserts, and prairies; in huddled traffic and busy streets; with groups of students or sitting with a friend, but more commonly alone in our home or office, with a glint of soft light streaming from a window. The result is always the same: a calm, centering force of stillness. We call it the Space.

### Invocation of the Violet Flame for Sunrise and Sunset
I invoke the Violet Flame to come forth in the name of I AM that I AM,
To the Creative Force of all the realms of all the universes, the Alpha, the Omega, the Beginning, and the End,
To the Great Cosmic Beings and Torch Bearers of all the realms of all the universes,
And the Brotherhoods and Sisterhoods of Breath, Sound, and Light, who honor this Violet Flame that comes forth from the Ray of Divine Love—the Pink Ray, and the Ray of Divine Will—the Blue Ray of all Eternal Truths.

I invoke the Violet Flame to come forth in the name of I AM that I AM!
Mighty Violet Flame, stream forth from the Heart of the Central Logos,
the Mighty Great Central Sun! Stream in, through, and around me.

(Then insert other prayers and/or decrees for the Violet Flame.)

# End Notes

1. The Rays are seven forces or qualities that demonstrate seven aspects of the Mother-Father God. The Ray Forces synthesize with life, quality, and appearance to produce all forms in the manifested universe.

2. A brief history of the historical events of United States from 1857 to 1869 shows the overtone of the Violet Ray through expressions of Brotherhood, freedom, open communications, unity, and the alchemy of the sciences for the good of humanity. Some striking examples can be found:

*1850.* When California applied for admission as a free state, pro-slavery interests felt threatened and sparked a series of senate debates. Henry Clay and Daniel Webster pleaded for compromise that would preserve the union. The Compromise of 1850 was enacted and most significant was a speech by William Seward declaring, "There is a higher law than the Constitution - the law of God." Subsequently, the extension of slavery into new states was stopped.

*1857.* The first stagecoach line is subsidized by Congress, linking the eastern and the western United States with the first mail line.

*1850 to late 1890.* Many practical inventions were given to humanity, such as surgical anesthesia, the sewing machine, the typewriter, McCormick Reaper, vulcanized rubber, electromagnetic telegraph, and the multi-colored press.

*1859.* The prophet John Brown stood as a national figure and martyr for the principle of equality and brotherhood.

*1861.* The Civil War was fought until Palm Sunday, April 9, 1865. Over 620,000 Americans were killed. President Lincoln wrote to a grieving mother who lost five sons, "I pray that our Heavenly Father may assuage the anguish of your bereavement, and leave you only the cherished memory of the loved and lost, and the solemn pride that must be yours to have laid so costly a sacrifice upon the altar of freedom."

*1869.* The final spike of the Transcontinental Railroad was malleted into place. The seventh overtoned Ray alchemized the marriage of east and west America.

3. The Great White (Light) Lodge is a fraternity of men and women dedicated to the universal spiritual upliftment of humanity. Their chief desire is to preserve the lost teachings and spirit of the ancient religions and philosophies of the world. They are pledged to protect against systematic assaults against individual and group freedoms that inhibit the growth of self-knowledge and personal choice. And, most importantly, their mission is to re-awaken the dormant ethical and spiritual spark that has almost disappeared among the masses.

4. Here, the author makes reference to the Hermetic Principle of Vibration. The Masters and Adepts apparently set aside the Laws of Nature and used one law against another to accomplish a change in vibration. This change in vibration, commonly known as a miracle, changes all forms of energy materially, emotionally, and mentally. The Three Initiates explain, in *The Kybalion Hermetic Philosophy*, "All manifestation of thought, emotion, reason, will, or desire, or any mental state or condition, are accompanied by vibrations, a portion of which are thrown off and which tend to affect the minds of other persons by 'induction.' This is the

principle which produces the phenomena of 'telepathy,' mental influence, and other forms of the action and power of mind over mind." This influence a Master Teacher may use with his or her students is explained further, "One may polarize his mind at any degree he wishes, thus gaining a perfect control over his mental states, moods, etc. In the same way, he may affect the minds of others, producing the desired mental states in them." This mental force, gathered at will by the Master Teacher is then carried vibrationally in the aura. It is the contact with the teacher's vibrations, through the aura, which then reproduce the same mental states in the student or chela. The Three Initiates further explain, "These mental states may be reproduced, just as a musical tone may be reproduced by causing an instrument to vibrate at a certain rate, just as color may be reproduced in the same way." (page 145-46) In this manner, the students of the Master's Ashram carry forward the objectives and intent of the Master Teacher.

5. Venus was a highly regarded planet of the ancients, as it was the only planet bright enough to cast a shadow. Since Venus is visible in the sky at sunset and arose before the Sun, it was called the false light, the star of the morning, or Lucifer, which means the light-bearer. Venus has also been called Isis or The Mother of the Gods because of this relationship to the Sun.

6. In traditional astrology, the first house, or ascendant, is the determiner of physical attributes. In this teaching, the Master Teacher K. H. is adding that the Venus position overshadows the first house, adding to or enhancing already existing characteristics.

7. The Master Years carrying numerological significance are: 33, 44, 55 and so on. According to Ascended Master teachings, when a candidate is prepared and readied, oftentimes Ascensions occur in these years. According to Pythagorean numerology, the three or triangle is the symbol of the creative aspect of God. The four is the fountain of nature and the most perfect number symbolizing the four powers of the soul as mind, science, opinion, and sense. Five is the number of nature herself. The Ascended Masters have always requested that five, five-pointed stars, be presented on all Earth Changes Prophecy maps. Manly Hall writes in *Secret Teaching Of All Ages*, "The pentad is symbolic of Nature, for when multiplied by itself, it returns into itself, just as grains of wheat, starting in the form of seed, pass through their own growth ... the pentad represents all the superior and inferior beings. It is sometimes referred to as the Hierophant, or the Priest of the Mysteries, because of its connection with the spiritual ethers, by means of which mystic development is attained. Keywords of the pentad are reconciliation, alternation, marriage, immortality, cordiality, providence, and sound. The tetrad (elements) plus the Monad equals the pentad. The Pythagoreans taught that the elements of earth, fire, air, and water were permeated by a substance called ether, the basis of vitality and life. Therefore, they chose the five pointed star, or pentagram, as the symbol of vitality, health, and interpenetration." (page 72)


8. Matthew 7: 16-20, "You will know them by their fruits. Grapes are not gathered from thorn bushes, nor figs from thistles, are they? Even so, every good tree bears good fruit; but the rotten tree bears bad fruit. A good tree cannot produce bad fruit, nor can a rotten tree produce good fruit. Every tree that does not

bear good fruit is cut down and thrown into the fire. So then, you will know them by their fruits."

9. Individualization is said to be one of the greatest achievements of consciousness. Animal consciousness is said to be a group consciousness; therefore, there is no need to teach certain skills. Animals acquire at birth, through collective group consciousness, skills known as "instincts." Cats, dogs, horses, and elephants are the most highly evolved and closest to obtaining individualization. In the human, because of the gift of individualization, certain skills must be re-acquired in each embodiment. The distinction made between the Mineral/Plant and Animal Kingdoms is the ability to generate audible sounds. The distinction made between animal and human is the ability to generate sound into the auditory and visual symbols of language.

Mineral Kingdom - Electricity

Plant Kingdom - Magnetism (color and sound)

Animal Kingdom - The power of instinct built on the sense of sound.

10. On the subject of Earth Changes, two distinct opinions have developed. One, Earth Changes are not necessary and, with the proper attitude and actions, devastation will be circumvented and an ensuing age of peace and prosperity for the Earth and her peoples will reign. The second opinion sees the necessity of Earth Changes to cleanse and purify the Earth and humanity's current state of self-destruction. In both scenarios, balance is the desired outcome. In the book, *Eternal Massage*, author and prophet, Jerry Canty, sees that change comes like a needed massage for our planet. It is this massage that balances both viewpoints and restores sanity and health to humanity and

the environment. "Within the next twenty years, the civilized nations of the Earth, to the very degree they have adopted the 'American Dream' and, thereby, Science and Technology as their God, will be utterly destroyed. The instrument of this destruction will not be the hydrogen bomb nor some similar creation of man's warped genius, though these will doubtless play a part in the play of Armageddon. Rather, we can expect uncontrollable physical and mental decay of the race, social and political upheaval, and finally, environmental catastrophe, summing into major climatic and seismic cataclysm. It is the purpose of this book to show that even these latter changes are instrumented by man, and are indeed a natural reaction to his actions.

The coming period of Great Change has been carefully and consistently described by the prophets, clairvoyants, and other men and women of inner vision of all ages and peoples. As is usually the case, however, the words of the prophets go unheard, while man of this age is quite unable to take stock in anything he can't see direct empirical evidence of, and for him "prophecy" remains a colorful bit of quackery. (Man's disregard for this gift is in direct proportion to his material sellout.)

It is for those of you who do believe (and those really rare souls who KNOW) who do see the obvious direction of this spiralling age of materialism, that I am writing this book. "THIS IS NOT THE END OF THE WORLD, BUT THAT VERY MASSAGE NEEDED TO KEEP THE WORLD FROM ENDING!" (page 6)

11. Desire is also known as Jurisdiction Nine, as presented in *New World Wisdom, Volume One.* In that teaching, Saint Germain and Sanat Kumara present desire as the soul's spark of creativity.

"Dear Ones, desire is your source! Without it you could not be. It is the seed, it is the spark, it is the source of origin. It is scientific and it is melodic." In *Eternal Massage,* Jerry Canty delivers a profound insight on desire. "A good way to get a better feeling for the universal desire I speak of is to consider the concept of weight. Weight is a measure of the desire in any given body to be in an equilibrium condition. A helium balloon has the same desire, but rises to find its balancing mate high in the sky. It is this same desire that motivates your actions, the seeming difference being that you intellectualize your desires and non-human creatures don't, they simply obey the law. (Ultimately, you do as well, as the process called "thinking" obeys the same law, and ultimately is the law.) The scientific name for the spiritual force of desire is "gravity." Is it any wonder science today has no grasp of the real nature of gravity? It is gravity that brings you to me, a bird to her nest, rain to the earth, and vapors to the sky, a rocket to the Moon, a bee to your forehead, you to MacDonald's for lunch, and Dr.'s into your life for cures." (page 57) Walter Russell summed it up, "Desire is the fulcrum of the Universe."

12. To hold back the truth or to adorn it as belonging to an individual or group is to adulterate it. The truth then remains hidden in ignorance, superstition, and fear. Manly Hall writes in, *The Secret Teachings of All Ages,* "Through education - spiritual, mental, moral, and physical - man will learn to release living truths from their lifeless coverings. The perfect government of the earth must be patterned eventually after that divine government by which the universe is ordered. In that day when perfect order is reestablished, with peace universal and good triumphant, men will no longer seek for happiness, for they shall find it welling up within themselves. Dead hopes, dead aspira-

tions, dead virtues shall rise from their graves, and the Spirit of Beauty and Goodness repeatedly slain by ignorant men shall again be the Master of Work. Then shall sages sit upon the seats of the mighty and the gods walk with men." (page 80)

13. This is in reference to seven Hermetic Principles. They are:

1) The Principle of Mentalism: The All is Mind; the Universe is Mental.

2) The Principle of Correspondence: As above, so below; as below, so above.

3) The Principle of Vibration: Nothing rests, everything moves, everything vibrates.

4) The Principle of Polarity: Everything is dual; everything has poles; everything has its pair of opposites; like and unlike are the same; opposites are identical in nature, but different in degree; extremes meet; all truths are but half-truths; all paradoxes may be reconciled.

5) The Principle of Rhythm: Everything flows, out and in; everything has its tides; all things rise and fall; the pendulum-swing manifests in everything; the measure of the swing to the right is the measure of the swing to left; rhythm compensates.

6) The Principle of Cause and Effect: Every cause has its effect; every effect has its cause; everything happens according to Law; chance is but a name for Law not recognized; there are many planes of causation, but nothing escapes the Law.

7) The Principle of Gender: Gender is in everything; everything has its masculine and feminine principles; gender manifests on all planes.

*The Kybalion: A Study of the Hermetic Philosophy of Ancient Egypt and Greece,* written by the "The Three Initiates" (the authors, otherwise remain anonymous), Chicago, 1940.

# Glossary

**Abundance:** The second of the Twelve Jurisdictions is the principle of overflowing fullness in all situations, based upon the Law of Choice. In Divine Destiny, Abundance, as a Meta-need, is defined as richness and complexity. Abundance, perceived as an Evolution Point, is synonymous with the Law of Choice, and develops the individual will; hence, the spiritual recognition of Universal Bounty and Manifestation leads the spiritual student to the discernment and the acknowledgement of the Hermetic principles of Cause and Effect through the Law of Attraction.

**Age of Cooperation:** The age humanity is currently being prepared to enter; it occurs simultaneously with the "Time of Change."

**Age of Transportation:** The age humanity is currently being prepared to enter; it occurs simultaneously with the "Time of Change."

**Angelic Realm:** The hierarchy or organization of Angels that includes Archangels, seraphim, cherubim, thrones, dominions, virtues, powers, and principalities. According to the Ascended Masters, seven unique Angels assist and protect each individual in their spiritual growth and evolution. This is referred to as the Angelic Host.

**Archangels** (the seven): The seven principal angels of creation. They include: Michael, the Blue Ray; Jophiel, the Yellow Ray; Chamuel, the Pink Ray; Gabriel, the White Ray; Raphael, the Green Ray; Uriel, the Ruby Ray; and Zadkiel, the Violet Ray.

**Astral body** or **plane:** The subtle light body that contains our feelings, desires, and emotions. It exists as an intermediate light body between the physical body and the Causal Body (Mental Body). According to the Master Teachers, we enter the Astral Plane through our Astral Body when we sleep, and many dreams and visions are experiences in this Plane of vibrant color and sensation. Through spiritual development, the Astral Body strengthens, and the luminosity of its light is often detected in the physical plane. Spiritual adepts may have the ability to consciously leave their physical bodies while traveling in their Astral Bodies. The Astral Body or Astral Plane has various levels of evolution and is the heavenly abode where the soul resides after the disintegration of the physical body. The Astral Body is also known as the Body Double, the Desire Body, and the Emotional Body.

**Ascended Master:** An ordinary human being who has undergone a spiritual transformation over many lifetimes. He or she has Mastered the lower planes—mental, emotional, and physical—to unite with his or her God-Self or I AM Presence. An Ascended Master is freed from the Wheel of Karma. He or she moves forward in spiritual evolution beyond this planet. However, an Ascended Master remains attentive to the spiritual well-being of humanity; inspiring and serving the Earth's spiritual growth and evolution.

**Ascension:** A process of Mastering thoughts, feelings, and actions that balance positive and negative karmas. Ascension allows entry to a higher state of consciousness and frees a person from the need to reincarnate on the lower Earthly planes or lokas of experience. Ascension is the process of spiritual liberation, also known as moksha.

**Astrology:** In esoteric terms, the language of the stars is also known as the science of the astral body. For example: the astral logic. Vedic astrology is commonly known as "Jyotish," which means the "science of light." The language of the stars seeks to explain the spirit of our destiny or fate. Because of this, astrology is considered one of the first applicable sciences of consciousness.

**Atlantis:** An ancient civilization of Earth, whose mythological genesis was the last Puranic Dvapara Yuga—the Bronze Age of the Yugas. Its demise occurred around the year 9628 BCE. Esoteric historians suggest three phases of political and geophysical boundaries: the Toltec Nation of Atlantis (Ameru); the Turian Nation of Atlantis (the invaders of the Land of Rama); and Poseid, the Island Nation of the present-day Atlantic Ocean.

The early civilizations of Atlantis were ruled by the spiritually evolved Toltec. Their spiritual teachings, ceremonies, and temples were dedicated to the worship of the Sun. According to Theosophical thought, Atlantis' evolving humanity brought about an evolutionary epoch of the Pink Ray on the Earth, and the development of the Astral-Emotional bodies and Heart Chakra. Ascended Master provenance claims that the Els—now the Mighty Elohim of the Seven Rays—were the original Master Teachers to the spiritual seekers of Atlantis. Atlantean culture later deteriorated through the use of nuclear weapons and cruelty toward other nations, including the use of genetic engineering. The demise of Atlantis was inevitable; however, modern-day geologists, archaeologists, and occultists all disagree to its factual timing.

Ascended Master teachings affirm that Atlantis—a continent whose geo-physical and political existence probably spanned well over 100,000 years—experienced several phases of traumatic Earth Change. This same belief is held by occult historians who allege that Earth repeatedly cycles through periods of massive Earth Change and cataclysmic pole shifts, which activate tectonic plates and subsequently submerge whole continents, creating vital New Lands for Earth's successors.

**Babajeran:** A name for the Earth Mother that means, "Grandmother rejoicing."

**Blue Ray:** A perceptible light and sound frequency. The Blue Ray not only resonates with the color blue, but is identified with the qualities of steadiness, calm, perseverance, transformation, harmony, diligence, determination, austerity, protection, humility, truthfulness, and self-negation. It forms one-third of the Unfed Flame within the heart—the Blue Ray of God Power—which nourishes the spiritual unfoldment of the human into the HU-man. Use of the Violet Flame evokes the Blue Ray into action throughout the light bodies, where the Blue Ray clarifies intentions and assists the alignment of the Will. In Ascended Master teachings, the Blue Ray is alleged to have played a major role in the physical manifestation of the Earth's first Golden City, Shamballa. Six of fifty-one Golden Cities emanate the Blue Ray's peaceful, yet piercing frequencies. The Blue Ray is esoterically linked to the planet Saturn, the development of the Will, the ancient Lemurian Civilization, the Archangel Michael, the Elohim Hercules, the Master Teacher El Morya, and the Eastern Doors of all Golden Cities.

**Breathwork:** The conscious, spiritual application of breath, often accompanied by visualization and meditation. Ascended Master teachings often incorporate various breathing techniques to activate and integrate Ray Forces in the Human Aura and light bodies.

**Chakra:** Sanskrit for wheel. There are seven separate spinning wheels that are human bioenergy centers. They are stacked from the base of the spine to the top of the head.

**Chela:** Disciple.

**Chohan:** Another word for Lord.

**Choice:** Will.

**Clarity:** The third of the Twelve Jurisdictions lends lucidity to our perceptions through the Law of Non-Judgment.

**Co-creator:** To create with the God-Source.

**Compassion:** Sensitivity and understanding for another's suffering and the desire to give aid to relieve human pain, distress, and anguish.

**Conscious:** Awake, aware, and thoughtful.

**Consciousness:** Awakening to one's own existence, sensations, and cognitions.

**Creator:** Fully empowered God-Source, affirmed through human thought, feeling, and action.

**Cup:** A symbol of neutrality and grace. The Ascended Masters often refer to our human body as a Cup filled with our thoughts and feelings.

**Causal Body:** The Fifth Dimensional Body of Light, which is affiliated with thought. Its name is associated with "cause," and is alleged to be the source of both the Astral and physical body. The Causal Body is also defined as the Higher Mind—superior to the Mental Body.

**Christ**, the, or **Christ Consciousness:** The highest energy or frequency attainable on Earth. The Christ or the Christ Consciousness is a Step-down Transformer of the I AM energies, which enlighten, heal, and transform all human conditions of degradation and death.

**Conscious Immortality:** Awareness, acceptance, and knowledge of the immortal, spiritual soul.

**Council of Elohim:** A category of Divine Beings who oversee the creation of worlds and planets.

**Dahl Universe:** Also known as the DAL Universe is a galactic star cluster that is said to exist beyond the Pleiades, approximately 415 light years away. It is claimed that many of the foundational spiritual teachings of the Great White Brotherhood originated from spiritual Masters who shared their insights with souls from the Pleiades, the moons of Jupiter, and the planet Venus. These teachings inevitably found their way to Earth.

**Decree:** Statements of intent and power, similar to prayers and mantras, which are often integrated with the use of the I AM and requests to the I AM Presence.

**Desire:** Of the Source.

**Deva:** A shining one or being of light.

**Devachan:** An afterlife where difficult and negative karmas cease, and only the positive forms of desires manifest. It is also known as "Paradise" and the "Summerland."

**Dharma:** Purpose.

**Divine Complement:** Each Ascended Master, Divine Being, and Archangel is alleged to be paired with a divine complement of energy. Each divine pair manifests and streams energies into the corporeal worlds through the Hermetic Law of Gender. Hence, one is masculine in quality, while the other is feminine. Similar to a Twin Flame, Divine Complements differ in that they are ascended and purposely divide their efforts to assist Earth and unascended humanity. In the higher realms they are ideally ONE energy, and serve upon one individualized Ray Force.

**Divine Mind:** The spiritual mind of the ONE Source, and the conscious, organized thought of God.

**Divine Plan:** The outcome of Creative and Co-creative processes that provoke spiritual growth and evolution. From a traditional viewpoint, the will of God.

**Divine Will:** The idea of God's plan for humanity; however, from the perspective of the HU-man, the Divine Will is "choice."

**Dove of Peace:** A symbol of universal peace; however, the Ascended Masters teach that the dove is also the symbol of one age shifting into a new one.

**Earth Changes:** A prophesied Time of Change on Earth. This includes geophysical, political, and social changes, alongside the opportunity for spiritual and personal transformation.

**Earth Plane and Planet:** The dual aspect of life on Earth. The Earth Planet is a reference to Earth as a conscious, evolving, and sentient being.

**Eight-sided Cell of Perfection:** An atomic cell located in the human heart. It is associated with all aspects of perfection, and contains and maintains a visceral connection with the Godhead.

**Eighth Energy Body:** A new light body that develops to assist the growth of Unity Consciousness.

**Eighth Ray:** A new Ray of both light and sound that emanates from the Great Central Sun and calibrates energies from Neptune. It is associated with Divine Heaven and Divine Man. Its qualities are unifying, perceptive, intuitive, cooperative, creative, and integrative. This Ray's colors are aquamarine and gold.

**Elemental:** A nature being.

**El Morya:** Ascended Master of the Blue Ray, associated with the development of the will.

**Elohim:** Creative beings of love and light that helped manifest the Divine Idea of our solar system. Seven Elohim (the Seven Rays) exist here. They organize and draw forward Archangels, the Four Elements, Devas, Seraphim, Cherubim, Angels, Nature Guardians, and the Elementals. The Silent Watcher—the Great Mystery—gives them direction.

**Embodiment:** Incarnated in a physical body.

**Emergent Evolution:** When the spiritual growth of an evolving life reaches a certain stage of conscious awareness, the soul forces itself into contact with higher streams of Divine Expression and Consciousness. The union of these two states of consciousness produces a new evolutionary being as an aspect of the manifestation of evolving life. This process is known as Emergent Evolution.

**Energy Body:** A distinct mass of energy that can be singular or independent; or dependent and interconnected to other diverse bodies of energy.

**Enlightenment:** The act of gaining spiritual wisdom and insight. According to the Spiritual Teachers, this process literally increases the light of the Human Aura. From a Buddhist perspective, it is a final state of spiritual growth and evolution, and is defined by the lack of desire and human suffering.

**Faith:** The tenth of the Twelve Jurisdictions, which places confidence and trust in our innate creative birthright.

**Father Ray:** A masculine energy.

**Feminine:** The Mother Creative principle as the highest expression of being. Femininity is akin to the Goddess. She comprises one half of the gender-neutral God force. Feminine energy represents love, beauty, seduction, sensitivity, and refinement—characteristics of the Goddess Venus. On the dark side, it reflects vanity, superficiality, fickleness, and exhaustion. Femininity is also the intuition—a nurturing force that, above all, produces the first creative spark in our Sun of Truth. The female essence serves as the inspiration and aspiration for life's goodness and purity—a devotion to truth.

**Flame of Desire:** The Ascended Masters claim that the physical presence of the Flame of Desire lies within the heart nestled inside the Eight-sided Cell of Perfection. As students and chelas perfect the Co-creation process, some teachings suggest the Flame of Desire evolves alongside the Three-Fold or Unfed Flame of Love, Wisdom, and Power into the Four-Fold Flame. In this physical, progressed state it develops as the fourth White Flame of Creation. The cultivation of the Jurisdiction Hope engenders and protects its development. The Flame of Desire is said to be another important innate link to the source of creation and is protected through chanting the "OM."

**Flame of Unana:** The conscious activity of the ONE that is cultivated and held as a physical, tangible flame within the light fields of an Ascended Master.

**Forty Pillars of Isis:** Small Vortices that are approximately forty to one-hundred miles in diameter where Divine Beings and Ascended Masters calibrate, stream, and leverage divine feminine energy throughout Earth for humanity's spiritual evolution and growth. It is alleged that there are forty feminine energy Vortices physically present on the Earth and they play a vital role for humanity's entrance into the New Age. Some of these smaller Vortices are located within larger Golden City Vortices. These Golden Cities are: Shalahah, Jeafray, Marnero, Andeo, Braham, and Tehekoa. Their energies help one to integrate both feminine and masculine energies to achieve the inner marriages. They are overseen and protected by Mother Mary.

**Forty Pillars of Zeus:** Small Vortices that are approximately forty to one hundred miles in diameter where Divine Beings and Ascended Masters calibrate, stream, and leverage divine masculine energy throughout Earth for humanity's spiritual evolution and growth. It is alleged that there are forty masculine energy Vortices physically present on the Earth and they play a vital role for humanity's entrance into the New Age. Some of these smaller Vortices are located within larger Golden City Vortices. These Golden Cities are: Gobean, Gobi, Adjatal, and Unte. Their energies hold the Divine Breath of our planet and prepare one to receive the feminine and cultivate the inner marriage. They are overseen and protected by Master El Morya.

**Freedom Star:** The Earth's prophesied new name as the Earth and humanity evolve throughout the Golden Age. Freedom Star is both a state of consciousness that is associated with Ascension and spiritual liberation, and is a new light body that planet Earth will develop in the New Times.

**Gobean:** The first United States Golden City located in the states of Arizona and New Mexico. Its qualities are cooperation, harmony, and peace; its Ray Force is blue; and its Master Teacher is El Morya.

**Golden Age of Kali Yuga:** According to the classic Puranic timing of the Yugas, Earth is in a Kali-Yuga period that started around the year 3102 BCE the year that Krishna allegedly left the Earth. During this time period, which according to this Puranic timing lasts a total of 432,000 years—the ten-thousand year Golden Age period, also known as the Golden Age of Kali Yuga, is not in full force. Instead, it is a sub-cycle of higher light frequencies within an overall larger phase of less light energy.

This Golden Age is prophesied to raise the energy of Earth as additional light from the Galactic Center streams to our planet. This type of light is a non-visible, quasar-type light that is said to expand life spans and memory function, and nourish human consciousness, especially spiritual development. There are many theories as to when this prescient light energy began to flow to our planet. Some say it started about a thousand years ago, and others claim it began at the end of the nineteenth century. No doubt its influence has changed life on Earth for the better, and according to the I AM America Teachings, its effect began to encourage and guide human spiritual evolution around the year 2000 CE.

The Spiritual Teachers say that living in Golden Cities can magnify Galactic Energies and at their height, the energies will light the Earth between 45 to 48 percent—nearly reaching the light energies of a full-spectrum Treta Yuga or Silver Age on Earth. The Spiritual Teachers state, "The Golden Age is the period of time where harmony and peace shall be sustained."

**Golden Thread Axis:** Also known as the Vertical Power Current. The Golden Thread Axis physically consists of the Medullar Shushumna, a life-giving nadi comprising one-third of the human Kundalini system. Two vital currents intertwine around the Golden Thread Axis: the lunar Ida Current, and the solar Pingala Current. According to the Master Teachers, the flow of the Golden Thread Axis begins with the I AM Presence, enters the Crown Chakra, and descends through the spinal system. It descends beyond the Base Chakra and travels to the core of the Earth. Esoteric scholars often refer to the axis as the Rod of Power, and it is symbolized by two spheres connected by an elongated rod. Ascended Master students and chelas frequently draw upon the energy of the Earth through the Golden Thread Axis for healing and renewal using meditation, visualization, and breath.

**Gondwanaland:** The ancient Arabian Continent that allegedly existed during Lemurian times was covered by huge tropical forests.

**Great Mystery:** The source of creation; all elements of life contain the sacred and are aspects of the Divine. In Ascended Master Teaching, the Silent Watcher represents the great mystery.

**Great Purification:** Primarily considered a Native American term, the Great Purification signals the end of one period of time for humanity and the beginning of a New Time. Contemporary prophets view the Great Purification as a time for humanity to heal and transform individually and collectively.

**Greening Map:** The second Map of Earth Changes Prophecies. It contains a total of seventeen Golden City Vortices and is sponsored by Ascended Master Kuan Yin. It entails all of Asia, Japan, and Australia. New land is prophesied to appear near New Zealand, New Guinea, Hawaii, and the Easter Islands, and is referred to as "New Lemuria" by the Spiritual Teachers. The Greening Map signifies personal and transpersonal healing of the feminine. It balances Mother Earth through the awakening of ecological alchemy. During the Greening Map's Time of Change, Earth is healed and rejuvenated with new flora and fauna appearing throughout the planet.

**Green Ray:** The Ray of Active Intelligence is associated with education, thoughtfulness, communication, organization, the intellect, science, objectivity, and discrimination. It is also adaptable, rational, healing, and awakened. The Green Ray is affiliated with the planet Mercury. In the I AM America teachings the Green Ray is served by the Archangel Raphael and Archeia Mother Mary; the Elohim of Truth, Vista—also known as Cyclopea, and Virginia; the Ascended Masters Hilarion, Lord Sananda, Lady Viseria, Soltec, and Lady Master Meta.

**Harmony:** The first virtue of the Twelve Jurisdictions based on the principle of the Law of Agreement.

**Heart's Desire:** The wellspring of abundance, love, and creativity. By identifying activities that yield personal joy and happiness, we may discover our Heart's Desire. Eastern philosophy often refers to this principle as the soul's specific duty or purpose in a lifetime—its Dharma. The Heart's Desire is analogous to the principle of desire—the Ninth Jurisdiction. This evolved perception of desire is based on the true etymology of the word. The French word "*de*" means "of," and the English word "*sire*" means "forefather, ancestry, or source." From this context, Sanat Kumara teaches, "The Heart's Desire is the source of creation." Since the Heart's Desire is one of the most influential principles underlying humanity's spiritual development and unfoldment, Ascended Master teachings give it utmost importance. It is considered a physical, emotional, mental, and spiritual presence that raises the unawakened animal consciousness into human consciousness, and then onward to the awakened aspirant and the devoted chela. The Ascended Masters claim that the physical presence of the Flame of Desire lies within the heart, nestled inside the Eight-sided Cell of Perfection. As students and chelas perfect the Co-creation process, some teachings suggest that the Flame of Desire evolves alongside the Three-Fold or Unfed Flame of Love, Wisdom, and Power, into the Four-Fold Flame. In this physical, progressed state, the Flame of Desire develops as the fourth White Flame of Creation.

**Heart of the Rose:** The self-actualized and realized balance of feminine energies.

**Helios and Vesta:** The masculine and feminine deities who reside in the heart of our solar Sun. In Ascended Master teachings, they are perceived as the divine parents of our solar system. Helios emits the quality of illumination for spiritual knowledge and enlightenment, while Vesta emanates energies of spiritual truth for self-actualization.

**Holy Comforter:** Spiritual consolation through devotion and purity.

**Horizontal Healing:** The healing of humanity through brotherhood, sisterhood, peace, and love is sponsored through the great Ascended Master Teacher and elder Kuan Yin.

**Human Aura:** The subtle energy field of luminous light that surrounds the human body comprised of different and distinctive energy bodies and layers and fields of light. When referring to the aura, the terms "light body," "layer," "planes," and "light-field" are often used. A "layer" is often an energetic portion of a "light body," defined through perceptible differences in both light and sound. A "plane" is a level within a "light body," often associated with vibration and the development of consciousness. "Layers" and "planes" exist simultaneously within a "light body." A "light-field" is yet another term for a portion of a "light body" and is sometimes an energy layer.

**I AM:** The presence of God.

**Illumination:** The sixth of the Twelve Jurisdictions, which gives light to our life without fear or judgment.

**Immortality:** Deathless and eternal. Ascended Masters often refer to two types of immortality: the immortality of the eternal soul (spiritual immortality), and physical immortality that is the acquisition of the deathless physical body, often taken on by will, by an Ascended Master.

**Karma:** Laws of Cause and Effect.

**Kuan Yin:** The Bodhisattva of Compassion and teacher of Saint Germain. She is associated with all the Rays and the principle of femininity.

**Kundalini:** In Sanskrit, Kundalini literally means coiled. It represents the coiled energy located at the base of the spine, often established in the lower Base and Sacral Chakras. Some scholars claim that Kundalini Shakti—shakti meaning energy—initiates spiritual development, wisdom, knowledge, and enlightenment.

**Kuthumi:** An Ascended Master of the Pink, Ruby, and Gold Rays. He is a gentle and patient teacher who works closely with the Nature Kingdoms.

**Lady Nada:** The Ascended Goddess of Justice and Peace who is associated with Mastery of speech (vibration), communication, interpretation, and the sacred Word. Nada is also known as a divine advocate of Universal Law, and she is often symbolized by the scales of blind justice. She is associated with the Yellow Ray of Wisdom and the Ruby and Gold Rays of Ministration, Brotherhood, and Service.

**Law of Acceptance:** A natural law of spiritual evolution which removes personal inner struggle and judgment of self and others. It dissolves conflict and separation and engenders freedom and joy.

**Law of Aggregation:** The Law of Aggregation is a function of the Yellow Ray and assists the conscious mind to receive direction, that results in conclusion and focus.

**Laws of Attraction and Repulsion:** Physical laws, as noted by the force of a magnet. When holding a magnet, like charges forcefully repel each other while unlike charges forcefully attract. Through the Spiritual Law of Allowing, like attracts like.

**Law of Divinity:** Every created form of life contains innate divinity and a connection to the Source. This is the Law of Divinity.

**Law of Involution:** As the inner process of spirituality develop and matures, one begins to express this profound change externally.

**Law of Life:** All life evolves and grows and is eternally seeking harmony. This great law is interwoven with the cycles of karma and reincarnation.

**Law of Love:** Per the Ascended Master tradition, to consciously living without fear, without inflicting fear on others. Perhaps every religion on Earth is founded on the Law of Love, per the notion of "treating others as you would like to be treated." The Fourth of the Twelve Jurisdictions instructs us that Love is the "Law of Allowing, Maintaining, and Sustainability." All of these precepts distinguish love from an emotion or feeling, and observe Love as action, will, or choice. The Ascended Masters affirm, "If you live love, you will create love." This premise is fundamental to understanding the esoteric underpinnings of the Law of Love. The Master Teachers declare that through practicing the Law of Love, one experiences acceptance, understanding, and tolerance, alongside detachment. Metaphysically, the Law of Love allows different and varied perceptions of ONE experience, situation, or circumstance to exist simultaneously. From this viewpoint, the Law of Love is the practice of tolerance.

**Law of ONE:** All of created life interacts with and is indelibly connected to the ONE.

**Law of Opposites:** Sir Isaac Newton's third Law of Motion, "Every action has an equal and opposite reaction." When this is understood according to Hermetic insight, everything has a pair of opposites, (e.g., hot and cold), and their difference is separated only by degrees.

**Law of Repulsion:** The opposite of the Law of Attraction, this action causes disintegration and metaphysically explains the idea of the space observed between opposites.

**Lemuria:** A continent that primarily existed in the Pacific Ocean before it was submerged by Earth Changes. It is deemed to have been the remaining culture and civilization of Mu—an expansive continent that once spanned the entire present-day Pacific Ocean. It is alleged that the lands of Lemuria, also known as Shalmali, existed in the Indian and Southern Pacific Oceans, and included the continent of Australia.

Thus, it is believed to have integrated with the Lands of Rama, and is to be considered one the earliest cultures of humanity. Sri Lanka is alleged to have been one of the empire's capital cities. Esoteric historians theorize that the tectonic Pacific Plate formed this lost continent. Asuramaya is one of the great Manus of Lemuria's Root Race.

Some esoteric writers place the destruction of Mu around the year 30,000 BCE; others place its demise millions of years ago. According to Theosophical history, the Lemurian and Atlantean epochs overlapped. The apparent discrepancy of these timelines is likely due to two different interpretations of the Cycle of the Yugas. It is claimed that the venerated Elders of Lemuria escaped the global tragedy by moving to an uninhabited plateau in central Asia. This account mirrors Ascended Master teachings and Lord Himalaya's founding of the Retreat of the Blue Lotus.

The Lemurian elders re-established their spiritual teachings and massive library as the Thirteenth School. Spiritual teachers claim that the evolutionary purpose of this ancient civilization was to develop humanity's Will (the Blue Ray of Power). Lemurian culture also venerated the Golden Disk of the Sun and practiced the Right-hand Path. It is claimed that these teachings and spiritual records became foundational teachings for the Great White Brotherhood of the mystical lands of His Wang Mu (the Abode of the Immortals) and the Kuan Yin Lineage of Gurus. Present-day Australia—once known by Egyptian gold-miners as the ancient Land of Punt—is considered the remainder of the once great continent of Mu and Lemuria, which likely existed in the time period of Dvapara-Yuga, over 800,000 years ago.

**Lighted Stance:** The Lighted Stance is a state of conscious perfection—a precursor to Ascension. It is observed in the tenth energy body and produces the alchemic ability to produce the Seamless Garment.

**Lords of Venus:** A group of Ascended Masters who came to serve humanity. They once resided on the planet Venus.

**Lotus:** An Eastern symbol of the maternal creative mystery—the feminine. The lotus signifies the unfolding of spiritual understanding, and the opening and development of the chakras. It also represents the growth of man through three periods of human consciousness—ignorance, endeavor, and understanding. This idea is mirrored in nature, too. In Oriental philosophy the lotus manifests in three elements: earth, water, and air. Thus, man exists on the material, intellectual, and spiritual planes. In Western culture, the symbology of the rose is similar to the lotus.

**Love:** "Light in action."

**Malton:** The second United States Golden City located in the states of Illinois and Indiana. Its qualities are fruition and attainment; its Ray Force is Ruby and Gold; and its Master Teacher is Kuthumi.

**Manu:** Any root race or group of souls inhabiting a vast time period (era or epoch) on Earth. Manu is also a mythical, cosmic being who oversees the souls during their incarnation process, throughout the duration of that specific time period. Some consider Manu a type of spiritual office, not unlike a "World Teacher." For example, one evolved cosmic being will serve as Manu for one world cycle, and when it ends, it will move on in the evolutionary process. A different entity will then serve as Manu for the next group. Each group of souls has a different energy and purpose. Seventh Manu children possess advanced capabilities—astute intellect, vast spiritual knowledge, and keen psychic abilities.

**Master K. H.:** An abbreviation for the Master Teacher Kuthumi; however, it is sometimes used as a description for Kuthumi's energies when united in threefold action in the physical, astral, and causal planes.

**Master Teacher:** A guru or teacher who has achieved a level of remarkable proficiency regarding a certain skill set. In Ascended Master Teaching a Master Teacher is often an Ascended Master who has individualized their energies to the light and sound of a specific Ray Force.

**Map of Exchanges:** The Ascended Masters' Map of prophesied Earth Changes for Europe and Africa. Its seventeen Golden City Vortices focus on the self-realization of the HU-man through the exchange of heavenly energies on Earth, which usher in the Golden Age. The Map of Exchanges is sponsored by Lady Nada, Kuthumi, and El Morya.

**Merkabah:** A triangular, geometric light body. This body can be cultivated through various visualization and meditation techniques and it is claimed that it can help with spiritual communication, spiritual travel, and the Ascension Proces.

**Monad:** Dynamic Will, or purpose and life, as revealed through human demonstration. It is also understood as the Father creative principle. It is also associated with the beginning and the totality of creation—the ONE.

**Monadic Body:** This energy body is associated with the Sixth Light Body and the Christ, or Christ Consciousness.

**Mother Mary:** Ascended Goddess of the Feminine who was originally of the angelic evolution. She is associated with the Green Ray of healing, truth, and science, and the Pink Ray of love.

**New Age:** Prophesied by Utopian Francis Bacon, the New Age would herald a United Brotherhood of the Earth. This Brotherhood/Sisterhood would be built as Solomon's Temple, and supported by the four pillars of history, science, philosophy, and religion. These four teachings would synergize the consciousness of humanity to Universal Fellowship and Peace.

**New Lemuria:** Ancient Lands of Lemuria, and entirely new lands, which will rise in the Pacific Ocean during the Time of Change. These new lands and continents are prophesied to appear near New Zealand, New Guinea, Hawaii, and the Easter Islands.

**Ocean of Balance:** A large ocean prophesied to be formed throughout Northern Russia, the Barents Sea, the Norwegian Sea, and large sections of Eastern Europe. Its waters are prophesied to flood France, the Netherlands, Poland, Ukraine, Denmark, Sweden, and Finland. The metaphysical and spiritual meaning of this massive ocean is that "balance begets life."

**Om Manaya Pitaya** or **Om Manaaya Patiya:** This Ascended Master statement has several meanings. Two spiritual translations are: "I AM the Light of God" and "I AM the Seer of the Lord." The Sanskrit translation means: "Amen, honored Lord."

**ONE:** Indivisible, whole, harmonious Unity.

**Oneness:** A combination of two or more, which creates the whole.

**Oneship:** A group or group mind that is based upon the notion of whole, harmonious Unity.

**Orgone:** Life-giving energy, prana, or chi.

**Outpicturing:** A spiritual technique, similar to visualization but differs in that its various methods often include the human aura or human chakras.

**Overshadowed:** The process of one distinct type of energy, i.e., a Ray Force, planetary energy, spirit guide, or Ascended Masters, morphs its energy with another distinct energy to assist spiritual development, growth, or evolution.

**Overtone:** The influence of one distinct type of energy upon another.

**Personality Ray:** According to Ascended Master Teachings, the personality protects each soul in their incarnation process. From this viewpoint, the Personality Ray cloaks each person in life, and protects the precious spark of life, often known as the Monad, or Unfed Flame.

**Pineal Gland:** A human gland that is located behind the brain's third ventricle that is associated with the Third Eye, rising of the kundalini energies, psychic ability, and many forms of spiritual development and growth. Researchers believe the pineal gland's production of pinoline is responsible for various psychic states of consciousness.

**Pink Ray:** The Pink Ray is the energy of the Divine Mother and associated with the Moon. It is affiliated with these qualities: loving; nurturing; hopeful; heartfelt; compassionate; considerate; communicative; intuitive; friendly; humane; tolerant; adoring. In the I AM America teachings the Pink Ray is served by the Archangel Chamuel and Archeia Charity; the Elohim of Divine Love Orion and Angelica; and the Ascended Masters Kuan Yin, Mother Mary, Goddess Meru, and Paul the Venetian.

**Prana** or **Prahna:** Vital, life-sustaining energy. The Master Teachers often refer to Earth energy as Prahna.

**Quality:** Considered the second characteristic of three creative builders. This esoteric energy translates spirit or consciousness into matter. It is analogous to feeling.

**Ray:** A force containing a purpose, which divides its efforts into two measurable and perceptible powers, light and sound.

**Ray of Transfiguration:** The Violet Ray.

**Rose:** The Western symbol of the maternal creative mystery—the feminine. It represents the chakra as a spiritual Vortex; a garland of roses typifies the seven chakras and their unfolding and attainment. In Eastern culture the symbology of the lotus is similar to the rose.

**Ruby Ray:** The Ruby Ray is the energy of the Divine Masculine and Spiritual Warrior. It is associated with these qualities: energetic; passionate; devoted; determination; dutiful; dependable; direct; insightful; inventive; technical; skilled; forceful. This Ray Force is astrologically affiliated with the planet Mars and the Archangel Uriel, Lord Sananda, and Master Kuthumi. The Ruby Ray is often paired with the Gold Ray, which symbolizes Divine Father. The Ruby Ray is the evolutionary Ray Force of both the base and solar chakras of the HU-man; and the Gold and Ruby Rays step-down and radiate sublime energies into six Golden Cities.

**Sacred Ray:** The Rays that overshadow the soul throughout the entire lifetime. In Jyotish—Vedic Astrology—these Ray Forces would be analogous to the atma karaka (soul indicator) and amatya karaka (helpful people), and Raja Yoga Ray Forces. In simple terms, Sacred Rays are associated with Saturn, Jupiter, Moon, and Sun. These are the color Rays of blue, yellow, and pink.

**Saint Germain:** Ascended Master of the Seventh Ray. Saint Germain is known for his work with the Violet Flame of Mercy, Transmutation, Alchemy, and Forgiveness. He is the sponsor of the Americas and the I AM America material. Many other teachers and Masters affiliated with the Great White Brotherhood help his endeavors.

**Sananda:** The name used by Master Jesus in his ascended state of consciousness. Sananda means joy and bliss, and his teachings focus on revealing the savior and heavenly kingdom within.

**Sanat Kumara:** One of the original Lords of Venus who founded the Great White Brotherhood at Shamballa. He is also known as Lord of the World. The Bible refers to him as Ancient of Days.

**Sattva:** Harmonious response to vibration; pure and spiritual in effect.

**School of the Four Pillars:** A mystery school associated with the Ascended Masters of the I AM America Teachings. The Four Pillars are associated with four Master Teachers. These teachers are El Morya, Kuthumi, Saint Germain, and Lord Sananda. They are the sponsors of the I AM America Teachings through their own lineage of gurus. In esoteric studies, the four pillars also represent the four seminal teachings of history, science, philosophy, and religion that are the foundation of the New Age. These tenents are meant to synergize the consciousness of humanity to Universal Fellowship and Peace. The shadow qualities of the Four Pillars are: disregard, ignorance, imprudence, and atheism.

**Seamless Garment:** The Ascended Masters wear garments without seams. This clothing is not tailored by hand but perfected through the thought and manifestation process.

**Sea of Grace:** A large European and Russian Sea, that is prophesied to exist within the Sea of Balance. It is allegedly formed when the Himalayan Mountains rise and the Black Sea, Azov, Sea, the Caspian Sea, and Aral Sea combine into the Sea of Grace. It is metaphysically and spiritually linked to humanity's spiritual transformation of greed into non-judgment, political freedom, and spiritual human rights.

**Self-Knowledge:** The idea of self-knowledge is key to many of the spiritual teachings of the Ascended Masters. It is associated with spiritual freedom and the Ascension Process as the spiritual maxim, "Know thyself." This involves the personal acknowledgement of our own doubts, limitations, strengths, and talents, and is a key component of personal freedom. The attainment of self-knowledge is further integrated by spending time in the Stars of Golden Cites that are associated with the planet Venus. Self-knowledge is considered a spiritual human right that is fiercely protected by the Spiritual Hierarchy that promotes the process of self-perfection, personal balance, and harmony.

**Serapis Bey:** An Ascended Master from Venus who works on the White Ray. He is the great disciplinarian—essential for Ascension—and works closely with all unascended humanity who remain focused for its attainment.

**Service:** The fifth of Twelve Jurisdictions. It is a helpful act based upon the Law of Love.

**Servile Ray:** Ray Forces that are created through combinations of the three primal color Rays of blue, yellow, and pink. The White Ray is considered a Servile Ray. Servile Rays literally "serve" the guardian Sacred Rays.

**Seventh Manu:** Highly evolved life streams that began to embody Earth between the years 1981 to 3650. Their goal is to anchor freedom and the qualities of the Seventh Ray to the conscious activity on this planet. They are prophesied as the generation of peace and grace for the Golden Age. South America is their forecasted home, though small groups will incarnate other areas of the globe. Their Manu or sponsor is Mother Mary.

**Shalahah:** The fourth United States Golden City located primarily in the states of Montana and Idaho. Its qualities are abundance, prosperity, and healing; its Ray Force is green; and its Master Teacher is Sananda.

**Shaman:** A shaman has developed the ability to leave their body to work for spiritual transformation at many levels. An intermediary between the natural world and the spirit world. Indigenous Shaman place a strong emphasis on their environments; nature spirits and animals play important roles and act as omens, messengers, and spirit guides.

**Shamballa:** Venusian volunteers, who arrived 900 years before their leader Sanat Kumara, built the Earth's first Golden City. Known as the City of White, located in the present-day Gobi Desert, its purpose was to hold conscious light for the Earth and to sustain her evolutionary place in the solar system.

**Shiny Pearl:** The present-day Ural Mountains form this prophesied islands, surrounded by the Ocean of Balance, with the Sea of Grace to the southwest. Its metaphysical properties help to hold the spiritual principle of balance for Russia, during the Time of Change and onward into the New Times.

**Silicon-based Consciousness:** A level or state of consciousness that humanity is moving toward. Silicon-based consciousness is a form of crystalline consciousness that quickly interconnects with others through compassion, empathy, and telepathy. It is associated with clarity, purity, and is uniquely humanitarian. This level of consciousness evolves from our current state of carbon-based consciousness.

**Sixth Manu:** The current group of souls who incarnated upon Earth during the Aryan epoch. This Manu or group of souls is actually the sixth sub-race of the fifth root race. They precede the Seventh Manu, the prophesied Seventh sub-race of the fifth root race.

**Six-Map Scenario:** A series of six maps of the United States. The Ascended Masters prophesied this schematic to illustrate choice, consciousness, and their relationship to Earth Changes.

**Soul Ray:** The Soul Ray is a protective, masculine energy that is esoterically calculated through observing the location of Mars within an astrology chart. It instigates currents of energy within the physical body for the interchange and exchange of the Seven Rays. This spark of life incites the biological functions to begin.

**Spiritual Awakening:** Conscious awareness of personal experiences and existence beyond the physical, material world. Consequently, an internalization of one's true nature and relationship to life is revealed, freeing one of the lesser self (ego) and engendering contact with the higher (Christ) self and the I AM.

**Star:** The apex, or center of each Golden City.

**Stillness:** The eleventh of the Twelve Jurisdictions, which produces motionless quiet as the foundation of the Law of Alignment.

**Subjective Energy Body:** This type of energy is similar to a thought-form, which causes behavioral changes when triggered. They are created through intense emotions, addictive behaviors, and the use of addictive substances, and often contain elements of lower consciousness.

**Swaddling Cloth:** An area of over a million square miles located in Brazil, South America. According to the Ascended Masters, this area is the primary prophesied physical location for the incarnation of the children of the

Seventh Manu. The Swaddling Cloth is protected by the Ascended Master Mother Mary.

**Sword of the Rose:** The philosophical notion that conflict can be overcome through the spiritual cultivation of justice, forgiveness, and healing.

**Time Compaction:** An anomaly produced as we enter into the prophesied Time of Change. Our perception of time compresses and time seems to speed by. The unfolding of events accelerates, and situations are jammed into a short period of time. This experience of time will become more prevalent as we get closer to the period of cataclysmic Earth Changes.

**Time of Change:** The period of time currently underway. Tremendous changes in societies, cultures, and politics, in tandem with individual and collective Spiritual Awakenings and transformations, will abound. These events will occur simultaneously with possibilities of massive global warming, climactic changes, and seismic and volcanic activity known to us as Earth Changes. The "Time of Change" guides the Earth to a "New Time," the Golden Age.

**Time of Testing:** In the year 2000 a new era, called the Time of Testing, got underway. While prophesied to last a span of seven years, the Time of Testing may occur for a longer time period alongside the Time of Change. This period is identified with unstable world economies and political insecurity alongside the convergence of personal trials and world change. Many may perceive the Time of Testing as a period of loss. This loss may encompass both the loss of financial and personal security; yet, simultaneously cause tremendous change within and the arrival of self-actualization, self-knowledge, and acknowledgment of the existence of the true self, and the consciousness of the ONE—Unana. These years are also defined by the spiritual growth of humanity; Brotherly love and compassion play a key role in the development of the Earth's civilizations as mankind moves towards the Age of Cooperation.

**Time of Transition:** A twelve-year period when humanity experienced tremendous spiritual and intellectual growth, ushering in personal and global changes. In the year 2000 a new era, called the Time of Testing, got underway. It's a seven-year span of time when economies and societies encountered instability and insecurity. These years are also defined by the spiritual growth of humanity; Brotherly love and compassion play a key role in the development of the Earth's civilizations as mankind moves toward the Age of Cooperation.

**Transfiguration:** A process of spiritual change, of form or appearance, to a more lighted state of consciousness. This change is instigated by a Spiritual Awakening or spiritual process; that is, the Ascension Process or use of the Violet Flame.

**Transmigration:** The metaphysical movement of souls. This movement may be across or through spiritual dimensions, from one planet to another, or from one Kingdom of Creation to another. (i.e., Angelic, Elohim, Animal, Plant, etc.)

**Tree of Truth:** The mystical Tree of Life that is associated with justice, balance, and protection.

**Twelve Jurisdictions:** Twelve laws (virtues) for the "New Times," which guide consciousness to Co-create the Golden Age. They are: Harmony, Abundance, Clarity, Love, Service, Illumination, Cooperation, Charity, Desire, Faith, Stillness, and Creation/Creativity.

**Unana:** Unity Consciousness.

**Unfed Flame:** The Three-Fold Flame of Divinity that exists in the heart and becomes larger as it evolves. The three folds represent: Love (Pink), Wisdom (Yellow), and Power (Blue).

**Universal Consciousness:** Collective Consciousness.

**Vibrational Shifting:** An energy anomaly that occurs more frequently as we move into the New Times. It is identified through these irregularities: fourth dimensional activities that increase activity with nature spirits and elementals; time compaction; assists the Ascension Process; problems with both emotional and mental balance.

**Violet Flame:** A spiritual process for Transmutation, Forgiveness, and Mercy. It is used to balance Karmas of the past. The result is an opening of the Spiritual Heart and the development of bhakti, the state of unconditional love and compassion. It came into existence when the Lords of Venus first transmitted the Violet Flame, also knows as Violet Fire, at the end of Lemuria. It was meant to clear Earth's etheric and psychic realms, as well as the lower physical atmosphere, of negative forces and energies. This paved the way for the Atlanteans to use the flame during religious ceremonies and as a visible marker of temples. The Violet Flame also induces Alchemy. Violet light emits the shortest wavelength and the highest frequency in the spectrum, so it induces a point of transition to the next octave of light.

**Violet Ray:** The Seventh Ray. It is primarily associated with Freedom and Ordered Service alongside Transmutation, Alchemy, Mercy, Compassion, and Forgiveness. It is served by the Archangel Zadkiel, the Elohim Arcturus, the Ascended Master Saint Germain, and Goddess Portia.

**White Flame:** The Flame of Desire develops as the fourth White Flame of Creation. It is associated with purity, freedom of expression, Unity Consciousness, and the New Children.

**White Ray:** The Ray of the Divine Feminine is primarily associated with the planet Venus. It is affiliated with beauty, balance, purity, and cooperation. In the I AM America teachings the White Ray is served by the Archangel Gabriel and Archeia Hope; the Elohim Astrea and Claire; and the Ascended Masters Serapis Bey, Paul the Devoted, Reya, the Lady Masters Venus and Se Ray, and the Group of Twelve.

**Yellow Ray:** The Ray of the Divine Wisdom is primarily associated with the planet Jupiter and is also known as the Divine Guru. It is affiliated with expansion, optimism, joy, and spiritual enlightenment. In the I AM America teachings the Yellow Ray is served by the Archangel Jophiel and Archeia Christine; the Elohim of Illumination Cassiopeia and Lumina; and the Ascended Masters Lady Nada, Peter the Everlasting, Confucius, Lanto, Laura, Minerva, and Mighty Victory.

# Index

## A

# E

# H

Hall, Manly 430, 433
harmony
  *definition* 443
healer
  *and the Five-fold Path* 93
  *and the Rays* 96
healing
  *a healing wave* 163
  *Horizontal*
    definition 443
  *"Love one another."* 174
heart
  *follow your heart* 277
  *I AM the Love of the Heart Decree* 168
Heart of the Dove
  *soul of compassion* 379
Heart of the Rose 170
  *definition* 443
Heart's Desire
  *definition* 443
Helios and Vesta 255
  *definition* 443
Hermetic Law
  *and Vibration* 428
  *Seven Principles* 434
Himalayan Mountains 344
Holy Comforter
  *and the White Ray* 34
  *definition* 443
Horizontal Healing
  *definition* 443
Houston, TX 381
HU
  *sound vibration* 385
HU-man 96, 387
  *and layers of consciousness* 269
human aura 182
humanity
  *and the Green Ray* 34

Hundredth Monkey Theory 208
Hungary 312

# I

I AM
  *Ameru, the Plumed Serpent* 376
  *definition* 444
I AM America Map
  *and collective consciousness* 370
  *for humanity's awakening* 186
  *the three Maps* 365
ice caps
  *melt* 195
Iceland 342
ice sheets 196, 340
  *and the North Atlantic* 197
illumination
  *definition* 444
illusion 269
immortal destiny 137
immortality
  *and perfection* 135
  *and the Law of Divinity* 180
  *and the Mental Body* 182
  *and the Unfed Flame* 133
  *conscious*
    definition 438
  *consciousness* 130
  *definition* 444
  *"The consciousness that beats your heart is
    immortal."* 308
incarnation 74
  *and the first breath* 82
  *through the Rays* 80
indigo
  *higher expression of the Green Ray* 35
Individualization 55, 73, 431
Initiate
  *and the Great White Lodge* 245
Initiation 55
inner kingdom 246

# M

# W

# Y

# Z

# About Lori & Lenard Toye

**Lori Toye** is not a Prophet of doom and gloom. The fact that she became a Prophet at all is highly unlikely. Reared in a small Idaho farming community as a member of the conservative Missouri Synod Lutheran church, Lori had never heard of meditation, spiritual development, reincarnation, channeling, or clairvoyant sight.

Her unusual spiritual journey began in Washington State, when, as advertising manager of a weekly newspaper, she answered a request to pick up an ad for a local health food store. As she entered, a woman at the counter pointed a finger at her and said, "You have work to do for Master Saint Germain!"

The next several years were filled with spiritual enlightenment that introduced Lori, then only twenty-two years old, to the most exceptional and inspirational information she had ever encountered. Lori became a student of Ascended Master Teachings.

Awakened one night by the luminous figure of Saint Germain at the foot of her bed, her work had begun. Later in the same year, an image of a map appeared in her dream. Four teachers clad in white robes were present, pointing out Earth Changes that would shape the future United States.

Five years later, faced with the stress of a painful divorce and rebuilding her life as a single mother, Lori attended spiritual meditation classes. While there, she shared her experience, and encouraged by friends, she began to explore the dream through daily meditation. The four Beings appeared again, and expressed a willingness to share the information. Over a six-month period, they gave over eighty sessions of material, including detailed information that would later become the I AM America Map.

Clearly she had to produce the map. The only means to finance it was to sell her house. She put her home up for sale, and in a depressed market, it sold the first day at full asking price.

She produced the map in 1989, rolled copies of them on her kitchen table, and sold them through word-of-mouth. She then launched a lecture tour of the Northwest and California. Hers was the first Earth Changes Map published, and many others have followed, but the rest is history.

From the tabloids to the *New York Times*, *The Washington Post*, television interviews in the U.S., London, and Europe, Lori's Mission was to honor the material she had received. The material is not hers, she stresses. It belongs to the Masters, and their loving, healing approach is disseminated through the I AM America Publishing Company operated by her husband and spiritual partner, Lenard Toye.

**Lenard Toye,** originally from Philadelphia, PA, was born into a family of professional contractors and builders, and has a remarkable singing voice. Lenard's compelling tenor voice replaced many of the greats at a moment's notice—Pavarotti and Domingo, including many performances throughout Europe. When he retired from music, he joined his family's business yet pursued his personal interests in alternative healing.

He attended *Barbara Brennan's School of Healing* to further develop the gift of auric vision. Working together with his wife Lori, they organized free classes of healing techniques and the channeled teachings. Their instructional pursuits led them to form the *School of the Four Pillars* which includes holistic and energy healing and Ascended Master Teachings. In 1995 and 1996 they sponsored the first Prophecy Conferences in Philadelphia and Phoenix, Arizona. His management and sales background has played a very important role in his partnership with his wife Lori and their publishing company.

Other publications include three additional Prophecy maps, twelve books, a video, and more than sixty audio tapes based on sessions with Master Teacher Saint Germain and other Ascended Masters.

Spiritual in nature, I AM America is not a church, religion, sect, or cult. There is no interest or intent in amassing followers or engaging in any activity other than what Lori and Lenard can do on their own to publicize the materials they have been entrusted with.

They have also been directed to build the first Golden City community. A very positive aspect of the vision is that all the maps include areas called, "Golden Cities." These places hold a high spiritual energy, and are where sustainable communities are to be built using solar energy alongside classical feng shui engineering and infrastructure. The first community, Wenima Village, is currently being planned for development.

Concerned that some might misinterpret the Maps' messages as doom and gloom and miss the metaphor for personal change, or not consider the spiritual teachings attached to the maps, Lori emphasizes that the Masters stressed that this was a Prophecy of choice. Prophecy allows for choice in making informed decisions and promotes the opportunity for cooperation and harmony. Lenard and Lori's vision for I AM America is to share the Ascended Masters' prophecies as spiritual warnings to heal and renew our lives.

## Books and Maps by Lori Toye

**Books:**

NEW WORLD WISDOM SERIES: Books One, Two, and Three

I AM AMERICA ATLAS: *Based on the Maps, Prophecies and Teachings of the Ascended Masters*

FREEDOM STAR: *Prophecies that Heal Earth*

THE EVER PRESENT NOW: *A New Understanding of Consciousness and Prophecy*

GOLDEN CITY SERIES
  *Book One: Points of Perception*
  *Book Two: Light of Awakening*
  *Book Three: Divine Destiny*
  *Book Four: Sacred Energies of the Golden Cities*

I AM AMERICA TRILOGY
  *Book One: A Teacher Appears*
  *Book Two: Sisters of the Flame*
  *Book Three: Fields of Light*

**Maps:**

*I AM America Map*
*Freedom Star World Map*
*United States 6-Map Scenario*
*United States Golden City Map*

I AM AMERICA PUBLISHING & DISTRIBUTING
P.O. Box 2511, Payson, Arizona, 85547, USA. (928) 978-6435

*For More Information:*
**www.iamamerica.com**
**www.loritoye.com**

# About I AM America

I AM America is an educational and publishing foundation dedicated to disseminating the Ascended Masters' message of Earth Changes Prophecy and Spiritual Teachings for self-development. Our office is run by the husband and wife team of Lenard and Lori Toye who hand-roll maps, package, and mail information and products with a small staff. Our first publication was the I AM America Map, which was published in September 1989. Since then we have published three more Prophecy maps, nine books, and numerous recordings based on the channeled sessions with the Spiritual Teachers.

We are not a church, a religion, a sect, or cult and are not interested in amassing followers or members. Nor do we have any affiliation with a church, religion, political group, or government of any kind. We are not a college or university, research facility, or a mystery school. El Morya told us that the best way to see ourselves is as, "Cosmic Beings, having a human experience."

In 1994, we asked Saint Germain, "How do you see our work at I AM America?" and he answered, "I AM America is to be a clearinghouse for the new humanity." Grabbing a dictionary, we quickly learned that the term "clearinghouse" refers to "an organization or unit within an organization that functions as a central agency for collecting, organizing, storing, and disseminating documents, usually within a specific academic discipline or field." So inarguably, we are this too. But in uncomplicated terms, we publish and share spiritually transformational information because at I AM America there is no doubt that, "A Change of Heart can Change the World."

With Violet Flame Blessings,
*Lori & Lenard Toye*

CPSIA information can be obtained
at www.ICGtesting.com
Printed in the USA
BVHW030210181121
621917BV00006B/154

9 781880 050699